Point Counterpoint

New Perspectives on People & Strategy

Edited by Anna Tavis, Richard Vosburgh and Ed Gubman

Published in association with the
Society for Human Resource Management
Alexandria, Virginia

HR People & Strategy
Chicago, Illinois

Published by HR People & Strategy
401 N. Michigan Avenue, Suite 2200, Chicago, Illinois 60611
www.hrps.org

Published in association with the Society for Human Resource Management.

Point Counterpoint: New Perspectives on People & Strategy

With Learning Guides for Discussion and Team Development

Edited by Anna Tavis, Richard Vosburgh and Ed Gubman

HR | People & Strategy

Part I: Talent Management

Talent Management is about the acquisition, retention, motivation and development of diverse talent to meet the current and future needs of the organization at all levels. It includes work related to career development.

This book contains 13 sets of Point Counterpoint debates addressing Talent Management, Organizational Effectiveness, Leadership Development, HR Strategy & Planning, and Building a Strategic HR Function. Each set of articles has a Learning Guide for the development of teams in organizations or students in classrooms. More than 120 authors, consultants, academics and practitioners from 14 countries contributed (China, France, Singapore, Austria, Spain, Germany, Japan, India, Slovenia, United Kingdom, Finland, United States, Switzerland, Australia), with many of the strongest Thought Leaders represented (Ulrich; Lawler; Boudreau; Buckingham; Cappelli; Goleman; Schein; Beer; Gratton; Goldsmith; Senge; Handy; and many more).

Point Counterpoint: New Perspectives on People & Strategy
With Learning Guides for Discussion and Team Development

Part II: Organizational Effectiveness

Organizational Effectiveness is about managing culture and organizational change, and includes organizational design. It involves the development of intellectual capital, organizational learning strategies, the development of a learning culture and work on organizational agility and organizational transformation. It also involves knowledge management.

Part III: Leadership Development

Leadership Development is about the acquisition, retention, motivation and development of leaders. It includes succession planning and results in providing a diverse and inclusive functional and organizational leadership to meet needs now and into the future.

Part IV: HR Strategy & Planning

HR Strategy and Planning is about aligning strategic business planning and HR planning. It involves linking business strategy to the HR implications and actions needed. It includes involvement in corporate governance and decision making and contributing to corporate social responsibility.

Part V: Building a Strategic HR Function

Building a Strategic HR Function is about enhancing the impact of the HR profession, with the goal to improve HR's functional excellence, impact, effectiveness, perception and reputation. It also includes measurement and reporting on efficiency, effectiveness and impact.

When You Come to the Cross Road, Take It

Anna Tavis

This selection of the Perspectives published within the span of three years from each other indirectly answers the much debated question about the future of human resources. The authors collectively lead us in the discovery of the solution for the future of the HR practice.

Fundamentally, and in the long run, the future of HR will not be defined by the same roster of leading issues that HR is facing now. Nor will the HR conversations of the future be dominated by the **"what"** of centrally controlled requirements answering to the HR compliance.

The future of HR will be about the **"how"** of the business first and foremost. It will be a question about the radically changing HR business world view and about the HR contribution to the innovative and customized solutions for the accelerating workforce challenges facing the business. HR's will be the conversation about **"how"** HR and Talent professionals will be solving for the business' emerging and unforeseen future challenges.

The power of Perspectives approach is in posing questions but withholding the definitive answers. More specifically, the Point Counterpoint format suggests solution options but does not name them directly.

It is sometimes difficult for people in HR to move away from our dependency on the familiar "best practices" and "best in class benchmarks." The Perspectives column promotes the radical idea that no one point of view is sacred, no matter how authoritative and dominant it may be at this point in time. Perspectives introduce us to the new world of discovery-based HR solutions, to the world of self-reliance and independent thinking about our business.

The Perspectives column introduces the new kind of HR debate. Name the "sacred cow" HR topic, and we took it on in these publications and opened it up for questioning. We brought the community of forward-looking consulting experts, seasoned practitioners, and the prominent academics into the same debate. We created an egalitarian platform for the broadly networked, self-directed, collaborative global team of experts that role modeled the new style of debate.

In other words, we came to the HR crossroads and we took it. Consider performance management: We invited Marcus Buckingham, the ultimate iconoclast in the HR world, to take on the topic. Sure enough, the fireworks started to explode on this focal topic in HR. Similarly, Karen Stephenson, the ultimate challenger of the received academic wisdoms, called on HR to learn to operate in the world of "heterarchies," not "hierarchies." And David Rock, the founder of global Neuroleadership movement, in his contribution questioned the established dominance of psychological explanations in the leadership development debate.

In summary, *People and Strategy* **Perspectives** role models a paradigm shift toward discovery-driven, evidence-based, context-specific HR thinking. Perspectives brings practitioners to the source of HR issues and invites them to co-create a solution in collaboration with a broader network of consultants, academics and HR gurus. The ultimate outcome is the emerging HR practice that is professionally sound, yet egalitarian and independent, and uniquely relevant to the emergent requirements of the business specific strategy and practice. **P&S**

Point Counterpoint Debates

Richard Vosburgh

One sign of a great leader is that they have a point of view; and for a mature leader that means a "teachable point of view." One of my most admired bosses and long-term mentors was more than once described as "sometimes wrong but never in doubt." He'd definitely always start with a pretty well-formed point of view, but to his credit he would also listen to logical arguments and continue to learn and grow. The Point Counterpoint debate series started with an understanding that in the strategic arena of HR, there often is "no one right answer" and that proper solutions evolve from the straightforward presentation of facts and points of view. It is in that context that we offer up this Point Counterpoint series.

The *People & Strategy* journal of HRPS has been a significant contributor to the ongoing evolution of the HR profession and has been published every quarter since 1977. Over the last few years a new section was developed titled **Point Counterpoint** where Thought Leaders and Practitioners debate key issues facing organizations and the HR profession. Just in this collection you will see the perspective of professionals from more than 13 countries, ranging from academicians to consultants to practitioners. You will recognize many of the names.

Almost 10 years ago, HRPS identified the five knowledge areas that define our focus, and this book assembles the Point Counterpoint debates under these five areas with one chapter per area:

1. **Talent Management**

2. **Organizational Effectiveness**

3. **Leadership Development**

4. **HR Strategy & Planning**

5. **Building a Strategic HR Function**

HR People & Strategy (HRPS), a nonprofit organization with headquarters in Chicago, has been the premier global association and network of strategic HR executives and thought leaders since 1977. In support of its worldwide membership, HRPS serves as a global forum for presenting the latest thinking and information about the HR implications of key business issues and strategic HR practices; offers a broad range of professional development programs with distinguished HR scholars, practitioners and business leaders; and builds networks of diverse individuals to exchange leading-edge HR ideas, information and experiences.

The Mission of HRPS is to help organizations enhance their performance through the strategic management of human resources. The HRPS Vision is to be the preferred provider of leading-edge HR knowledge in key strategic areas. In service to this mission and vision, we added a Learning Guide for each Point Counterpoint set of articles—essentially a discussion guide that can be used within organizations for Lunch 'n' Learn team development and within classrooms for management education.

The Learning Guides are each structured as follows:

1. **Discovery Questions:** What are we dealing with in our organization today that relates to this content area?

2. **Selected Facts:** What new facts that were presented got your attention?

3. **Key Discussion Points:** What were the key points being made in this Point Counterpoint presentation?

4. **Review of Solutions:** Identify two to three Big ideas that are worthy of exploring for our organization.

5. **Recommendations Summary:** Identify one thing that we are all going to do differently based on what we learned.

6. **Learning Outcomes:** What one new piece of information did you learn that will be important to you?

A note on the authors—As is true of all areas within HRPS, the three volume editors have been volunteer contributors for many years. The Point Counterpoint series for the *People & Strategy* journal began under the five-year Executive Editorship of Dr. Richard Vosburgh; Dr. Anna Tavis developed and grew the concept over the last four years; and for the last three years Dr. Ed Gubman has been the Executive Editor for the journal. The authors of the Point Counterpoint articles represent a global Who's Who of thought leaders and practitioners. **P&S**

The Five HRPS Knowledge Areas

HR Strategy and Planning
Aligning business and HR planning; linking business strategy and HR strategy; involvement in corporate governance and decision making; contributing to corporate social responsibility; HR measurement and analytics

Talent Management
The acquisition, retention, motivation and development of diverse talent to meet the current and future needs of the organization at all levels; workforce planning; career development

Leadership Development
The acquisition, retention, motivation and development of leaders; succession planning and management; providing diverse and inclusive functional and organizational leadership

Organization Effectiveness
Managing culture and organization change; building a learning culture; organization design; intellectual capital and knowledge management; organization learning, agility and transformation; sustainability; social networks

Building a Strategic HR Function
Enhancing the HR profession; the CHRO role; improving HR excellence through greater impact, effectiveness, efficiency; perception and reputation; HR functional measurement and reporting; outsourcing and technology advances

Point/Counterpoint

Executive Editor's Note: With this issue of the journal we introduce the new **Point/Counterpoint** section. We chose and "pre-published" a short article from a thought leader and invited up to 750-word responses to it from our Editorial Review Board. Responses may be in radical agreement or disagreement, or have a story to symbolize and support it or to refute it. Some may add a global or cross-cultural perspective. Some are informally conversational and humorous while others are more formal and serious. We believe this approach will advance the debate on key topics. If our members find this valuable we'd like to make this a regular feature of the journal and open the Counterpoint debate to our membership. We see it as one more way of bringing forward the best thinking related to **people and strategy**.

The first article chosen for this was written by an old friend of HRPS (and for many years in the '80s my dotted line boss at PepsiCo), Dr. Bob Eichinger--whom we know to have both innovative and at times controversial fact-based opinions! Many thanks to Bob for being willing to try this. We hope you enjoy the article and the many well thought out responses to it. We were pleased with the quality and quantity of the responses.

Our new Perspectives editor, Dr. Anna Tavis (anna.tavis@aig.com), will own this section and manage this process. We'd like to hear from you. Please also consider this an open invitation to offer up a short article that could be used to generate Counterpoints!

Richard Vosburgh
Executive Editor

POINT

Is "Build On Your Strengths" The Best Advice?

So I Was Thinking...

Bob Eichinger
CEO, Lominger International
A Korn/Ferry Company

We are all getting ready for the second world war for talent. We all know the script. Demographics. Oldies are retiring and the youngish are taking over. Global. Everything is getting more complicated. Speed. Everything is getting faster. CEOs are under pressure to deliver Growth. Jobs are getting bigger, more complex and more global and the pool of senior talent is dwindling. As if that weren't bad enough, CEO's are stumbling at a greater pace. Freshly minted GM's are failing in their first assignments. Derailment is mostly fueled by a lack of "EQ" (emotional intelligence) and adaptability (learning agility). CFO's are leaving because of the new regulatory environment. So what to do?

So that set me to thinking. There are two big things rummaging around the competency space. One is the finding that most successful managers and executives have somewhere between 5-7 strengths around which they build a highly successful career. Specifically, they have 5-7 of the most mission critical skills for the jobs they have, have no noise (that is, they are at least average) in the rest of the mission critical skills and have no glaring derailers. That means, as it always has, that no one is expected to have all of the competencies listed on the executive success profile. Success is not cloning. They need 5-7 of the 9-15 that comprise a typical success profile. The other buzz in the competency world is the so called "strengths movement." This movement tells you to find your strengths. Build your strengths. Use your unique strengths to build your career. Find a place and a role that fits your unique strengths. There's no need to address your weaknesses.

So I was thinking … what should I tell my two newly minted college graduate children about how to plan for their careers? What should I tell the youngish up and comers about how to prepare for their future careers?

So I was thinking… How many people have enough (let's say five just to pick a number) strengths?

Well, that sort of depends upon how you define a strength.

Simply stated, a strength might be what you personally are best at. If you need five strengths to succeed, it's your five best skills.

But is that definition adequate? Is it enough to win? Is it enough to be as successful as you want to be? Even if an individual has five strengths, are those five strengths strong enough to win, to be effective and successful? To be competitive?

If your highest grades in school were math and biology but those grades were C grades and all your other grades were D grades, would you have what it takes for a successful career in science?

What kind of strength do you need to win? How athletic do you need to be to medal in the Olympics? How good do your acting skills need to be to win an Oscar? An Emmy? A Tony? What ERA stats do you need to be considered a top pitcher? What team batting average is required to consistently win your division and play in the World Series? To what level must you develop golf skills in driving, chipping, putting, sand shots, composure under pressure, etc., to win a major tournament?

So while everyone has five relative strengths (five skills that are stronger than other skills), the question is this: are those five strengths really strong enough to compete?

You can't answer that question unless you compare and contrast those strengths with others doing the same work. Who are you competing with? Perhaps it's enough to be in the top ten percent of the competitive population, those doing the same job at the same level, to be the best one out of ten doing the work you do. To be the best one out of ten strategists. Upper ten percent of negotiators. Top ten percent of motivators. Top ten percent of team builders. Top ten percent of innovators. Top 10 of 100 change managers.

If you're out to create the best marketing department in your industry, what level of talent will you seek? If you aim to achieve the best supply chain efficiency in your industry, what level of talent do you need to design and manage the supply chain? To consistently beat your competition and to support the CEO's growth agenda, what level of talent do you need in your key positions?

With this thought in mind, we wanted to see how many people have five competitive strengths compared to the manager/executive population at large. We looked at a database of 2,045 who were rated by others on 67 individual contributor, manager and executive competencies or skills* (refer to the sample description). We asked a simple statistical question, how many individuals have any five competitive strengths among the 2,045. In theory, any individual could have 67 competitive strengths meaning scoring higher than the other 2044 managers on all 67. We assumed that most would have five strengths.

Since others might have a different idea or standard about what represents a competitive strength, we looked at the top 2% and top 5% – very stringent interpretations of a strength. We also looked at the top 10% and top 15% as more reasonable standards. Finally, we also looked at the top quarter (25%) and top third (33%) – relatively liberal or loose definitions of what a strength might be.

The following table presents those results. *Note.* N = 2045

Cut Off Point			5 Strengths at or above the cutoff point	No Strengths at or above the cutoff point
Standard Deviation	Percentile	TOP		
2.06	98	2%	4.8%	69.9%
1.65	95	5%	15.1%	46.7%
1.29	90	10%	33.4%	26.3%
1.04	85	15%	51.4%	15.1%
0.68	75	25%	74.0%	5.3%
0.44	66	34%	85.0%	2.6%

As you can see from the results in that table, if you use the definition of top 10% as the cutoff or standard to represent a competitive strength, 33.4% of 2,045 have five or more strengths, and 26.3% of the sample have none. Zero. Zilch. Nada. At that level.

If you use the more stringent definition of top 5% to define competitive strength, then only 15.1% have five or more, and over half (46.7%) have none.

If you use the looser, top quarter, definition of a competitive strength, then 74% have five or more competitive strengths and 5.3% have none.

That's an interesting finding. So, if you have to make a career out of five strengths, you better first make sure your strengths are indeed competitive strengths.

So I was thinking... Are the five top strengths the right ones? If 33.4% have five strengths, are they the ones they need to excel as managers and executives? To have a fulfilling career? To be at the top of their game?

To answer that question, we looked at the most and least frequently achieved strengths using the more lenient top quarter data.

At the 75th percentile, 1520 people have five or more competencies (74% of the population). The seven most frequent strengths people have are:

Rank	Competency
1	Organizational Agility
2	Decision Quality
3	Career Ambition
4	Peer Relationships
5	Interpersonal Savvy
6	Caring About Direct Reports
7	Integrity and Trust

Not bad competencies to have. But maybe not the most critical ones.

The ten (some are tied) least frequently demonstrated strengths are:

Rank	Competency
58	Political Savvy
59	Sizing Up People
60	Innovation Management
61	Business Acumen
62	Total Work Systems
63	Managing & Measuring Work
64	Planning
65	Fairness to Direct Reports
66	Directing Others
67	Problem Solving

Some pretty important management and executive competencies are in the bottom ten of 67. These are skills related to developing people, strategy, creativity, and adaptability.

So I was thinking... How many managers and executives have five of the more critical competencies required to succeed at the top? Looking at our studies over the last 15 years, we selected eight competencies that our analysis has shown repeatedly to be highly correlated with success for managers and executives and are the best differentiators of effectiveness. The "Big 8 Critical Competencies" are:

- Creativity
- Dealing with Uncertainty and Ambiguity
- Building Effective Teams
- Innovation Management
- Motivating and Inspiring Others
- Planning
- Strategic Agility
- Managing Vision

Arguably, a very necessary set of competencies for managers and executives.

We again went back to our data base of about 2,045 made up mostly of managers and executives and asked how many had five of those eight mission critical skills using the same multiple cutoff scores. The table below presents those findings.

Cut Off Point		5 Strengths at or above the cutoff point	No Strength at or above the cutoff point
Standard Deviation	Percentile		
2.06	98	0.1%	90.9%
1.65	95	0.5%	79.1%
1.29	90	1.6%	66.7%
1.04	85	4.1%	53.7%
0.68	75	9.3%	35.5%
0.44	66	17.8%	24.9%

Note. N=2,045 rated on BIG 8 mission critical competencies

Using the same top 10% definition of a competitive strength, 1.6% have five of the critical eight, and 66.7% have none of them. None. Even using the least stringent definition of a competitive strength, 17.8% of the sample have five strengths in the upper 1/3 and 24.9% have none.

So, if you plan to succeed by focusing on strengths, make sure you do more than just discover your strengths (your top best skills). You've got to see if your strengths are competitive. Determine the level you think you need to achieve to be competitive and see if your skills are at or above that level. Then, and just as important, you need to see if your strengths are the ones you really need for long term career success.

Our review of the data shows that most managers and executives do not have strengths that are competitive. For those who do, almost none have the strengths that matter most. That might have something to do with why such a high percentage fail.

So I was thinking... If that's the case, almost everyone better start developing things they're not good at now.

So I told my children to discover their strengths, then gauge how they compared to the people they would be competing with, find out which strengths they are going to be needing to fulfill their career dreams and to start working on the ones that are not up to par.

And yes, I would also tell the up and coming youngish HIGH POTENTIALS to discover their strengths, then gauge how they compare to the people they are and would be competing with, find out which strengths they are going to be needing to fulfill their career dreams and to start working on the ones that are not up to par.

I'm done thinking. What do you think?

COUNTERPOINTS

COUNTERPOINT
Michael Beer
Professor Emeritus
Harvard Business School

I like Bob Eichinger's carefully crafted article. He is using a unique data set and his conclusions progress cleanly and logically to a final recommendation – ambitious individuals who want to progress up the managerial hierarchy better identify their strengths and their weaknesses. And they better work on their weaknesses.

It was very interesting, even shocking, to learn that so many mangers have so few of the strengths that Eichinger argues are needed to succeed in senior executive positions. While, I don't disagree with the individual development implications of Eichinger' argument *it got me thinking* about an interpretation of Eichinger's findings he does not articulate. I explore these below.

Eichinger's findings and my own observations suggest that corporate developmental practices are largely non-existent or ineffective. This in my view comes from the transactional view of talent – it is fungible, comparable across firms and therefore ought to be acquired rather than developed. This conventional wisdom *human capital* perspective suggests that talent management is about comparing your own people to that of other firms, weeding out the least talented and hiring the most talented – those with more and higher level of requisite competencies available in the market. While there is of course some truth in this perspective, it is not the whole truth. It misses the importance of *social capital* illustrated by Boris Groysberg's recent research on the transportability of "stars."

By social capital I mean the positive impact that team cultures have on individual and firm performance. Groysberg's studied what happens to highly rated investment banking analysts (stars) on Wall Street who move to another firm. He finds that their performance declines significantly and does not recover to its former level even after five years. In effect, investment banks that believe they can improve the performance of the firm by find-

ing people with more talent compared to their current talent will not enjoy a good return on money invested in higher salaries needed to attract stars. Individuals who believe that their performance is solely a function of their competencies and think of themselves as "free agents" in a market for the best talent will fail to sustain their performance and suffer the psychological consequences of being overpaid.

Eichinger's article has a Darwinian tone – not surprising given that through Korn Ferry, Eichinger is now in the executive search business - that implies that all managers are competing in the same single market. Because talent must fit the situation there are in fact different labor markets that serve different types of organizations. Again, Groysberg's research suggests otherwise. The skills required for success in one business and culture is not the same as those in another. Following the implication of his findings regarding the portability of talent on Wall Street, Boris Groysberg and Nitin Nohria studied what happens to GE executives who moved to another company. Not surprisingly they did not all succeed. Success was related to whether their business experience at GE and GE culture fit the new firm. Competence cannot be assessed or exercised without regard to context.

experiences is horizontal as opposed to merely vertical, managers are "forced" to learn from the challenges they meet as the skills that have made them successful prove to be insufficient in the new situation.

Horizontal career progression across different companies is not as valuable, however, as developmental assignments in the same firm. By embedding their development in single firm, managers develop relationships – they become part of a team - that enable them to receive essential support from others with complementary skills. Eichinger might want to suggest to his children that they find a team and developmentally oriented company to attach to as much as simply focusing on their weaknesses.

In summary, the relatively narrow set of competencies Eichinger found executives possess suggests that performance is a function of more than individual talent. It is a function of the organization in which the manager is embedded and must be developed in that context. Firms must develop a team culture and they must focus on making rather then buying talent. Individuals might think about their own development as more than simply working on their weaknesses. Their success is tied to becoming part of an organization's culture and learning to work with people whose talents complement theirs.

> The fact that outstanding talent and performance are deeply embedded in the organization has implications for both firms and individuals. Firms ought to pay more attention to developing talent than buying talent.

The fact that outstanding talent and performance are deeply embedded in the organization has implications for both firms and individuals. Firms ought to pay more attention to developing talent than buying talent. Management development, as Morgan McCall and his colleagues at the Center for Creative Leadership showed, is largely dependent on a progression of job experiences and stretch assignments that both test managers and at the same time develop the manager's capabilities. If that progression of

COUNTERPOINT
John Boudreau
Professor & Research Director
University of Southern California

Bob's finding that many of the least-common strengths relate to sound thinking about work systems and talent certainly fits with our research at the Center for Effective Organizations. Organization leaders are better at decisions about resources like money, techology and customers than they are about their talent.

Should this surprise us? When I earned my MBA degree almost 30 years ago, and even today when I teach MBA's and business executives, it's striking how much deeper and more systematic are their concepts regarding finance, operations, and marketing, than about talent and organization effectiveness. Everyone has the same concept of "net present value," but everyone has a different concept of "employee motivation."

Bob correctly suggests that we are entering an era where talent-related strengths will be more important. Why is that? Because talent will be scarcer, more pivotal, and more amenable to thoughtful analysis than ever before. These are precisely the conditions that motivated the emergence of the Finance decision science for money, and the Marketing decision science for customers, in earlier eras.

It's also true that we'll need to get much more precise about which strengths matter, among our leaders and among our employees generally. Just as customer segmentation revolutionized marketing, talent segmentation will revolutionize the competition for competencies. Generic solutions work less effectively.

For example, when Boeing decided to compete by building the 787 using composite-based engineering rather than traditional metal-based engineering, the strength of leaders who could build global supplier teams became more pivotal than it had ever been. Winning organizations will get very good at such logic. It's going to be increasingly important for organizations to look beyond generic lists of strengths and competencies, and to compete for and with leadership talent — indeed for all talent — in unique strategic ways.

COUNTERPOINT
Paula Caligiuri
Director, Center for HR Strategy
Rutgers University

I'd like to focus on early career development for future global careers. Bob Eichinger's advice for his newly graduated college-age children (and all aspiring high potentials) is timeless, universal and highly practical. I whole-heartedly agree that an accurate self-awareness is the necessary starting point for positive professional growth and that the best way to Carnegie Hall is still practice – practice - practice. If Bob's children are like most

other well-educated twenty-somethings around the world, another good piece of advice might be "check that your passports are up-to-date." Analyzing data from a Universum Communications survey of over 100,000 newly-minted college graduates globally, we found that "having an international career" is one of this generation's top professional goals and part of the "dream career" for many[1].

Beyond the needs for a passport, plane ticket, and paying job there are other useful "strengths" for those whose "career dreams" will take them across national borders. From my own research and the research of my colleagues, we know that those who are successful tend to have certain personality characteristics (e.g., openness, emotional strength, and extroversion), have the ability to learn languages, manage complexity, form relationships across cultures, and the like. (I should also mention that those in successful global careers also tend to have a supportive spouse, a supportive organization, healthy parents, and the absence of teenage children...but let's focus on the individual.)

We believe it was Socrates who gave us the sage advice approximately 2,500 years ago to "know thyself": This is especially great advice for those interested in successful global careers. I have had the opportunity to work with many organizations in developing their strategic global assignment processes. In each company, while implemented in a variety of ways, the process begins with an opportunity for candidates to self-assess their profiles against what we know is typically necessary for international assignments[2]. This first step is self-discovery, not evaluation – giving candidates an opportunity to consider their

strengths and weaknesses relative to what it will take to live comfortably and work successfully in another country (including their dispositional characteristics, competencies, experiences, motivations, and personal situation related to general success and cross-cultural adjustment). **Self-awareness of personal strengths is not a small first step.**

Discovering the best international route from Delphi to Carnegie Hall – from self-awareness to professional success – is a challenge for both high potentials and the HR professionals trying to develop them. After a dozen years and countless opportunities to work with high potentials who are striving for global careers, I have three observations related to Bob's suggestions:

(1) Not everyone will internalize self-awareness data accurately. Listen to karaoke or a group of MBAs after their job interviews and you can quickly hear that some people have an overly-inflated perception of their strengths. At the opposite extreme, some people refuse to believe they possess the raw talent that others see in them. Given that global success often requires a fair dose of humility, the arrogance end of this continuum concerns me more. Low self-efficacy for international work can often be enhanced appropriately when presenting clear evaluations relative to what it takes to be successful (despite the fact they currently do not possess a passport). In either direction, **internalized accuracy about personal strengths is needed.**

(2) Not everyone can fully develop useful strengths. Try as I may to be a professional basketball player I will not overcome my 5'3½" stature and the fact that I have difficulty catching a cold. (Being selected last in gym classes since the 1st grade was my first

> The skills required for success in one business and culture is not the same as those in another. Following the implication of his findings regarding the portability of talent on Wall Street, Boris Groysberg and Nitin Nohria studied what happens to GE executives who moved to another company. Not surprisingly they did all succeed.

dose of 360° feedback.) Volumes have been written about the relative mutability of knowledge, skills, abilities, and other personal characteristics: At minimum, we know that some are easier to change than others (e.g., gaining knowledge about the rules of basketball is easier than improving my eye-hand coordination). For most international assignments, personality characteristics including openness, extroversion and emotional stability, underlie many necessary competencies. Personality, however, is typically more difficult to change in the traditional organizational development context. It is important to **consider the level of mutability which underlies the various strengths to be developed.**

(3) Opportunities to develop strengths are not always readily available. Developmental opportunities to build necessary strengths can happen in traditional venues such as organizational development programs, training centers, and universities – or through a variety of self-initiated situations. In the case of global careers, our research has found that the best global business leaders have, among other competencies, cultural flexibility – and that cultural flexibility is often gained in non-traditional ways (e.g., living abroad, being raised in a bi-cultural household, marrying a person from another culture)[3]. Some of **the best ways to develop strengths may occur in non-traditional places – and experiencing them may be bound by time, money, or opportunity.**

I agree with every piece of Bob Eichinger's advice. Applying his advice to the global "dream career" I would supplement his advice with the following: Self-assess against the characteristics most often found in successful global leaders; be honest with yourself regarding whether you are hard-wired for this type of work – and what you can do to excel in it; seek opportunities in non-traditional places to test your own cultural assumptions; seek opportunities to take cultural risks to understand the limits of your knowledge cross-nationally. (For Bob's children specifically, ask for Dad's credit card, take a few years off before work and explore this amazing world.)

REFERENCES

[1]This research has been conducted with Saba Colakoglu (Rutgers University) and Universum Communications.

[2]Caligiuri, P. M., & Phillips, J. (2003). An application of self-assessment realistic job previews to expatriate assignments. International Journal of Human Resource Management, 14 (7), 1102-1116.

[3]Caligiuri, P.M. (2006). Developing global leaders. Human Resource Management Review, 16, 219-228. These ideas were further tested and are currently under review in a manuscript with Ibraiz Tarique entitled "Predicting effectiveness in global leadership activities".

COUNTERPOINT

Donna Dennis
Managing Partner
Leadership Solutions Consulting

Definitions can be tricky. People say one thing but mean another. This is the problem that Dr. Bob Eichinger falls victim to in his article "So I Was Thinking" and one of the major stumbling blocks in the coaching world today.

According to Encarta Dictionary, a skill is the ability to do something well that is gained through some sort of training or experience; strength is an extremely valuable or useful ability, asset, or quality. Dr. Eichinger does what many have done in this field and uses these words interchangeably. In his article, he says a skill is something "you are personally best at." Then he says, "If you need 5 strengths to succeed, it's your 5 best skills." The confusion between a skill which can be taught or improved or learned and a strength which is innate begins.

In 1998 Don Clifton of the Gallup Organization studied strengths with a measurement he called his "Strength Finder" (Rath, 2007). What Clifton and others in the "strengths movement" suggest is that it may be possible, with a lot of hard work, to add a talent or strength where one does not exist. But it is infinitely better to add skills, knowledge and practice to a natural talent because then the raw talent becomes the multiplier that leads to "strength." This is what is meant by the term "building on strengths." It is about building on a person's natural talents. Not only does this approach work better, it builds real career satisfaction as well.

In the countless interviews I have done with managers after they have completed the *Strengths Finder*, anecdotally it is those managers that are aligned with their core strengths that are happy doing what they are doing and pay is not a factor for judging their personal success.

Dr. Martin Seligman found that a person can become lastingly happier by using "character strengths"—things like creativity and curiosity—more often and in different ways (Seligman, Steen, Park and Peterson, 2005). If an employee can incorporate their

character strengths into their work they are more fulfilled.

Creativity is not a skill; it is very difficult to "teach" someone to be creative if he or she is not. Dr. Eichinger mixes strengths like integrity and trust with skills like planning and problem solving. It is this semantics problem that leads to the confusion in his argument.

So what do I suggest to young people? I tell them to take a strengths inventory and find out what their natural talents are, then add skills and knowledge through education and practice so that these natural talents become competitive strengths. Developing all the competence in the world will not make for a successful career if the skills are not aligned with the natural strengths. It's important to identify natural strengths and talent then work to enhance them. This will lead to a successful, fulfilling career in whatever field is chosen.

REFERENCES

Rath, T., *Strengths Finder* 2.0 (2007). Gallup Press, New York.

Seligman, M., Steen, T., Park, N. And Peterson, C. (2005). "Positive Psychology Progress, Empirical Validation of Interventions." *American Psychologist, Vol. 60. No 5, 410-421.* The American Psychological Association, Washington, D.C.

COUNTERPOINT

Fred Frank
CEO
TalentKeepers

I was thinking—A very dangerous thing for me to do. This is a response to Bob Eichinger's article. And unlike Bob's, it is not data based, although in my heart of hearts, it is – based upon data I and my organizations have accumulated over the past approximate 31 and a half years (see the mythical sample description below)[1].

Funny thing, I agree with Bob. What Bob is saying is the following: If you were going to give your grown kids some "early" career advice, it would be something like "discover your strengths", compare yourself with others with whom they will be competing and start working on the competencies that are not up to par. And Bob would also tell similar things to the up and coming youngish HIGH POTENTIALS.

Well, I agree totally with Bob. The only difference is that I wouldn't give any career advice to my three grown children – I would just be messing them up. That being said, why would you simply work on developing your weaknesses – as some "experts" have claimed? Here is what I think makes sense.

Yes, first discover your strengths. I don't care how you do this but you need to do it. Whether it is through a 360 survey, and/or a test, etc. just do it. But it shouldn't be what you think your strengths are, or what your parents or best friend think they are. My mother thought there wasn't a thing I couldn't do. How wrong she was. And how wrong I would have been if I had relied on her judgments.

Now that you know what your strengths are, find out what areas you need to develop and start developing them. And if you are too weak in a given competency area, give up the thought of getting good at it. No way. It is what it is. Just mask it through your other strengths or fake it as well as you can. No matter what, you are not going to turn a horrible communicator into Bill Clinton or Ronald Reagan. Or the opposite might work — perhaps, you could become Jimmy Carter or Richard Nixon, but that is another story — all politics aside.

So Bob, thanks for your great thoughts. My one additional thought of course, is don't try to work on your weaknesses if they are too weak to begin with. Contemplate a different career.

REFERENCES

[1] Sample Description: The total sample size is in the millions, from hundreds and hundreds of organizations encompassing every conceivable industry. The data come from the years 1976 through 2007. The gender composition: probably 70.13 % male and 29.87% female. The mean age is likely 40. The position level composition: I have no idea but would logically be individual contributor, 30%; supervisor, 40%; manager, 20%; director/executive, 5%; and senior executive, 5%. The average number of years of experience in management would be about 15 years and about 80% would have college degrees.

COUNTERPOINT
Ed Gubman
CEO
Strategic Talent Solutions

Bill Russell, Magic Johnson and Michael Jordan all were great basketball players, maybe the three greatest of all time. They each led their teams to multiple championships, and yet they each played the game very differently. Russell was a tenacious defender and rebounder; Johnson was a passer first, some-

one who preferred to set up his teammates but could score when needed; and Jordan, the greatest scorer of all time, could close out a game like nobody else. Each had very different strengths, and each played to them to ascend to the highest levels of achievement.

What do three basketball players have to do with Bob Eichinger's insightful ruminations and research on competencies? Plenty, as it turns out, since trying to find a common set of competencies across organizations that lead to executive success, to me, invariably leads down the wrong path. And trust me, it's not just basketball—pick out any three or four successful corporate leaders, politicians, coaches or managers in other sports—any walks of life, and you'll realize the same thing. The commonalities are not really there unless you get to very broad categories—so broad they may not mean much. Success is far more individual than that, and, as a result, a lot more variable.

I must admit that I feel a little guilty writing this since I am a big fan of Bob's work and often quote it (with proper attribution of course) when I do workshops and speeches. Bob's presentations at our HRPS conferences are always among the highpoints for me. However, when it comes to looking for the holy grail of a set of definitive success competencies, Bob and other researchers are destined to fall short.

Put simply, **who you are, is how you lead.** Successful leadership, particularly at the highest levels, is more about personal characteristics than about competencies. Characteristics are that combination of intelligence, attitudes and beliefs, values, personality traits and habitual ways of interacting that go deeper than competencies or skills. Competencies are still important at leadership levels, but they tend to pale in impact compared to characteristics. In other

words, when it comes to leadership, how you do things is less important than who you are.

I see this all the time in our work assessing and selecting CEOs and other "C" level executives. In a recent CEO selection assignment I was blessed to work with a slate of

> Put simply, who you are, is how you lead. Successful leadership, particularly at the highest levels, is more about personal characteristics than about competencies.

three highly capable candidates. Each one demonstrated enough of the requisite competencies that we identified for the job, including strategic ability, decision-making, accountability, innovation, marketing orientation, motivation and interpersonal skills to do an effective job. Each would have made the company money, kept the Board happy and been an effective steward of the culture. But they were very different people. They differed in how smart they were; their values about personal ambition, career success and how long they stayed in jobs and companies; how they had experienced the ups-and-downs of life and the resulting impacts on their levels of personal maturity; how far "above and beyond' the norm they were willing to go to treat employees right and other key dimensions. I've been working with competencies since early in my career—1982 to be exact—and I've never seen those expressed as competencies on a typical success profile.

In our efforts to build common approaches and tools to help manage performance, we often overlook the most important aspect of people. We are infinitely variable. This is the major reason most tools and programs fall short and leave managers frustrated. It's the individual differences that make us interesting and account for the great achievements and achievers we see throughout history. Corporate leadership is no different. My advice to Bob's children: Find your passion and become as good at it as you can be. And the more unique you are, the more likely you are to stand out from the crowd and be successful. Good luck.

COUNTERPOINT
Gerald E. Ledford, Jr.
President
Ledford Consulting Network, LLC

Let's buy the conclusions, but not the analysis. I am impressed by the degree to which unsupported assertions are Teflon-coated, while data attracts counter-arguments like a magnet. I often have seen a speaker make sweeping, unsupported, overblown generalizations, and have seen the audience respond by nodding, smiling knowingly, and complimenting the speaker on his or her wisdom and insight. Another speaker makes the same arguments with data, the response is often nit-picking about how the speaker collected and analyzed the data. In part, this is because the data are almost never as convincingly one-sided as the sweeping generalizations. In part, data analysis just gets those critical thinking, left-brain processes going, and many of us can't stop the process if we take the data seriously. As a result, the forest (lessons learned) is often lost in trees (the data).

have some pretty big and important weaknesses.

I agree with all of these points. Indeed, if Bob had made his main points in this form and supported them with a few folksy stories, I would have nodded, smiled, and agreed with him. Since he used data, I'm hooked, and I have a few problems with whether the data, however extensive, really prove his points.

Bob's first analysis addresses the common advice, that managers build their career around 5-7 strengths. Is this possible? The analysis indicates to me that it is, at least for many managers. In looking at the table, I would use the 90th percentile as a cut point. A manager at or above this cut point will be superior to nine out of ten fellow managers on at least five competencies. Becoming excellent at just five of 69 competencies would not seem to be a formidable challenge for any manager with ambition and talent. Indeed, the table shows that *one-third* of managers meet this criterion. The fact that just over a fourth have no strengths at which they are superior to 90 percent of their peers did not

pool of 69 competencies because they were the most strongly correlated with a measure of effectiveness. If a correlation is high, people high on a given competency also scored high on effectiveness; those in the middle on the competency were middling in effectiveness; and those low on the competency were low in effectiveness. The higher the correlation, the more perfectly we match this pattern. When the analysis says that few people are high on at least five of the "Big 8", all we are doing is proving that the Big 8 are good measures. A competency is not a good differentiator if a great many people are high on it. Therefore, concluding that relatively few people are high on any five of the Big 8 is somewhat tautological; if there were too many people were high on the competency, it would not have been one of the Big 8 in the first place.

However, although I don't buy the data, I do buy the lesson: make sure that the effort you expend on increasing your competencies is spent on competencies that make you more effective.

> Therefore, concluding that relatively few people are high on any five of the Big 8 is somewhat tautological; if there were too many people were high on the competency, it would not have been one of the Big 8 in the first place.

My reactions to Bob Eichinger's piece show me that I'm just like that guy in the back of the room who can't let go of the data. Therefore, to make sure that I don't miss the forest, I would begin by summarizing his main points as follows:
1. Most managers do not have as many as five competencies on which they are superior to (that is, have a competitive advantage over) other managers.
2. Even fewer managers are high on as many as five competencies that are critical to success; many managers are good at things that don't matter very much.
3. Managers (and the rest of us) should work on overcoming weaknesses that get in the way of their success, because most of us

surprise me at all. I find these data somewhat encouraging. At least a third of managers have, relatively speaking, great strengths as managers. The pool of managers who are superior on at least five competencies is larger than I would have guessed.

The second analysis poses a more serious problem. It restricts the analysis to the eight out of 69 competencies that prior research has shown to be the best differentiators of effectiveness. The "Big 8" include such competencies as creativity, managing vision, and building effective teams. Bob finds that very few managers are high on at least five of these competencies.

Here, however, a statistical artifact gets in the way. The "Big 8" were selected from the

COUNTERPOINT
Bill Stopper
Partner
The Walker Group

Normally, I would never presume to dispute the doctor's diagnoses, but I had to read Bob Eichinger's article a number of times to discover the couple of things that bothered me about it. So I was thinking. . . .
1. In describing the "strengths movement," he concludes, "There's no need to address your weaknesses." Everything I read about the concentration on strengths and the strengths movement says you should recognize your weaknesses and manage around them. That's different than not addressing them, and sounds pretty reasonable.
2. The advice to HIGH POTENTIALS to "find out which strengths they are going to need to fulfill their career dreams" led me to think about another view of the strengths movement: make career choices based on your strengths. There are probably a fair number of high potentials who are trapped in a career that after some time in the job—in the field—is not what they really want. Before working on weaknesses that are not up to par competitively, they really should rethink

their dreams in terms of their strengths before they do what Dr. Bob says. A change in career may lead to a whole other analysis of strengths and weaknesses.

Other than that, I was thinking I like what the good doctor has to say. As usual, he's got the data to make his point.

COUNTERPOINT
Dave Ulrich
Professor
University of Michigan

As always, Bob's ideas cut to the chase. He has a unique ability to challenge popular thinking and offer innovative approaches. The tag line "build on your strengths" has such emotional appeal. I like to think that what I do well is what others want me to do well, that when I can do better and even become the best at what I do I will succeed. Bob has highlighted the flaw in this thinking.

In college, I majored in English. I was superb at sitting in a chair reading novels. Few could read novels much better than me. I was good at it, even (in all humility) great. But, I found that as I finished my novel-reading degree, few would really pay me for being the best at this strength. I learned a simple truth, that value is defined by the receiver not the giver. If my strength in reading novels is not what others would enjoy, no matter how well I did it, it was not a strength that had an impact.

Building on our strengths, if taken to the extreme, is an internally focused development agenda. Defining what I want and what I am good at is a good and valuable question, but if it is not coupled with reality, it is not a useful question. Companies that are superb at marketing in a product driven world need to focus on product innovation not just advertising. At times this means finding new strengths that meet real business realities.

Reality sometimes forces clarity. Nokia has mastered an incredible supply chain for building and selling over 800 million devices in the last decade. But, as the internet looms, the company executives have learned that they must find strengths in providing services on these devices. The emerging Nokia focus is not one of their current strengths, but the market demands that it become one. As their executives recognize these emerging market trends, they will develop current employees, attract new employees, and ally with new partners to source future strengths.

Starting a discussion of leadership or talent from the outside in helps clarify strengths that are required to succeed. Rather than doing competency models based on what successful vs. non-successful leaders have done in the past, we suggest involving key custom-

Starting a discussion of leadership or talent from the outside in helps clarify strengths that are required to succeed.

ers to identify what they will need in the future. Customer expectations can then be turned into employee actions through high quality leadership. We have called this building a leadership brand, where external demands frame leadership delivery. If target customers affirm the accuracy and power of leadership competency models, then leaders will build strengths that really deliver value.

Again, Bob's prescient ideas will help leaders and organizations deliver future value.

COUNTERPOINT
Kathryn Zukof
Director-Learning & Organizational Development
New York University

So only 1.6% of managers and executives would get an A on at least five of the eight competencies critical for success in a leadership role? Feels about right, based on the churn and burn I've seen in my walk around the organizational neighborhood. Yeah, it is a smart strategy for today's "high pot", at least from a competitive perspective, to focus on developing the strengths their desired job demands, whether that's five strengths, or eight, or fifteen. Won't hurt getting you in the leadership door – if that's your desired destination - and sure might help keep you there.

But maybe the real message isn't for employees seeking to discover, leverage or develop their strengths, but for employers trying to cope with their apparent shortage. I've seen enough CEOs develop crushes on this year's crop of high pots, only to banish them to the wood pile when deficiencies are revealed, to know that most leaders don't

have anything close to all the skills they need to excel in the role (and I'm talking here about a skill gap in both the disbarred high pots and in the CEOs who have done the disbarring). This is especially true in today's flat organizations where we expect managers to demonstrate intrapreneurial, fiercely humble, emotionally intelligent, voice-finding, service championing, black belt wielding, knowledge managing, global thinking, team building, generationally-sensitive, servant-based, execution-driven leadership, while simultaneously excelling at a few individual contributor functions. Knowing that only 1.6% of managers live up to these expectations, at least from a competitive perspective, should we so quickly dispense with a leader when a competency gap is discovered? Why swap out a faltering incumbent for the next star, when the odds are that this new super luminary will have warts hiding beneath the glow of his or her halo too? I don't mean we should tolerate under-performance. I do mean that when expectations are so high and pickings are so slim, we need to really invest in development, whether this means helping high pots and leaders find and leverage their strengths, fill skill gaps, or identify other means of compensating for their deficiencies.

Perhaps the strength of the strengths-based perspective has nothing at all to do with its message to individual employees, and perhaps it's even wrong in the message it's sending to them. No, perhaps the strength of the strengths-based approach is in the message it sends to employers about restraint and forgiveness. In a world where 98.4% of us fail the test, maybe we should agree that I won't quite so readily throw you under the bus for your imperfections if you won't throw me there either.

Of course, to be on the safe side, and for my own personal satisfaction, I'm going to keep chipping away at some of those areas where I don't quite measure up. Just in case.

learning guide

People & Strategy 30.4 Point Counterpoint:

Is "Build on Your Strengths" the Best Advice— "So I was Thinking. . ."

Discovery Questions

- What are we dealing with in our organization today that relates to this content area?

- Learn about the misunderstandings and misinterpretations of the Strengths movement and Competency models.

- Be able to compare and contrast Skills, Strengths and Personal Characteristics.

- Develop a point of view regarding when and how to use competency models.

- Learn more about methodology, data analysis and how conclusions are drawn.

- Understand the different interpretations put to the Strengths Movement.

Selected Facts

- What new facts that were presented got your attention?

- In a large sample (2,045), 51% had 5 of 67 competencies in the upper 15% of all scores but only 4% were in the upper 15% of 5 of the 8 most critical competencies.

- Global jobs require a larger dose of openness, emotional strength and extraversion.

- Competencies vary in "mutability"—the likelihood of being able to improve in them.

- A Skill is an ability gained through experience; a Strength is a valuable innate asset.

- Building on and using natural talents (strengths) leads to fulfillment and happiness.

- Value is defined by the receiver not the giver—how does this relate to Strengths?

Key Discussion Points

- What were the key points being made in this Point Counterpoint presentation?

- What defines the "second world war for talent"?

- Discuss the issue of "relative" vs. "absolute" level of a strength in a person.

- What are "the Big 8 Critical Competencies"?

- What flaws in the methodology or logic presented by Dr. Eichinger were pointed out?

- What does Beer teach us about the "transportability" of talent?

- Is it individuals or teams that most greatly determine organizational performance?

- What does Caligiuri reveal regarding global success factors across cultures?

- Awareness is a key first step to growth, but what does Caliguiri teach us about the potential pitfalls of self assessment?

- What does Dennis show us regarding how Skills and Strengths are different?

- How did Bill Russell, Magic Johnson and Michael Jordan play the game? So what?

- What does Gubman mean by "Who you are is how you lead"?

- What does the Strengths Movement say you should do about Weaknesses?

- What does Ulrich mean by developing a talent strategy "from the outside in"?

- What does it mean to show intrapreneurial, fiercely humble, emotionally intelligent, voice-finding, service championing, black belt wielding, knowledge managing, global thinking, team building, generationally-sensitive, servant-based, execution-driven leadership?

- On what basis does Zukoff argue that the Strengths movement teaches us restraint and forgiveness?

Review of Solutions

- Identify 2-3 Big Ideas that are worthy of exploring for our organization.

- How could "talent segmentation" be used rather than generic competency lists?

Recommendations Summary

- Identify one thing that we will do differently based on what we learned.

Learning Outcomes

- What one new piece of information did you learn that will be important to you?

Point/Counterpoint

POINT

One More Time—Focus on Your Strengths (And Implications for Performance Management)

Marcus Buckingham
Author, independent consultant and speaker

The Inconvenient Facts

Study performance within any organization and you discover consistent and meaningful differences in performance among teams doing exactly the same work. Unit profitability, individual productivity, employee retention, customer satisfaction, an employee's likelihood to have an accident, to sue, or to steal—all these vary significantly within organizations.

We don't hear much about this range because it implies a lack of control and unpredictability, and for most organizations, particularly publicly traded organizations, lack of control and unpredictability are perceptions they would rather avoid.

Nonetheless, the discovery reappears whenever research is done: Some teams consistently outperform other teams who are doing exactly the same work within the same organization.

This discovery forces leaders within organizations to confront two key questions:

a. What is causing this range in performance?

b. How can we create more teams like our best teams?

The answer to the first question is that, no matter what work the teams are doing, and no matter which organizations or countries they are doing it in, this range in performance is significantly influenced by whether or not the employees on the team believe their strengths are being called upon every day. It doesn't seem to matter whether the employees are "right" in identifying what their strengths are. **What matters is simply whether the employees *feel* that their strengths are in play most of the time.**

This conclusion is drawn from a large body of research conducted over the last 15 years by the Gallup Organization. Gallup's methodology was straightforward. The researchers asked the employees in the high-performance and low-performance teams long lists of employee survey questions. Then they threw out all those questions where employees in both the high- and low-performing teams answered the same. Instead they focused on those very few questions where the high-performing teams strongly agreed and the low-performing teams did not.

After repeating this process across more than 2 million employees, tens of thousands of teams, hundreds of companies, and more than 20 countries, Gallup landed on 12 questions that showed the strongest positive correlations to team performance. (The complete list of 12 questions can be found on page 28 of the book, *First, Break All The Rules*, by Marcus Buckingham and Curt Coffman.) These questions measure the basic conditions that must be present for a team to excel. However, subsequent research reveals that one of these questions is more powerful than all the others. One of these questions shows the strongest and most consistent links to the performance of the team:

"At work, do you have the opportunity to do what you do best every day?"

The teams where most of the employees answer Strongly Agree or Agree outperform their peer teams consistently and significantly.

Obviously, getting people to feel that their strengths are being used is not the only lever a team leader should pull to build a high performing team—the leader should, of course, set clear expectations, give people the materials they need to do their work, praise them when they excel, help each person learn and grow, and draw clear connections between the work of the team and the mission of the organization as a whole.

However, the master lever is getting people to feel they are playing to their strengths most of the time. Pull it, and everything else a team leader does to build a high performing team will be multiplied. Fail to pull it and every other action to improve performance will be diminished.

Why? Because the feeling that your strengths (whatever you happen to believe them to be) are not recognized and used undermines everything else. If you feel that the best of you is not called upon every day at work, expectations always will be unclear for you; praise, even when it comes your way, will be discounted; you never will feel that your leader truly understands you or cares about your growth and development; your motivation suffers, your resilience diminishes, your performance falls, and your sense of victim-hood ("No one here really gets me") rises.

Given this finding, the answer to the second question, "How can an organization build more teams like the best teams?" now becomes: **"How can we build more teams where each person feels that his or her strengths are understood and used every day?"**

At present, organizations have shown themselves to be surprisingly ineffective at grappling with this question. The last five polls of nationally representative samples of the working population of the United States, the United Kingdom, Australia, India and China reveal that none of these countries has more than 12 percent of workers who believe that they play to their strengths at work most of the time.

Repeated surveys within individual companies reveal a similar figure. Of course, when this research is conducted with a specific company, you discover a significant range—on some teams more than 80% of people say they play to their strengths most of the time, while on other teams, teams that are doing exactly the same kind of work, 0% say they do. But those teams where the majority says they play to their strengths still outperform those teams where the majority says they don't.

However, overall, the data are unequivocal: Organizations do a poor job of addressing the single most important driver of team performance.

Let's restate this positively: Those organizations, which succeed in identifying, focusing and deploying the strengths of each employee, will immediately gain a significant competitive advantage. They will be more attractive to talent; and they will accelerate turning this talent into sustained performance.

The Performance Management Implications

Thus, to build high-performance teams, organizations need an integrated human capital system that is designed explicitly to make people feel their strengths are being called upon at work.

In the end, this integrated system will include the way the organization

- recruits people;
- selects people;
- conducts performance reviews/appraisals;
- plans succession and readiness for advancement;
- compensates people; and
- promotes people.

This is too much to tackle all at once.

In an ideal world, and following the practice of every professional sports team the world over, the best place to start would be with the recruiting and selection systems. Hiring the best makes everything go easier. However, in the world of large organizations you rarely have the luxury of filling an empty roster from scratch. Nor do you have the time to wait until candidates from your new strengths-based recruiting and selection system have filled your entire team.

Instead you are compelled to play the game right now, and to win it with the team you have. Given your situation, the best place to start is with your **performance system**.

Your performance system—the ritual of goal setting, rating and coaching that happens between each employee and his or her manager—is your pivot point. Here, during these regular conversations, is where you can make the best of the team you already have. Here is where you can instill across the entire organization the same strengths-based approach to performance. Here is where you can accelerate turning each employee's strengths into performance. Here is where you can best collect the information for identifying where each person should fit within the organization, both today and into the future, and so here is where you'll collect the information you need for accurate team-building and succession planning.

Here, finally, is where you will see the greatest and fastest turnaround.

Why? Because the performance system in most organizations is among the least productive and least popular of organizational rituals. It tends to be disappointing to the employees, frustrating to the managers, and nets little productive output for the organization. It is the equivalent, one might say, of a visit to a bad dentist: Before it happens, you don't look forward to it; while it's happening, you wish it were over; and when it's done, you rarely get the outcomes you wanted.

Five Flaws

What is wrong with most performance systems?

1. They are **remedial**. Either implicitly or explicitly, they communicate to the employees that the best way to increase their performance and their chances of promotion is to identify their areas of greatest weakness and work on improving them.

2. They are **paternalistic**. Employees are told that they are not the best judges of their strengths and weaknesses. Instead the manager is. Some performance systems do allow the employees to rate themselves, but even here the not-too-subtle message is that the manager is the ultimate authority on where the employees' strengths and weaknesses truly lie.

3. They are **infrequent**. Most performance systems are built around a once-a-year evaluation/goal setting session. Others opt for a twice-a-year rhythm. A few rely on once-a-quarter conversations. In each of these cases, the time span between conversations is so great that both the manager and the employee struggle to recreate the previous months' work and arrive at appropriately detailed examples of what the employee actually has been doing.

4. They are **isolating**. The most effective organizations are communities of mutual trust and complementary partnerships. Most performance systems do little to foster these kinds of connections. When you have your performance conversations with your manager, you know you are there to discuss *you* and *your* performance and *your* career. Rarely are you encouraged to talk about anyone else, and, even if you are, you certainly don't get a chance to see your colleagues' strengths, weaknesses, goals, plans or aspirations.

5. Finally, they are **outdated**. Generation Y is entering the workforce. Unfortunately, most performance systems, **remedial**, **paternalistic**, **infrequent**, and **isolating** as they are, appear deeply unfamiliar to this generation; and so they are rejected or, at best, passively resisted. The psychographic data on Generation Y are clear, and they resonate with the anecdotal "data." This is one of the most praised and pampered of generations—they received an award for coming in 7th on the sports field; a graduation ceremony for graduating from 2nd to 3rd grade. It is also one of the most narcissistic—their cameras are filled with pictures of themselves; they spend hour upon hour on sites such as MySpace, YouTube, and Facebook, telling the

> And now this huge cohort—twice the size of Generation X, bigger than the Boomers—is storming the workplace. Given its size, it is much more likely that this generation will change the world of work rather than the other way around.

world who they are and what they've done. This is an instinctively interconnected generation, whether IMing each other, or linking up to form virtual gaming teams, or reaching out online to find those with similar interests, fascinations, strengths. This is also a significantly more positive and volunteerist generation than either Generation X or the Boomers—they believe they can make the world a better place, and are more likely than their elders to engage in community-oriented and charitable activity. And now this huge cohort—twice the size of Generation X, bigger than the Boomers—is storming the workplace. Given its size, it is much more likely that this generation will change the world of work rather than the other way around. Those organizations that fight against this narcissistic/community-seeking/volunteerist generation—"Get back into your cubicle and pay your dues"—will lose out to those organizations that can find the right way to channel it.

> The performance system should challenge each employee to make specific commitments each week.

Four Design Principles

What should an effective performance system look like?

1. It should be **strengths-based**. Extensive research reveals that the most effective managers operate from the logic that the fastest way to turn an employee's personality into performance is to identify each employee's strengths and then target these strengths toward the goals of the team. Of course, they don't ignore a person's weaknesses, but neither do they view weaknesses as "areas of opportunity." Instead they see weaknesses as "areas of least opportunity." Weaknesses can be neutralized, but rarely, if ever, will they be transformed into consistent performance strengths.

2. It should be **employee-driven**. When employees join the organization they should be given access to a Web-based application—a series of customizable, interconnected, searchable Web pages—in which they are encouraged to capture their discoveries about their strengths and weaknesses, their recent successes, their weekly performance commitments, and their learnings. This application, and the content within it, must be interesting, useful and "sticky" enough for the employees to want to regularly update it—it will only be as useful as its currency. Of course, there can be some organizational coercion, such as "You *must* keep your pages up-to-date." But, this won't sustain. What will sustain is an application that plays into the narcissism/community-seeking/volunteerism of this generation and makes them actively want to share what they are doing and learning.

3. It should be **fast and frequent**. Performance is not something a manager and an employee should be thinking about once or twice a year. Instead, it should be perpetual. Inside the highest performing teams you find a constant and intense focus on what each person's goals are and what can be done now to reach these goals faster and with higher quality. The performance system should challenge each employee to make specific commitments each week about what he or she can do to put strengths into play this week. This ritual must be fast and simple, or it never will become habitual. It must be specific, or these commitments rarely will be completed. And the data within it must be able to be archived and retrieved, so that when, at the end of each quarter, the manager and the employee discuss performance over the last three months and goals for the next three months, both can refer to the vividness of the employee's week-to-week commitments.

4. It must reveal the strengths of the entire **community**. Both employees and managers should be able to view each employee's pages. The employee will be invigorated by realizing how many and varied are the strengths of the team, and will feel more intense accountability when he or she sees the kinds of commitments every other employee is making each week. The manager will get to know the current team much faster, and will be able to search the database for people who have strengths, skills and values that might improve the team. Senior managers will be able to scan the entire organization and gain a current, vivid and specific perspective on the state of their human capital.

In sum, the benefits of such a system are:

- It places responsibility for performance, learning and planning where it belongs—with the employee.
- It creates an intense and constant focus on performance—"Look what everyone else is committing to! What am I going to commit to this week?"
- It makes an organization more relevant, more in-touch with, and therefore more attractive to the incoming generation of talent.
- It invigorates the employee—"Look at the strengths of people I am surrounded by!"
- It is user-driven and therefore more likely to gather information that is current, specific and vivid—information that can be used either in coaching conversations between manager and employee or during succession planning discussions.
- It is user-driven and therefore less costly to sustain.
- It enables managers to build teams faster and with greater accuracy.

Most performance systems, which so often lapse into bureaucratic "going-through-the-motions," are the antithesis of this. The alternative is a system that fits the design principles just described, strengths-based, self-directed, and explicitly interconnected. We are developing just such a system—we call it an iStrengths system—and we look forward to hearing and learning from the comments of other professionals about our ideas and approach.

COUNTERPOINTS

COUNTERPOINT

Edward E. Lawler III
Distinguished Professor of Business, University of Southern California Marshall School of Business. Founder and Director of the Center for Effective Organizations (CEO)

I find myself in agreement with most of the points in Buckingham's piece, but worry that they are a bit simplistic. Unfortunately, it just is not as easy as he makes it seem to improve the effectiveness of organizations. Let's start with his point that high performance is linked to people doing what they do best.

Yes! Decades of research by others than the Gallup Organization have shown this to be true. But my work with Richard Hackman in the 1960s showed that this is only one factor that leads to high job performance. We found that in order to be motivating, work needs to provide feedback, involve a whole or complete piece of work, and provide individuals or groups with meaningful autonomy with respect to how the work is performed. Unfortunately, it is not always possible to create jobs that are engaging and motivating. Technology, customers and cost factors get in the way, but when you can do it, the evidence is clear that it is worth doing.

Buckingham's points about performance management are generally on target, but incomplete. I couldn't agree more with the point that organizations don't do a good job of designing and implementing performance management systems. The same goes for his comment that these systems need to be part of an integrated human capital system. This point is at the core of my new book, *Talent*. What I am not sure of is that performance management is the best place to start an improvement effort. Getting it out in front in a change effort runs the risk (indeed, the likelihood) of a failure from which it may be difficult to recover.

I agree that the five flaws Buckingham cites are common and often fatal, but they are not necessarily the most critical. For example, one he doesn't mention is senior leadership. All too often performance reviews are what the top level in an organization tells the middle to do to the bottom. As a result of this, it doesn't work for anyone.

I am in general agreement with Buckingham's four design principles, but I would state them a bit differently. For example, with respect to their being strengths-based, I would say they should be skill and competency based in a way that recognizes the organizational capabilities and competencies that are needed to make the business successful. It cannot be all about what the strengths of individuals are. I should add I am a big believer in using pay for skills rather than jobs because it motivates individuals to develop their skills: People can learn and develop!

Finally, I agree that feedback should be ongoing and that the Web can help. My research strongly supports that ongoing feedback is a key determinant of the effectiveness of a performance management system. Moving performance management to the Web has the potential to make performance management an integral part of the way work and people are organized and managed. It can lead to efficient, self-organizing systems and goal-based organizations. I don't think we are very knowledgeable about how to do this yet, but I think we are learning that performance management, which has not worked well in hierarchical organizations, can actually be key in creating less bureaucratic organizations.

COUNTERPOINT

Lynda Gratton
Professor of Management Practice,
London Business School

When Gary Hamel and I asked a group of 20 CEOs at London Business School what was the process that was most broken in their companies, we expected them to talk about production or quality—or even perhaps some manufacturing process. They did not. Almost all said that the process that most irritated and annoyed them was performance management. The emotion in the room was running really high. It was not just that they believed it was broken—they absolutely hated it. They hated the bureaucracy, they hated the form filling, and they hated the ranking.

I have occasionally reflected on this conversation. It is clear that while many companies have been great at innovating their services and products—few (if any) have really innovated management practices such as rewards or performance management. If we have third generation technologies, we also have second-generation managers—and first generation performance management practices. They feel arcane to me as a "Baby Boomer"—and when I talk to my MBA students recently recruited to companies - they describe these processes as positively Neanderthal.

How did we get into this mess—for as the CEOs testify so clearly, it is indeed a mess.

We have always known that good managers, as Drucker pointed out decades ago, give clear, frequent, positive feedback. My own research on cooperation supports this. One of the most crucial organizational levers in the creation of cooperative working environments and collaborative teams is managers who coach and mentor others. This simple action has a profoundly positive effect on others. It demonstrates caring and builds trust and is perhaps one of the most important gifts managers can give to their colleagues—the gift of their undivided attention.

Across the world people engaged in what has been called "positive psychology" have shown that good management practice—supporting others, providing an opportunity for people to flourish and encouraging their development—makes for happier people, better functioning teams and higher performing companies.

The question HR professionals face is how to realize and act on this simple truth.

In his point article Marcus argues that strengths-based integrated system will be a way out of this morass—and that a strengths-based performance system is a good place to start. His analysis of the five flaws is spot on—as the CEOs that Gary and I spoke to will attest. There is no doubt in my mind that his four design principles would make a real difference.

The question the design principles raise is "how can we transform a company so these principles are lived on a day-to-day basis." Here are some thoughts:

- *Excite through good practice:* Take a look at where some of these practices are already building. Consider for example professionals in the consulting firm McKinsey & Company who are required to complete an annual description of what they have done to build their human capital, or the performance management process at Goldman Sachs that meticulously collects feedback data from a whole community of peers and colleagues. These good practices can provide inspiration and insight.

- *Experiment at the margins:* Make sure that you are continuously experimenting with new ways of working. For example, BT's innovative approach to managing the performance of a team would never have become widespread without a series of experiments in their Cardiff office that showed how this innovation could work.

- *Create signature processes:* As Tammy Erickson and I argued in a recent *HBR* article (March 2007), good practice can be a real spur to action—but great companies also invent their own "signature experience" that sets them apart. By explicitly communicating what makes your firm unique, you can dramatically improve employee engagement and performance.

Performance management is way past its sell-by date. As Marcus argues, now is the time to reinvigorate, refresh and renew.

COUNTERPOINT

Arthur Yeung
Associate Dean and Philips Chair Professor,
China Europe International Business
School, People's Republic of China

Drawing upon an extensive database of more than 2 million employees from hundreds of companies in more than 20 countries, Marcus Buckingham and his associates at Gallup discovered that the single most powerful question that explains and predicts an employee's performance is: **"At work, do you have the opportunity to do what you do best every day?"** It is indeed an interesting and provoking insight as it challenges management scholars and practitioners to rethink and redesign management practices that can capitalize on employee strengths for better performance, instead of wasting unnecessary energy and efforts to fix their weaknesses or work on tasks that underutilize their talent.

processes to capitalize on their strengths; c) encouraged and challenged to accurately understand what their strengths and weaknesses really are rather than basing their understanding on an inflated

kinds of tasks? Will such a performance system universally be applicable to all organizations and employees, or only relevant to specific kinds of companies or jobs? My preliminary judgment (without empirical support) is that such a system would work better for knowledge intensive workers who can perform their tasks relatively independently. For manufacturing workers who need to work interdependently in a production line, it seems that such a system would be less relevant. Also, will such a performance system work well in different national cultures? Will it work in countries like Japan or China where paternalistic cultures still prevail? It would be helpful if Buckingham could be more specific in defining in what kinds of industries, jobs, or national cultures such a performance system will be most effective.

> Will such a performance system universally be applicable to all organizations and employees, or only relevant to specific kinds of companies or jobs?

Along the same line of thought, Buckingham's practical concern is, then, to address the question: **"How can companies build more teams where each person feels that his or her strengths are understood and used every day?"** In Buckingham's opinion, the most important lever companies should work on to capitalize on employee strengths is a brand new performance system that is strengths-based, employee-driven, fast and frequent, and community-oriented. The system is designed to place greater responsibility and initiative for performance, learning, and planning with employees (instead of being over-managed by managers) and to enhance employee control (at least, feeling) that their strengths are in play most of the time. If that happens, Buckingham believes that employees can achieve better performance.

Buckingham has indeed clearly laid out his arguments with solid empirical data. He also has attempted to introduce an innovative performance system with interesting promises. To provoke discussion and to think through such an innovative performance system from a variety of perspectives, I would like to highlight some of my concerns and challenges, as follows:

1. While I strongly concur that creating an environment where employees can capitalize on their strengths for better performance is the right approach for companies, I don't think such an end-state can be achieved primarily through employee initiative. I believe managers (not employees) still should be ultimately held accountable for creating such an environment by making sure employees are: a) assigned tasks, projects, and responsibilities that they are good at; b) provided with adequate decision-making authority, IT support, and streamlined

confidence in their capabilities (as argued by Buckingham, potential problems of Generation Y); and d) stretched to go beyond their comfort zone and what they are currently good at (avoid over-capitalizing on their current strengths). At least in rapidly emerging economies like China, where employee maturity is still lacking (especially in the new generation workforce who are raised as the single child in their families), I believe it will take a lot of time and support before the ideal of such an employee-driven performance system can be realized.

2. A performance system, no matter how great it is, has limited impact unless it is aligned with and supported by other HR systems simultaneously. Given the kind of radically different performance system Buckingham is proposing, companies also need to dramatically realign and redesign other HR systems at the same time to ensure the effectiveness of the new performance system. HR professionals also need to carefully think through other design questions like: How to translate company goals into individual employee goals in a systematic and coherent way if employees are allowed to decide their performance plan? How to determine an employee's salary increase, promotion, and bonus in a fair and consistent manner based on the new performance system?

3. While the proposed performance system that is strengths-based, employee-driven, fast and frequent, and community-oriented appeals greatly to me intuitively (though I somehow feel that it is too good to be true), I wonder how applicable such a performance system is to companies operating in different industries and to employees performing different

Once again, I believe capitalizing on employee strengths for better performance is a great approach that companies should explore further and work towards. Buckingham has made a good step to introduce a new performance system that may be able to put such a strengths-based approach into action. However, as in any other management innovation, it also entails significant risks and possible pitfalls that should be fully assessed and considered. Having said that, it doesn't mean human resource management should stop innovating. On the contrary, I think our field desperately needs great breakthroughs to keep up with changing business realities created by globalization, technological advancement, and changing employee demographics.

COUNTERPOINT

Ranjan Acharya
Joseph George Anjilvelil
WIPRO, Ltd.
Bangalore, India

The refrain of positive psychology comes through strikingly on reading Marcus Buckingham's proposal to replace remedial, paternalistic, infrequent and outdated performance management systems with strengths-based, employee-driven, community-generated designs. That such a refrain should sound somewhat familiar is due to the flood of visionary writing that recently has engulfed our managerial senses, Gary Hamel (2007) being one of the more radical protagonists.

Since the premise is that strengths seem to determine performance accomplishment, we think it useful to dip into some reflected wisdom from our experience. There is a strand of trait-based thinking that permeates the strengths-based fabric of performance management. So, why is it, we wonder in our part of the world, that our workplace neighbor can be expected to repress his emotions with his colleagues and yet yell his heart out at a cricket stadium? We think that emotional restraint is not merely a function of inner personality traits, but a veritable interaction between the person's inner need and the situation in which it is to be exhibited. Hence, what may be a sure strength may at times be suppressed, and in turn give rise to multiple strengths based on the role one is expected to play in a work context. The samurai warrior need not, therefore, keep smashing every conceivable person on the street to prove his or her combat prowess.

Human beings are known to be amazing learners, and learning accentuates some strengths, while suppressing others with several possible variations in behavior. Hence the question before us becomes, "Do strengths by themselves facilitate requisite behaviors?" Of late, we also have begun to appreciate that behaviors are not so much caused by learnt consequences, as much as by the perception of consequences, and most significantly, by the antecedents to that behavior. On not being able to achieve sales targets, and consequently being negatively rewarded, a sales manager's commitment to the next year's planning exercise is moderated downwards. The antecedent for this consequence that lay in planning is now the more causative influence of this behavior. Over time, the certainty of the consequence and its immediacy qualifies one's choice of behaviors. The faster and more frequent such a performance management practice becomes, the more certain and immediate will be the eventual perception of consequence. In fact, certainty of a consequence would outweigh the positive and/or negative nature of any eventual reward.

Marcus quotes national samples from diverse nations such as USA, UK, Australia, China and India to point out that not more than 12% of workers believe that they play to their strengths at work most of the time. Now, for what patterns we read of cultures, say by the Hofstede traditions (1980), we quickly may note that high power-distance and relatively high collectivistic cultures like India and China seem to be no different on performing to one's best than their apparently opposite cultures like the U.S. and the U.K. From Trompenaars' framework, even rules of thumb like Particularism (India, China) and Universalism (U.S., U.K., Australia) seem to be irrelevant differentiators to working to one's strengths.

Additionally, Gilmore and Pine (1999) captured the dilemma of engagement as the challenge of managing employee energy. Is it possible that organizations carry different levels of employee energy, and that not more than 12% need to feel engaged for overall success? Perhaps a survey respondent to the Gallup questions might stop to reflect, *Do I know what my best for today should be?* To be able to get 100% involvement everyday is not commonplace. Nature would have its ways for such phenomena. Astrophysicists do not come across new galaxies on an everyday basis.

Csíkszentmihályi's (1996) treatment of creativity is what informs us about what really sets apart the also-rans from the ones who tend to arrive. Creativity, as we may like to see in performance management paradigms, can occur only in the interrelations between the three main parts of a system: 1) The Domain—a set of symbolic rules and procedures that distinguishes one domain from another; 2) The Field—composed of individuals who act as gate-keepers to the domain; and 3) The Individual—the person who has a new idea or recognizes a new pattern to change a domain or establish a new one. "There is no way to tell whether a new thought is valuable, until it passes social evaluation." Ringing in a new paradigm is a systemic phenomenon, however incidental or influential individual thought leaders may be to a new practice of systemic proportions. The confrontation of paradigms with performance management based on strengths may be seen when stock market vagaries determine top management behaviors.

Explicitly unambiguous inputs to a defined process of reaching an end that is fixed and ideal are what lie in notions of stability amidst change (Lawler and Worley, 2006). Such processes do not take away from the positive nature of developmental processes, but inherently call for more tolerance for, and competence with, variety and perspective in our lives. Marcus thus makes a timely reminder of emergent online communities. There are more variants of such goings-on in virtual environments. For example, Intranet blogs are a veritable treasure of how employees behave in written expressive formats. Insights into mindsets and generational differences from such avenues are invaluable in mapping the performance contexts of a range of demographic groups. Beyond electronic networks in the form of the Facebooks and LinkedIns of the Internet era, social networks need to reflect the community of purpose, process and people sensitivity.

To conclude, performance management is not a problem that can be oversimplified. Merits of positivism and positive thinking around interventions notwithstanding; we must recognize at least two things: 1) Although much remedy emerges from individual awareness for action, the stronger forces that shape behavior are systemic in nature; and 2) the strengths-based approach needs to be integrated with conscious recognition of what may get in the way of effective performance. Significantly, as we started out reasoning our point of view, we concluded the strengths-based approach, if overused in the worship of effectiveness, will be derailed by environmental, cultural, structural and learning process elements within an organization.

Performance in contemporary organizations is about managing behaviors to expectations that are already set by an organization's leadership. Otherwise, leadership loses its capacity to entice its workforce to the insurmountable and employees are in danger of peaking ahead of him/her occupying a significant role. Strengths are but one view from a prism of soft data that human beings represent. Their overuse or under-utilization is a function of both the internal needs of the person and the demands of the situation or environment. If we master the manner in which to appreciate people as a collection of strengths and yet hold room for allowable weaknesses in them, the chances are that we could use strengths in a fungible manner. Role models need to stoke the passion for positive attitudes and self-correcting behaviors. Then, taking the strengths-based approach to performance management may indeed be beneficial in the long run.

REFERENCES

Csíkszentmihályi, Mihaly (1996). *Creativity—Flow and the Psychology of Discovery and Invention.* London: Harper Perennial.

Gilmore, J. and J. Pine (1999). *The Experience Economy.* Boston, MA: HBS Press

Hamel, Gary (2007). *The Future of Management*. Boston, MA: HBS Press.

Hofstede, G. (1980). *Culture's Consequences: International Differences in Work-Related Values*. Newbury Park, CA: Sage.

Lawler, Edward and Christopher Worley (2006). "Winning Support for Organizational Change: Designing Employee Reward Systems that Keep on Working." *Ivey Business Journal Online, March 2006.*

COUNTERPOINT

Niko Canner
Managing Partner, Katzenbach Partners

Organizations tragically fail to leverage the strengths of their people. They leave on the table the best of what individuals can offer and disengage employees in ways that impact every aspect of their performance. A great many people have read Buckingham's excellent books; few have been willing to make the hard choices required to create strengths-based organizations.

The human resource processes—selection, performance management, and incentives—represent only one battalion in the army arrayed against the strengths-based approach. Buckingham begins with the observation that there is too little focus on the "inconvenient fact" of performance variability. Our own observation is that

most companies are *so* afraid of variability that they fall prey to the *prescriptive fallacy*. They devote tremendous analytical resources to finding the best process, the best policy, the best script that they can dictate from the center to large numbers of employees with inconveniently divergent identities and skills. They enforce adherence to this recipe, and wait for variability to decline. (Ironically, this approach structurally resembles the kind of research that finds the one best question—the strengths question—that differentiates strong teams from weak teams across a two million-employee database.)

Best practices are important to know, and large-data-set analysis is a powerful tool. But the strengths-based organization

needs to begin with a willingness to allow employees to exercise judgment and to apply different strengths in different ways within some reasonable set of boundaries. What is difficult about this, which has very little to do with HR as traditionally conceived, is summoning the willingness to bear the organizational anxiety that comes from variability in practices in return for the results that come from highly-engaged, highly-accountable employees striving to achieve clear performance targets in diverse ways.

Human resource processes do have an important supporting role in creating the strengths-based organization. Buckingham's encouragement to reinvent the stale ritual of traditional performance management is part of the answer. For the most part, what differentiates the very best performers in any given role from their "merely good" peers are behaviors and mindsets that come so naturally to the stars as to be introspectively invisible. There is huge incremental value in understanding at an operationally actionable level what these differentiators are and making them teachable. At T-Mobile, we analyzed what differentiates a great retail representative from a merely good one, and turned this analysis into a comic strip sequence shared with every US employee.

The objective was not just to share a finding—and certainly not in the traditional language of competencies—but to begin a discussion at the front lines about what great retailing looks like, face to face with the customer.

Applying strengths in a more consistent way is a significant driver of improved performance within a role. Development over the long arc of a career is much about *unlearning* certain strengths and the dominant behaviors that go with those strengths in order to meet new challenges in new, more senior roles. In the words of my colleague Marshall Goldsmith, "what got you here won't get you there." HR functions often fail the leaders they intend to support *both* by taking the developmental spotlight

away from their strengths *and* by neglecting to help leaders unlearn what used to work as roles change, strategies change and the essence of a leader's work evolves.

Buckingham's focus on strengths is powerful. Too many of his followers in HR, however, implement the Q12 and shy away from the essential work, much of it beyond the traditional boundaries of the HR function, of 1) addressing the barriers that operating processes present to the exercise of strengths, 2) teaching broadly the behaviors and mindsets that underlie the strengths of stars, and 3) facilitating the "unlearning" that will enable their highest-potential employees to break through the limits of where their strengths alone can take them.

COUNTERPOINT

Andy Liakopoulos
Karen McDonald
Deloitte Consulting LLP

While, for the most part we agree with Mr. Buckingham's points, as his design principles align with many of the effective performance management practices Deloitte recommends, we believe there are additional design principles upon which an organization's performance management approach should be based. Specifically, the performance management approach should also:

- **Align to the Company's Business Strategy.** While measuring employee strengths may increase employee commitment, a performance management process must primarily measure individual, team and business performance results that are aligned to their business strategy.
- **Align to a Holistic Talent Program.** Organizations implementing a strengths-based approach would do well to fully integrate the talent processes and place a priority on implementing the strengths-based approach throughout the suite of talent management processes.
- **Support Pay-for-Performance.** A highly regarded performance management process is a direct input into a total rewards process that supports pay-for-performance. Buoyed by a sound performance management process, organizations can use total rewards to differentiate pay and achieve their strategic ends. Further, recognition as part of a total rewards process is especially germane to a strengths-based approach. By using considerations other

> Best practices are important to know, and large-data-set analysis is a powerful tool.

than pay (e.g., taking time off to participate in community service), recognition can be used to encourage the development of a strengths-based culture.

- **Measure Results (What) and Competencies (How).** Our experience indicates that a performance management process also must include quantitative results to be fully effective

- **Reveal Information Only When Needed.** The real value of gathering information on employee strengths is that employees can use knowledge of their own strengths to help them make career choices.

- **Strive for Consistency and Accuracy.** Organizations should use calibration meetings to increase the consistency and accuracy of performance ratings. The investment will be rewarded when employees demonstrate an increased commitment to an improved performance management process.

Any organization implementing a performance management process, strengths-based or otherwise, should migrate the remaining talent processes to a strengths-based approach as soon as possible. Key implementation components should:

- **Align Career Development Capability.** Integrate the career development capability into the performance management process. Employees will need access to a career development process and tools with guidance from their managers and other coaches. Consequently, organizations must invest in their career development processes and coaching training in order to prepare managers to engage in an ongoing "career conversation" tied to long-term career goals rather than just a performance discussion, no matter how frequently.

- **Identify Critical Workforce Segments (CWS).** By implementing the strengths-based approach across CWSs (Segments of the workforce that deliver disproportionately higher value), organizations can realize the benefits of enhanced productivity from increased commitment within these segments.

- **Develop a Coaching Culture.** Deloitte's research on Gen Y indicates that while they are open to adhering to the current talent programs such as performance management, Gen Y (as do all four generations in the workplace) value coaching and mentoring.

- **Remember to Utilize Technology.** By fully leveraging technology, employees

and managers can capture data once and at the source. Once this data is captured, it can be used to develop a richer picture of an employee's career than would otherwise be available.

Finally, prepare the organization for an effective transition through a coordinated training and communications program that builds skills and communicates the business case for change.

COUNTERPOINT

Lee J. Konczak
Olin Business School,
Washington University

If given the choice between two personal investments of similar risk, one having a high probability of returning 4-5% and the other having a high probability of paying 10%-12%, which would you choose? The answer is obvious but yet when it comes to investing in the time and energy of employees, managers focus heavily on skill deficits and competency gaps—foregoing potentially higher-ROI solutions and more substantial performance improvements. As Peter Drucker (1999) noted, "one cannot build performance on weaknesses, let alone something one cannot do at all" (page 66). Drucker also noted that most people think they know what they are good at, but they are usually wrong.

Shifting the focus to an individual's strengths when assessing performance, making job assignments and placement decisions and determining promotions in line with succession plans makes good business sense, but how can an organization increase the likelihood that managers change their behaviors and pull the "master lever" more consistently? Buckingham aptly chronicles the problems with many performance management (PM) systems and offers some viable and creative solutions along these lines, particularly for those employees in the Generation Y age group. The observations that most PM systems focus on weaknesses and provide infrequent feedback driven primarily by the manager are certainly sentiments that would be shared by many HR professionals. But these are *transactional* aspects of PM. There are two other critical factors that need to be in place to help managers put Buckingham's ideas to work and *transform* their own thinking and the performance of their teams.

Culture Change. Implementing a new performance management system in a

culture that thinks and behaves in the "old way" won't result in positive change or add sustained value. Senior leaders have to ensure that the organization's culture supports the new system. Recent research by Hewitt Associates (2007) suggests that a key driver of successful talent management initiatives is senior leader involvement and support. I've experienced numerous initiatives that change rating formats, feedback schedules and manager training that result in "surface" changes but no underlying shift in the desired mind-set and behaviors of managers. In order for talent management systems to be optimized, culture change must occur and must be driven by senior leaders to ensure enduring behavior change.

Accountability and Reinforcement. It follows that managers must be held accountable and then recognized and rewarded for adapting new approaches and behaving differently in managing individual and team performance. I'm not referring solely to monetary rewards. Managers have to feel that their performance management responsibilities are valued and recognized for them to become engrained practices in the organization. This sense of accountability must be modeled by senior leaders and reinforced continuously for best practices in performance management to be sustained.

One final point concerns generational differences and performance management. Buckingham offers some interesting suggestions on how to engage Generation Y in the performance management process. Though generational differences are top-of-mind for many practicing managers, studies comparing different generations on workplace values and factors that facilitate work motivation find few if any significant differences (Deal, 2007; Giancola, 2006). This suggests that the real PM challenge is to create flexible systems that address the needs of the different generations in the workplace and can evolve as demographics continue to change.

REFERENCES

Deal, J. (2007). *Retiring the Generation Gap: How Employee Young and Old Can Find Common Ground.* San Francisco: Jossey-Bass.

Drucker, P. (1999). "Managing Oneself." *Harvard Business Review*, March-April, 64-74.

Giancola, F. (2006). "The Generation Gap: More Myth Than Reality." *Human Resource Planning*, 29(4), 32-37.

Hewitt (2007). "Top Companies for Leaders: Research Highlights—North America." Lincolnshire IL: Hewitt Associates.

One More Time: Focus on Your Strengths (And Implications for Performance Management)

Discovery Questions

- What are we dealing with in our organization today that relates to this content area?

- Discover ways to energize the performance of teams in our organization.

- To explore what is meant by the "inconvenient fact" of performance variability.

- Recognize what tends to wear down the commitment and engagement of employees.

- Consider the redesign of HR systems so they build up people and relationships, not tear them down.

- To think strategically about how a positive, energizing performance system could be designed.

- Recognize the importance of coaching and mentoring.

Selected Facts

- What new facts that were presented got your attention?

- Across over 2 million respondents, the item that most predicted performance was: "At work, do you have the opportunity to do what you do best every day?"

- Across the US, UK, Australia, India and China, no country has more than 12% of respondents believing they play to their strengths every day.

- Those organizations that succeed in identifying, focusing and deploying the strengths of each employee will immediately gain a significant competitive advantage.

- What different expectations do Generation Y employees have?

- Generation Y is twice the size of Generation X.

Key Discussion Points

- What were the key points being made in this Point Counterpoint presentation?

- How do you account for meaningful differences between teams doing the same work?

- Lack of control and unpredictability of performance—how do public companies react?

- How can we create more teams like our best performing teams?

- How do you respond to the assertion: "the performance system in most organizations is among the least productive and least popular of organizational rituals."

- Assess your organization's performance review system on the issues of: "Remedial; Paternalistic; Infrequent; Isolating; and Outdated."

- Assess how well our performance management system addresses the following design principles: Strengths Based; Employee Driven; Fast & Frequent; and Show the Strengths of the Entire Team.

- Does our system try to convert weaknesses to strengths? Is that a good idea?

- What does it mean to appeal to the narcissistic, community seeking, volunteerism of Generation Y?

- Lawler presents research from the 1960s that showed that for work to be motivating, it needs to provide feedback, involve a whole or complete piece of work, and provide meaningful autonomy on how work is performed. Is that still relevant today?

- What do you think of the assertion: "All too often performance reviews are what the top level in an organization tells the middle to do to the bottom; and as a result it doesn't work for anyone"?

- Why do you think that a group of CEOs had such a strong negative reaction to the design of performance management systems that requires extensive form filling, bureaucracy and ranking?

- Do organizational "Best Practices" too greatly restrict and smother the creativity of employees finding new and better ways?

- Discuss the issue: "Organizations should use calibration meetings to increase the consistency and accuracy of performance ratings."

- What can our senior leaders do to model the importance of effective feedback?

Review of Solutions

- Identify 2-3 Big Ideas that are worthy of exploring for our organization.

- Should we redesign our performance management system?

Recommendations Summary

- Identify one thing that we will do differently based on what we learned.

Learning Outcomes

- What one new piece of information did you learn that will be important to you?

Perspectives—Point/Counterpoint

Anna Tavis, Perspectives Editor

This *Point/Counterpoint* focuses on the broadly debated topic of talent management in the 21st century. We invited Peter Cappelli of the Wharton School to lead the discussion with this provocative thesis: *A Supply Chain Model for Talent Management*. Cappelli launches a spirited debate among the diverse group of human resources consultants, academics and corporate practitioners from the United States, Europe and Asia. Also joining in the HR debate is Jamie Flinchbaugh, a supply-chain and lean-manufacturing specialist and the founder of the Lean Center. Together the discussants present an emerging picture of talent management as a customized, agile and business- and culture-aligned process. The bottom line is a shared responsibility among HR, business leadership, management—and employees themselves. Your response to this discussion will be much appreciated. Please write to us at **perspectives@hrps.org**.

A Supply Chain Model for Talent Management

Peter Cappelli, University of Pennsylvania

Talent management is the process through which employers anticipate and meet their needs for human capital. Getting the right people with the right skills into the right jobs—a common definition of talent management—is the basic people-management challenge in any organization. While talent management often focuses on managerial and executive positions, the issues involved apply to all jobs that are difficult to fill.

Failures in talent management may be more recognizable than the concept itself. Those failures include mismatches between supply and demand: on the one hand, having too many employees (leading to layoffs and restructurings), and on the other hand, having too little talent or not being able to find the skills that are needed. These mismatches are among the biggest challenges that employers face. During the past generation, many employers have lurched from surpluses of talent to shortfalls and back again. Something is wrong with this picture.

Most talent-management practices, especially in the United States, fall into two equally dysfunctional camps:

- The first and most common is to do nothing. Make no attempt to anticipate your needs and develop no plans for addressing them. Recent survey data suggest that about two-thirds of all U.S. employers are in this category. Making no attempt to anticipate and plan for needs means relying on outside hiring, a reactive approach that has begun to fail now that the costs and difficulty of finding candidates has risen.

- The second strategy, which is common among older companies, relies on complex bureaucratic models of forecasting and succession planning from the 1950s. These legacy systems grew up in an era when business was highly predictable. These models fail now because they are inaccurate and unresponsive. They also are costly in the face of uncertainty.

A New Way to Think About Talent Management

Helping the organization achieve its goals begins with recognizing that the most important problem faced by virtually all employers is uncertainty. This results in a need for a more rapid response to changes in competitive environments. Employers now change strategies, structures and operations quickly and repeatedly in answer to customer demands, competitor innovations, regulatory changes and other outside factors. The developments driving these responses are difficult to predict, and mistakes in responding—waiting too long to change or planning for circumstances that fail to pan out—are costly.

There are two great risks in talent management:

- First, there are inherent costs in a mismatch of employees and skills (not enough talent to meet business demands, or too much, leading to layoffs or a poor fit between individual attributes and requirements).

Second, the costs of losing your investments in talent through the failure to retain employees.

The risk-management problem facing talent management is analogous to problems already analyzed in the field of operations research. For example, the practical definition of talent management, getting the right person in the right job at the right time, is identical to the basic task of supply chains. Perhaps not surprisingly, it is newer companies—and often those outside the United States where the talent crunch is greatest—that are the innovators because they have no stake in the older practices. Their innovations, along with basic lessons on managing risk from supply-chain management, led me to formulate four key principles for managing talent in the contemporary environment, where uncertainty is the major challenge.

Principle 1: "Make and Buy" to Manage Demand-side Risk

Risk has two aspects: the uncertainty of a given outcome occurring and the costs of that outcome. It may be possible to reduce somewhat the uncertainty associated with business outcomes through better forecasting, but it is easier to make progress in managing risk by understanding and then reducing the costs of mistakes.

Over the past generation, many employers have lurched from surpluses of talent to shortfalls and back again. Something is wrong with this picture.

For example, it is difficult to forecast with accuracy how many units of some product will be needed, but it is relatively easy to know the costs of not having enough product and services to meet demand (losing opportunities as a result) versus the costs of exceeding demand (producing inventory). Cost effectiveness demands that we choose the amount to supply that minimizes both costs. In other words, it is not enough simply to estimate the demand. To minimize costs you need to know what the costs will be when you are wrong, as you inevitably will be in an uncertain world.

A deep bench of talent is inventory. Unlike other forms of inventory, talent does not willingly stay on the shelf until it is called on. It walks out the door for better opportunities elsewhere.

Producing too little talent may be less of a concern than in the past because it is almost always possible to hire from the outside to make up any shortfall in talent.

Although the cost of outside hires typically is greater than the cost of candidates developed internally, that difference pales in comparison to the cost of losing a developed candidate to a competitor.

Producing too much talent, or having a "deep bench" as some describe it, is now very costly. A deep bench of talent is inventory. And unlike other forms of inventory, talent does not willingly stay on the shelf until it is called on. It walks out the door for better opportunities elsewhere.

The way to deal with the costs of uncertainty above is "make *and* buy," choosing the mix of internal development and outside hiring to minimize the risk and associated costs of being wrong in our forecasts. In most cases, that means beginning with the best workforce forecasts we have and then planning a level of internal development to make certain that we minimize the risk of "inventory," or overshooting the actual demand for talent and then making up any shortfall through excess hiring.

Principle 2: Reduce the Uncertainty in Talent Demand

The business needs we must predict are more complex than any contemporary forecasting techniques can handle: markets contain more competitors that innovate faster, businesses react to their competitors' strategies more quickly and the options for doing business (outsourcing, joint ventures, acquisitions, etc.) are greater. Long-term succession plans in particular are mistakes because they assume that we know what jobs will need to be filled in the future and what current employees will be around to fill them. Many companies update their succession plans every year to try to keep up with the fact that jobs change and individuals leave. As a practical matter, how useful is a plan if it must be changed every year? What problem is it solving?

A better approach is to take that uncertainty as given and find ways to manage it. One way to reduce the effects of uncertainty is to use the principle of portfolios. To apply this concept to talent management, consider the ➤

part I: talent management

idea of talent pools, where you avoid developing employees to fit narrow, specialized jobs. Instead, you develop a group of employees with broad and general competencies that should fit into a range of jobs. Once the candidates are developed, you can allocate them to the actual vacancies, as opposed to trying to guess years in advance where vacancies will occur and what individuals should be slotted into them. The fit between candidate and specific job may be less than perfect. But just-in-time training and coaching can help close the gap.

Principle 3: Earn a Return on Investments in Developing Employees

How can we recoup investments in employees when the need for their skills is uncertain in the long run and they can walk out the door, taking those skills with them? One way to improve the payoff from development is to rely on shorter, more accurate forecasts and improve the odds that the investments will pay off. Lessons from supply chain management can help here as well.

Consider the problem of bringing a new class of candidates into an organization. For those employers who hire people directly out of college, an alternative arrangement hires half the new class in June and the other half at the end of the summer in September. Instead of 100 developmental assignments, now the program needs to find only 50 in June and then rotate the new hires through them in

three months. The June cohort steps out of those roles at the end of the summer when the September cohort steps into them. Then rather than having to find 100 permanent assignments in September for the June cohort, the organization need find only 50, and so on. The more important advantage is that hiring forecasts can be shorter and more accurate. This eases the match with the first developmental assignment and then with every set of assignments along the progression of that cohort.

An important way to deal with the problem of recouping investments in development is to get employees to share the costs. Employees are now the main beneficiaries of investments in their development because of their ability to cash them in on the open market. The simplest way that individuals contribute to the costs of their own development is by taking on learning projects voluntarily, perhaps in addition to their nor-

mal work. Assuming that the candidates are more or less contributing their usual performance in their regular jobs and their pay has not increased, they essentially are doing these development projects for free.

Several companies now offer promising employees the opportunity to volunteer for projects working with their leadership team sometimes restricting them to projects outside their current functional area to broaden their experience. The employees get access to company leaders, a broadening experience and good professional contacts, all of which will surely pay off later. But they pay for it. Similarly, tuition reimbursement programs in which employers pay college tuition and the employees attend classes on their own time offer another way to share the investment in development.

The most important approach to developing employees increases the value of employee contributions by speeding the process that gets them to jobs that add greater value to the organization. This approach requires that you spot talent and potential early on and then give the employees opportunities to advance faster than they otherwise might. Many companies are moving away from the difficult task of

> Long-term succession plans in particular are mistakes because they assume that we know what jobs will need to be filled in the future and what current employees will be around to fill them.

> An important way to deal with the problem of recouping investments in development is to get employees to share the costs. Employees are now the main beneficiaries of investments in their development because of their ability to cash them in on the open market.

their ability to cash them in on the open market. The simplest way that individuals contribute to the costs of their own development is by taking on learning projects voluntarily, perhaps in addition to their nor-

attempting to predict who is ready for what new job and toward a self-nomination model. The best of these provide opportunities to literally try out a role to see how they do. If you want to see who can lead a team, here is nothing better than giving various people the chance to try it. Finding opportunities like these, in which candidates can fail quickly and inexpensively, is a key element of developing talent and an important task for line managers in the talent management process. That takes us to our final talent management principle.

Principle 4: Balance Employee Interests by Using an Internal Market

Career decisions—making matches between individuals and jobs—used to be the most important task performed by the executives and managers in charge of talent management. Internal job boards, where employees bid on posted openings and through which virtually all internal job moves now take place, coincided with employers giving up on career planning. They effectively turned over the problem of managing one's career to employees. Employees, rather than the employer, now initiate job changes and drive career paths.

Although there are many benefits to this new approach, one drawback for employers is

that they have much less control over their internal talent. Programs that attempt to mitigate that risk by negotiating a balance between the employee's and the employer's interests in career advancement are one of the truly new developments in talent management. Some of these efforts simply involve providing information about career paths and descriptions of how individuals have advanced in the past. Others go much further, attempting to negotiate compromises between the preferences of the organization and those of the employee.

It is fair to say, though, that most organizations have not yet thought through how to handle the challenge of managing a more open internal market for talent. Whether employers are willing to let it become a real market, where internal hiring managers are allowed to compete for internal talent by raising wages or making their jobs more attractive, is an open question.

How to Manage Talent on Demand

The new way of managing talent described here is fundamentally different from what has

come before it, first because it takes as its starting point organizational goals and not human resource targets. Its purpose is to help the organization perform, and it does that by managing the talent risks that are generated by uncertainty in business demand and the new, more open labor markets. The new approach to talent management may help to resuscitate the development of managerial talent, something that risks being choked off because employers cannot envision how to make it work in the current environment.

The lack of internal development of talent has increased the demand for outside hiring, which in turn causes retention problems elsewhere, undercuts the ability to develop talent internally and creates a vicious circle that erodes managerial talent. The only way forward is to recognize these problems and adapt to the uncertainty that drives them.

Peter Cappelli is George W. Taylor Professor of Management and the director at the Center for Human Resources at the Wharton School, University of Pennsylvania.

THE U.S. PERSPECTIVES

An Agreement, a Disagreement and an Added Risk

Don Ruse, Axiom Consulting Partners

I find myself in agreement with much of what my esteemed colleague, Peter Cappelli, has to say about the need to think and act differently when managing talent and the benefits

of applying the concepts of supply chain management to do so.

I think the most important point Cappelli makes, and one that I hope everyone who reads his perspective takes to heart, is that managing talent should not just focus on managerial and executive positions. This is a myopic and failed approach that does not recognize the importance of roles outside the management ranks. In today's information- and innovation-based business world, scientific, technical, creative and customer-facing roles often have a greater impact on a

company's success than do managerial and executive roles.

Companies such as Corning, Inc. and 3M have taken this to heart and applied two additional key business concepts from marketing and finance—segmentation and portfolio management—to understand and manage the relative value and impact that roles (not people) have in achieving their strategic objectives. This understanding enables them to effectively manage their talent as a portfolio of assets and make informed decisions regarding investments and divestments in tal-

➤

part I: talent management

ent segments (i.e., roles) based on their relative value and contribution to strategy.

While I agree that the complexity of our global business environment makes it more difficult to forecast future talent needs, I respectfully disagree that contemporary workforce planning processes cannot handle them. What may have been true for static and inflexible approaches developed in the last century is not true about today's planning processes: they are different. Axiom Consulting Partners (along with other firms such as Aruspex) has helped companies implement strategic workforce planning processes that are fully capable of forecasting future talent needs across a variety of scenarios within today's complex business environment.

These processes, modeled after strategic planning processes, provide complex analytic capabilities as well as the foresight and insight necessary to make informed decisions regarding the type and allocation of talent investments needed to execute strategy. They enable companies to strategically and tactically manage their talent portfolio—even in the most global of business environments.

Finally, Cappelli states that the greatest risks in talent management are the cost of mismatches in employees and skills and the cost of losing your investments in talent through turnover. While I agree with both, I believe there is a third and maybe even more significant risk that should be added—the cost of paying for a disengaged workforce that has both the capability and capacity to contribute but chooses not to because the organization fails to provide an environment and value proposition that motivates employees to give their very best. I have seen many clients make significant investments to improve their ability to attract, develop and retain talent while at the same time scratch their heads about the top- and bottom-line results these investments *fail* to return.

A key tenet of supply chain management is to develop strong partnerships with your suppliers that result in their working not only for, but with, your organization to deliver great products and services to your customers. Companies should apply this lesson in managing talent.

Developing a true partnership with your employees requires that you create a win-win relationship by meeting the key needs and desires of employees as well as those of the company and its shareholders. Creating and maintaining such a partnership can significantly improve the creativity, flexibility, productivity and retention of your talent—all of which are critical to your ability to match talent supply with talent demand.

> **Don Ruse** is a partner with Axiom Consulting Partners.

Dialogue: The Critical Element

Kim Nugent

Peter Cappelli presents a holistic, systems approach to addressing talent management with his supply chain model. Perhaps at no time in recent memory has the "brokenness" in talent management and a need for a different approach been found than in this economy. However, based on my experience, many employers have not reached the point of sophistication to embrace this supply chain approach.

Optimizing the match of supply and demand to get the right people in the right jobs hing-

es on the workforce planning component of talent management. However, this process, according to a 2004 Conference Board Study, "Integrated and Integrative Talent Management," is one of the talent programs that is least mature and least integrated with other talent processes in many organizations.

Many would benefit from Cappelli's system view; however, many are not there because

> Managing talent should not just focus on managerial and executive positions. This is a myopic and failed approach that does not recognize the importance of roles outside the management ranks.

executives still look at talent management as an HR versus business process. To have talent on demand, one cannot underestimate the required executive commitment and involvement or what might be needed for them to disengage from the current state. Executives must own workforce segmentation and their "make or buy" talent decisions. They also must make their philosophy real through their actions, such as "talent management is a shared responsibility among the employer, managers and employees versus an employee's responsibility alone."

In addition, many employers invest time in the data definition and collection aspects of talent management (i.e., "What are we going to track and rate? How can we pull up facts about people to match them to openings?") at the expense of investing in effective dialogue. Dialogue is where decisions about the talent supply play out. Through dialogue, employees thoughtfully create and discuss their self-assessment, focusing on aligning strengths, values and interests with opportunities. Dialogue is where leaders become aware of their derailers, and dialogue, when done poorly, can have unintended consequences on the motivation levels of the best performers.

Furthermore, these discussions, which are the foundation of shaping employees' performance and development, can be made richer by embracing some of the "portfolio" and development concepts Cappelli identifies. In particular, employers need to improve their ability to coach and broker assignments around a desired future "portfolio" of capabilities that the organization needs (versus having back-ups identified for a list of destination positions). Employers would further benefit from understanding how different programs, such as compensation, are shaping their capability portfolio. For example, compensation design can sometimes reinforce what roles and assignments individuals pursue, leading to further unintended mismatches between supply and demand.

Last, employers cannot achieve meaningful dialogue if they are not strategic about their HRIS approach, including the development and/or purchase of their talent management applications. If technology is overly cumbersome with disconnected applications, data feeds and outputs for decision making, employers will never get to the rich discussions. Also, employers need to focus on designing integrated processes first before jumping to the technology solutions and data elements.

Kim Nugent is a Boston-based independent human capital consultant.

Optimizing Workforce Planning Processes

Elise Freedman, Watson Wyatt Worldwide

I agree with many of the points Peter Cappelli made in his article. First and foremost, a vast majority of companies could optimize the way they are doing workforce planning. Companies cannot afford to bring in employees whose skills and competencies are not a match for what the organization needs nor can they afford to let their key employees walk out the door. While it is very challenging to predict the future, especially in these economic times, there are still many ways an organization can improve its workforce planning practices—to predict what is needed and determine the best ways to obtain talent.

Our research also supports Cappelli's recommendations on creating pools of talent versus simply identifying specific people for specific positions. I also agree that career development needs to be a shared process. The

also need to guide employees on how to develop the skills required to obtain these opportunities—especially how to close specific skill gaps. In addition, organizations need to communicate the process for pursuing other internal options to grow one's career. For example, will it be against company culture if an employee openly pursues an opportunity in another business unit or function? This type of issue should be addressed to encourage a culture of strong engagement and growth, and companies must have the right systems to support internal career boards and expressions of interest.

It is a business decision to "make or buy" talent and it starts with a clear understanding of your business needs and the makeup of your current workforce. Making this decision is difficult if you do not have all the information required, such as how difficult will it be to hire specific roles externally or the level of investment needed to develop talent. Organizations have tended to focus their measurement activities on elements that are easiest to measure but with lower business value (e.g., average age and service) as opposed to areas with greater business value (e.g., productivity and costs).

During events such as downsizing and restructuring, it is especially important to consider workforce planning. Workforce planning considerations typically are included only after the process has begun and to a limited extent. As a result, many companies take a reactive rather than proactive approach to their staffing strategy and decision making. The economic crisis has heightened this. Too many companies have made workforce decisions to cut costs without properly considering the long-term impact on their ability to meet future business demands.

Adding to what Cappelli has mentioned, Watson Wyatt also has found the following critical to the success of workforce planning:

- Workforce planning must be viewed as a business process versus an HR process.

Many employers invest time in the data definition and collection aspects of talent management at the expense of investing in effective dialogue. Dialogue is where decisions about the talent supply play out.

A supply chain systems view is the right view when owned by executives. However, in absence of this ownership, talent management could remain an HR data collection effort and result in limited energy focused on elevating the richness of the dialogue, so critical to shaping talent supply and aligning it with demand.

organization and the employee both need to provide inputs and outputs to the process. Gathering information about employees' skills, interests and experiences is critical.

Organizations need to communicate clearly the job opportunities (including key requirements) that are available and possible. They

part I: talent management

- Start with a few critical positions; do not try to "boil the ocean."

- The talent acquisition (recruiting) group in the organization must play a critical role both in providing input to the process and utilizing the output.

- Workforce plans must be reviewed and updated at least quarterly to truly be effective in today's environment. Annually is not enough.

- Technology is needed to do workforce planning well. This does not mean that technology is a substitute for a strong process but rather that it enables the process.

By taking steps now to further optimize workforce planning processes, organizations can better predict what is needed and determine the best ways to obtain talent. Taking the time and obtaining the tools needed to truly do this well are essential investments in the future of the organization.

A workforce plan that addresses economic fluxes, shifting employee demographics and critical talent shortages can allow employers to make smart investments in human capital and proactively manage business risks and costs.

Elise Freedman is senior consultant, Talent Management, with Watson Wyatt Worldwide.

You Cannot Overinvest in Talent

Jamie Flinchbaugh, Lean Learning Center

Peter Cappelli captures many valid points about talent management, but the fear of an overinvestment in talent development is overblown. A truly capable lean-thinking organization focuses on building people first and does not draw a line in the sand where you have had enough.

The major flaw in the argument for not over-investing is that it assumes that the cost of incremental talent development is fixed, when in fact it is not. When an organization focuses on developing people every day through everyday activities, it learns how to learn. Toyota, the hallmark of lean companies, believes that it is "building people before building cars." Every person has a coach, a teacher. The primary objective for a manager

A truly capable lean-thinking organization focuses on building people first and does not draw a line in the sand where you have had enough.

is developing the person. In fact, managers in Toyota will not be promoted until they can demonstrate that they have developed their team to be able to perform the boss' job.

A lean organization does not do most of its talent development through training but through coaching and everyday learning. Experimentation is a powerful method within the learning process. As problem solving and improvement work is performed, instead of only validating a solution, a real hypothesis is developed. The hypothesis is not anything more than an "if I make this change, then I expect this result" statement.

By requiring hypothesis development, individuals are forced to put their knowledge, assumptions and understanding into a statement. When the hypothesis is then tested, that knowledge is validated or invalidated, creating a much better method for testing knowledge than an actual test. By doing this thousands of times over, the talent for improvement and problem solving far exceeds that without it. And the only "investment" is the time that a coach takes to help someone through that learning process.

Another powerful method a lean organization utilizes to drive embedded learning in the organization is reflection. As an exam-

ple, the U.S. Army developed the After Action Review as a training tool at the National Training Center.

This is beyond the typical post-mortem gripe session. It does not need to be more complicated than four questions:

- What was supposed to happen?

- What did happen and why?

- What can we learn?

- How will we change?

What is important is that you enter the activity with intent to learn. You observe what is happening during the event to have ground truth data to help you reflect. And you turn that reflection into action. Every cycle of action also generates learning and talent, and again the only investment is the time required to perform the reflection.

Many organizations have leaders who coach. But there is a difference between coaching someone toward the solution (or the "right" answer) and coaching someone toward the method (how to get the answer). Most organizations coach toward the solution. A lean organization generates talent and learning through coaching on the method. An organization that develops its talent through action and improvement cannot overinvest in talent, because to stop that investment is to stop improving.

Jamie Flinchbaugh is co-founder and partner of the Lean Learning Center.

Value Chain Focus: The Human Touch

Kathleen T. McCarthy, American Express Company

Peter Cappelli is right—well, at least half right. He discusses human capital and its management as a supply chain. I want to expand his thesis beyond the supply chain to include the value chain. Although they are complementary views of how integrated business processes can improve an enterprise's performance, the primary difference between a supply chain and a value chain is a fundamental shift in focus from the supply base to the customer base.

Today, human resource practitioners need to create a differentiated employee experience while reducing the cost of delivering that experience. The way that workforce planning is evolving suggests it could help bring together the supply chain and value chain to have the most impact for a company's talent management strategy.

- formalization of talent governance mechanisms (planned moves, succession management); and

- evolution of HR capabilities (competencies, systems, information insights).

A differentiated employee experience—when it is done well—promotes flexibility and responsiveness, reduces talent acquisition and development costs, enhances communication and provides for the efficient transfer of information and talent across business units. But it always must focus on the human element. As an HR function, we are accountable for the employee experience.

Let us consider talent acquisition as an example. From a supply chain perspective, a well-structured global recruitment model can improve recruiting performance, reduce costs, increase the quality of hires, improve ability to meet global talent requirements and promote business agility and flexibility. But we cannot look at this just mechanically. Supply chain helps you with the processes, but

percent lower time-to-fill, 34 percent better quality of hire and 21 percent higher intent to stay. [Source: Recruiting Round Table Executive Summary—Realizing Breakthrough Gains in Recruiting Effectiveness (2007).]

As human resource practitioners, the principles of supply chain and value chain management can (and need to) help our businesses achieve their goals and create shareholder value in these unprecedented times. Again, what we cannot forget is that the human element always will be a key driver of success.

Kathleen T. McCarthy is senior vice president, Recruitment and Workforce Planning, at the American Express Company.

Additional Talent Management Lessons

Scott Brooks and Jeffrey Saltzman, Kenexa

Comparing talent management to supply chain challenges, Peter Cappelli guides us toward four handy lessons. Set aside for a moment the tempting reaction to his comparison of employees to manufactured widgets, Cappelli's points are useful. So let us plunge into the supply chain metaphor to find additional talent management lessons from the modern industry icons of Amazon.com, Google and the Wildlife Conservation Society.

(What, you say? What about the Wildlife Conservation Society, a 114-year-old organization known for running the Bronx Zoo and worldwide conservation efforts, as a modern industry icon? While even the whiff of comparing employees to caged animals will get us into trouble, bear with us.)

1. **Amazon.com**—a disruptive leader in the retail supply chain and e-publishing.

> The way that workforce planning is evolving suggests it could help bring together the supply chain and value chain to have the most impact for a company's talent management strategy.

Managing workforce planning is a complex activity. It involves all functions of a business; it is a part of all levels of planning and execution; and it can be influenced by both rational and irrational decisions. There are a number of significant trends that drive the need for workforce planning, including the following:

- business complexity;

- human capital importance;

- pressure on talent human capital costs;

- globalization of talent supply and demand;

there has to be a human touch that creates brand ambassadors for the business.

From a value chain perspective, talent acquisition needs to invoke a powerful set of emotions. It needs to be about a promise to the candidate for a certain kind of experience—values, heritage and reputation. It is not just the way candidates feel toward the company but also the way they feel about themselves when they interact with it. It is this marriage of the supply chain and value chain that can define best-performing recruiting organizations and drive results such as a 54

part I: talent management

- *Customized portals that learn from our history and interests work spectacularly well.* Amazon introduced many of us to the convenience of online shopping, including the shopping cart, product suggestions and virtual storefronts. Brought together under one portal is an impressive coalition of businesses (including mega brands like Target mixed in with auctions and used

- *Talent management must reflect organizational strategy.* Not even Google is immune to the impact of the recession on a "world's best workplace." But stepping back, it is clear that Google's impressive talent management pipeline is managed to match its core business: rigorous, intense and scientifically minded. Google's talent management style honors its value proposition.

Scott Brooks, Ph.D., is the director of the Consulting Center of Excellence for Kenexa's Global Survey Practice. Jeffrey Saltzman is a principal at Kenexa.

PERSPECTIVES FROM EUROPE/ASIA

Balance is the Key in the Global Context

Jürgen Rohrmeier, Pape Consulting Group AG

> As an HR function, we are accountable for the employee experience… It is not just the way candidates feel toward the company but also the way they feel about themselves when they interact with it.

merchandise). Employees are not books, yet this portal has parallels for how we might shop for talent in the future. (And let us not think of employees as "used;" maybe just transitioned from other careers or semi-retirement.)

- *Ambidexterity is required.* Organizational ambidexterity is the simultaneous maintenance of traditional businesses focused on efficiency (e.g., shipping books) alongside radical innovation (e.g., Kindle). Talent management efforts need to balance get-it-done efficiency with the disruptive change that fuels an organization's future.

2. **Google**—no widgets to warehouse and distribute, yet information to share.

- *Search algorithms work better than organized directories.* The world generates an ever-changing, organic blob of information. Google has taught us that we can organize this blob and make it accessible. As Cappelli implied, perhaps formally structured succession planning needs to give way to a more organic, ongoing flow of information.

3. **Wildlife Conservation Society**—a venerable, yet reinvented non-profit dedicated to "help people imagine wildlife and humans living in sustainable interaction."

- *"Supply chains" are about more than widgets.* WCS supplies experiences and education, nothing physical for a traditional supply chain to manage. Correspondingly, the intangibles of the talent management experience matter.

- *A sustained supply of wildlife interactions requires working with the rhythms of the natural world.* Modern wildlife husbandry deals with permeable organizational boundaries. Similarly, as the management sciences continue to mature, we uncover more about the natural rhythms of organizations as well as individuals. Talent management strategies must keep these synchronized.

Thus, when building from the supply chain metaphor, we can learn additional lessons from how organizations deliver not just physical goods, but information and experiences. This helps to calibrate Cappelli's advice and to promote overall organizational vitality.

Two things came to my mind looking at the title of Peter Cappelli's article. The first was a discussion we had at one of the European HR Forum events in Lugano, Switzerland, when more than 20 HR professionals from various countries tried to define talent management—and failed! We were not able to agree to a common definition of what talent and talent management really mean. We finally decided to agree to disagree as it seemed there was value and reason behind all the arguments, driven by different national and corporate cultures and also different legal systems.

The second thought was the question whether a supply chain model is indeed a feasible notion when talking about managing human resources. After having finished reading the piece, I found a number of great ideas and statements that I could not agree with more: the need for balancing internal and external solutions, for balancing the needs and interests of both employer and employees, the necessity of focusing more on organizational goals, and for more flexibility and creativity in talent management. Yes, that is what we need, and that is all well stated. However, the article also raised some questions—especially from a European/German point of view—which I would like to share.

The current economic situation has caused a rather schizophrenic scenario when it comes to talent management. We see short-term crisis measures again through cost cutting, iring freezes, restructuring, layoffs, etc. However, there is also a continuous demand for certain talent, especially in engineering, that requires further attention.

Unfortunately, when it comes to possible solutions, we cannot ignore the fact that companies everywhere in the world face restrictions in managing their talent, such as legal systems, cultural aspects and other influencing factors. Some labor markets here in Europe are certainly significantly less volatile than the United States (Germany, but also France, Italy, Sweden and others). In Germany, laws such as the Works Constitution Act or the Termination of Employment Act have a significant influence on creative solutions for talent management—sometimes restrictively and yet sometimes supportively.

One of the more creative solutions, for example, is the idea of so-called "transfer companies," where employees would be transferred instead of being laid off, primarily to find a new job while being employed or to be taken back if business improves. There are several reasons why balancing between internal and external solutions is a given in Germany: Posting vacancies internally is a legal requirement, so companies do not necessarily have a choice to opt for internal or external hiring (this does not apply for executives, however). They are forced to go internal first, thoroughly monitored by works councils. It is also not that easy to make up for a shortfall in talent through hiring from the outside as we are facing a shortage of specific technical talent on the market and also because employment contracts are often coming with notice periods of up to six months—meaning talent from the outside is anything but immediately available.

The solution of developing a talent pool for allocation to vacancies when and where needed also is not too feasible here in Germany as there are cultural and legal barriers that make it difficult simply to transfer employees to other locations or to jobs that are not at least equal or preferably better than the recent job.

So focusing on internal solutions does not seem to be the big challenge here: We actually might focus a bit too much on it. Looking for talent externally also is not just something a company should focus on because of lack of internal development. Sometimes it is recommendable to hire from the outside to bring in new ideas and competencies as well as competitive and complementary business and market knowledge—not a reactive but rather a proactive approach.

When working with my clients, I try to convince them not to get lost in short-term cost cutting even in times of crisis, but rather to also think about the future by investing in developing talent both through internal and external means. Hiring talent from the competition and strengthening your employer brand today might be exactly what you need to do to ensure your success tomorrow. As suggested, the balance is the key—and knowing about the varieties of different cultural, legal, market and business aspects in the global context!

On a last note, getting and retaining talent in the right quantity and quality at the right time is important and yet not enough: We need the talent we have invested in to be as committed,

spectives and ensuring that employees work on challenging tasks, which is one of two main aspects of engagement. The other main aspect is who you work for, your boss! This seems to be a major issue: Where are the inspiring leaders that can motivate and coach their people so that they are, and stay, engaged? That might be an even more important talent management issue for which we need solutions.

Jürgen Rohrmeier is senior partner and member of the executive board, Pape Consulting Group AG, Munich, Germany. He is a member of the faculty/visiting lecturer for HR management and leadership, FOM University of Applied Sciences, Essen/Munich, Germany.

People Are Not Commodities

Peter Bedford, ABB Group

Peter Cappelli's article draws parallels between supply chain and talent management

---

More than 20 HR professionals from various countries tried to define talent management—and failed!... it seemed there was value and reason behind all the arguments, driven by different national and corporate cultures and also different legal systems.

---

productive and creative as possible, in one word "engaged." The most recent Gallup Institute engagement survey in Germany shows that only 13 percent of the German workforce is truly engaged at their jobs—a sad and worrying result.

Talent management as discussed in Cappelli's article can be very helpful through offering development opportunities and career per-

issues and proposes the adoption of supply chain principles to one of the most fundamental of HR practices. He defines talent management as getting the right people with the right skills in the right jobs. This is indeed true, although, and especially for those of us who practice talent management in global companies, it also is important to add "at the right time and in the right place." Truly strategic talent management practices ➤

include analyzing business strategies and determining the capabilities required; then identifying the capability gaps and surpluses which are resolved through development, redeployment, exit and, as a last resort, external hiring.

This implies a joined-up approach in HR processes that often is more difficult in larger, geographically diverse organisations. As Cappelli identifies, symptoms of talent management failure include mismatches of supply and demand. And in a large company, failure also can manifest itself as talent blockage (practices and/or organization structures that make it difficult for employees to develop their careers through, for example, not making vacancies open to all) or, worse, managers taking a local, rather than a global, perspective and declining to release an employee—who will then leave anyway.

Contrary to the implication that a "deep bench" of talent is unhealthy, in practice there is no substitute for a wealth of talent in a successful company. Providing as many career-development opportunities as possible—and in larger companies these can include similar roles on different continents—is one form of retention. And if some of your best employees ultimately decide to move on, alumni management processes should keep tabs and in due course, they may well return and bring with them enhanced skills and experience. And what they say about your company in the meantime will enhance your reputation as a great employer.

To further challenge the supply chain analogy, unlike commodities purchased to the same specification, some people fit companies better than others. It matters not how technically competent a candidate is if he or she does not have the ability to work successfully within a particular company culture.

Operating with a surplus of talent means there is a pool of "cultural maturity" that is more difficult to find through external hiring; and "hire for attitude, train for skills" has long been the mantra in some successful companies where cultural preferences are assessed

along with technical skills during the selection process. The issue becomes more complex in some large organizations where there exists a variety of cultures that may militate the ability to offer international career development opportunities.

Finally, the suggestion that graduate hiring may be phased to smooth the internal logis-

Contrary to the implication that a "deep bench" of talent is unhealthy, in practice there is no substitute for a wealth of talent in a successful company. Providing as many career development opportunities as possible is one form of retention.

tics around providing assignments assumes that, just like goods procured by purchasing, the quality will be the same at each intake. In reality, graduate trainee programs need to be aligned with the academic calendar in each country: Waiting three months after the prime hiring period, or asking the intake to wait for three months, significantly reduces the pool of top-quality talent.

HR has much to learn from supply chain principles, but let us never, ever forget that people are not commodities.

Peter Bedford is head of Global Resourcing for the ABB Group in Switzerland.

Employee-centric Markets: A Different Direction

Nicholas Kemsley, Group VP Org Effectiveness at Travelport, UK

Aspects of Peter Cappelli's article are echoed by U.K. businesses. At the same time, I would

make some points in respect of markets like the United Kingdom where better people despite the recent downturn, continue to have the upper hand over businesses that might wish to retain them for longer than they wish to stay.

We need flexibility, but the approach described is one where the benefit for the employer is

perhaps easier to see than that for the individual. In the United Kingdom, traditional "talent pools" are often viewed with caution and some cynicism. The best people have jumped into the career saddle, seeing organizations with whom they work as deliberate and managed pieces of their career/life jigsaw. Talent pools, as described in the article, risk feeling too ambiguous and paternalistic to these people. The U.K. model needs to be less about retention in potentially stagnant talent pools and more about individual solutions and a "mutual exchange of value" so long as the individual and the organization are in partnership.

Some U.K. businesses have put in place approaches that are far more informal and partnership-oriented. For them, it is about understanding how business need, individual capability and longer-term aspiration fit together over time to create value for both individual and business. Such an approach allows connections between demand and supply to still be made swiftly, which Cappelli quite rightly sees as vital.

However, it also *requires* flexibility, not so much in resource deployment, but in capability. It requires us to move away from one-size-fits-all leadership development, and toward solutions which are both individual and contextual, because what it will take to unlock each of these individual "value equations" will differ from person to person.

My own experiences leading such approaches have changed my perspective on the issue forever. They deliver whole new levels of insight and engagement, the ability to focus laser-like on the real issues, while still being able to manage the breadth of development support required within sensible and economical limits.

As to an internal talent market, this again feels like a model that would work best in employer-centric markets. From a U.K. perspective, the signs are that the market should not be developed as either "internal" or "external," but as a single market spanning both, effectively erasing the organizational boundaries when it comes to both recruitment and development. The best people are increasingly just passing through organizations within a system which they increasingly control. So why is it that organizations still feel these people can be retained for 20 years within their walls?

A few businesses in the United Kingdom already are swimming with this tide, rather than against it. They are forming loose cooperatives and swapping employees with the other businesses to drive pertinent development that will benefit them in the future, but that they find hard to provide themselves. As the realities of employee-centricity and cost-effectiveness continue to bite, surely this is a trend that will only grow and become more organic.

So, there is much to be said for taking elements of supply chain management into talent development, but in employee-centric markets this may need to be done differently. In these markets, some organizations are waking up to the realities of the situation and setting off in an exciting direction from which many, irrespective of location, might benefit.

Nicholas Kemsley is former head of Learning, Prudential U.K., and is an OD, Talent and Leadership consultant.

Talent Management: Quantifying Risks and Returns

Richard Arvey, National University of Singapore

Peter Cappelli makes several observations and remarks that are quite insightful. He argues that there is a new way to think about talent management, and he particularly discusses the role of risk in viewing possible mismatches between the talent needed in an organization (the demand side for labor) and the talent available to meet the organization's needs (the supply side of labor). He suggests a number of different approaches and practices to understand the risks and costs associated with mismatches. Interestingly, he draws on other disciplines such as supply chain management and operations management to draw practical approaches.

I am in great agreement with what he says and would amplify a little on some of his concepts. Suppose an organization needs to ensure that talent in the organization is performing at or above a threshold level. There are a variety of ways or choices with regard to increasing the probabilities (or reducing the risk) of meeting this goal:

- the organization can hire the talent or ensure that external markets fulfill the need;
- the organization can develop the talent relying on internal labor markets within the firm; and/or
- the organization can engage in performance management to ensure that the labor is performing up to par.

Each of these choices involves risks (the uncertainty that the needs of the organization will be met) and each has associated costs.

How is the organization to decide what to do? Cappelli suggests using multiple choices and strategies (a mix and match perspective). However, Cappelli essentially is silent on quantifying the various risks and returns; perhaps we could learn and/or borrow a set of principles and techniques from the field of finance when it comes to looking for the "right" combination. The field of finance has developed a model or technique called capital asset pricing where optimal combinations of various assets can be observed balancing or optimizing both the risks (measured by the variance in performance) and the returns (or costs). The technique is fairly straightforward where what is needed is quantitative data on the variance, the returns and the covariances or correlations between different assets with regard to their returns. Perhaps we could pursue this strategy as well when managing talent.

Importantly, Cappelli makes the central argument that we need to review talent management—and really all HR practices—to engage in serious risk assessment and management. We should be reviewing the costs and probabilities of achieving the talent goals of the organization, be it hiring new employees, deploying employees overseas, compensating executives, putting money into expensive development programs and the like. It is obvious that I am drawing from the field of decision making and focusing on the basic problem associated with the latest financial meltdown in our economies because of inattention to appropriate risk management in the financial world. **P&S**

Richard Arvey is a professor and head of the Management Department at the National University of Singapore.

learning guide

People & Strategy 32.3 Point Counterpoint:

A Supply Chain Model for Talent Management

Discovery Questions

- What are we dealing with in our organization today that relates to this content area?

- Deeply understand the concept of "mismatches" in talent supply and demand.

- Recognize the relative contribution to workforce planning of HRIS data collection and "the right conversations".

- Develop creative new ways of thinking and talking about talent management.

- Be able to describe talent management as yet another business process.

Selected Facts

- What new facts that were presented got your attention?

- Why are there so few "facts" presented in all these articles?

- Talent management is the process through which employers anticipate and meet their needs for human capital.

- Uncertainty is created when employers change strategies, structures and operations quickly and repeatedly in response to customers, competitors and regulators.

- High performing recruiting organizations are 54% faster in time to fill; 34% higher quality hire; and 21% higher intent to stay.

- Only 13% of German employees are "engaged" per Gallup data.

Key Discussion Points

- What were the key points being made in this Point Counterpoint presentation?

- What do you think of the conclusion: Long term succession plans are mistakes because they assume that we know what jobs will need to be filled in the future and what current employees will be around to fill them.

- What can be done to reduce the uncertainty in predicting talent requirements?

- What is the employee engagement lesson that can come from an understanding that great supply chain management treats their vendors as partners who share common goals?

- What does it mean to say that talent management requires more than data collection and reporting—that it's quality depends on the dialogs that occur?

- How can workforce planning be positioned as a business process, not an HR one?

- How could you use "hypothesis development" (if I make this change I expect this result) for talent development?

- What is the difference between coaching toward a solution and coaching toward the method?

- How does McCarthy differentiate between the "supply chain" and the "value chain"?

- How does Amazon show ambidexterity—both efficiency and radical innovation?

- How is Google's talent management style consistent with their value proposition?

- What are the legal restrictions in Europe or Germany impacting talent management?

- Is it possible to have too deep of a bench strength?

- Where does the supply chain analogy break down when applying it to real people?

Review of Solutions

- Identify 2-3 Big Ideas that are worthy of exploring for our organization.

- Principle 1: "Make and Buy" to manage demand side risk of too much inventory (that is, a deep bench).

- Principle 2: Reduce the uncertainty in Talent demand: Plan to talent pools not to specific positions.

- Principle 3: Earn a return on investments in developing employees—shorten the development cycle and add employee accountability.

- Principle 4: Balance employee interests by using an internal market.

- Use the US Army's After Action Review to develop organizational learning agility.

Recommendations Summary

- Identify one thing that we are all going to do differently based on what we learned.

Learning Outcomes

- What one new piece of information did you learn that will be important to you?

Redesigning Your Organization for the Future of Work

Tamara J. Erickson, nGenera Innovation Network

The work world of the next several decades will be significantly different from the work world of the last two decades in at least three key ways:

- There will be a dramatic and rapid shift in the capabilities of technology that reduces the costs of coordinating activities and sharing ideas.

- There will be a set of economic activities that is shifting away from the 20th-century industrial or manufacturing-based model and mass-consumer brands to a model based on knowledge and co-creation between consumers and suppliers.

- There will be new patterns of demand for talent and skills in which many individuals, particularly those with higher levels of education, will have the leverage to create work arrangements that are more conducive to adult growth than were possible before.

The changes underway, including demand for skilled talent, will provide the catalyst required to create a new way of working and challenge many of the fundamental assumptions that underlie the structure and design of today's organizations.

Many of today's organizational principles are centered on the premise that the workforce is shaped like a pyramid—with a small number of older workers, a medium number of mid-career workers and many young people. This indeed *was* the shape of the workforce in most countries throughout the 20th century. As a result, a number of standard organizational practices that are deeply embedded in our assumptions about how "it's always done" make no sense today. For example, we assume that over the course of their careers employees will be promoted "up"—at least until they reach their maximum challenge or, if you believe in the Peter Principle, one step beyond it—in order to provide variety (something new and interesting to do) and increased compensation.

Today the workforce is not pyramidal in shape (it is more like a diamond, with a large middle group) and it is rapidly evolving into a rectangle, with nearly the same number of workers at each major life stage. Going forward, many of our deeply ingrained assumptions about the course of a person's lifetime career will not be *mathematically* possible. For example, there will be too few "higher" level positions to provide everyone in the workforce with sufficient opportunities for variety, learning or increased compensation—particularly as the generational cohorts become more eager for frequent change and less willing to remain in one position for extended periods of time.

If you overlay the changing demographic patterns with the changing nature of value creation—the growth in knowledge-based work—our common design parameters around time and job design come into question. Most jobs today still are described in terms of a unit of time—a 40-hour workweek, an eight-hour day. But the majority of workers of the western world are now employed in service industries; and already more than half of those are knowledge workers, paid for writing, analyzing, advising, counting, designing, researching and countless related functions, including capturing, organizing and providing access to knowledge used by others. Time-based jobs make little sense for these workers. Who's to say how long it will take an individual to write a report, conduct an analysis or produce a piece of software?

And, of course, people's needs and values are changing. At some point, the tightening labor market will motivate even the most traditional companies to change or face the likelihood that their growth will be constrained by a lack of talent. At the core, the relationship between employees and employers—or perhaps more accurately, between workers and the organizers of work—will be redefined. These shifts will reinforce and will

enable the desires of individual workers, allowing greater personal flexibility, autonomy and participation.

There's a strong need to rethink our organizations' design and practices. HR has an important role to lead the redesign of organizations better suited for the future of work.

Here are some of the questions I encourage you to ponder.

- *Is it time to redesign career paths for lateral moves, with less dependence on promotion?* Many employees aren't particularly interested in "up"—they want challenge and variety. "Up" is out. But most approaches to compensation are heavily tied to vertical status—and people do want opportunities to earn more money. Can we redesign career paths and compensation programs around lateral movement—tie variety, recognition, learning and compensation to the development of capabilities that are not necessarily related to hierarchy? Can we create attractive individualized paths that maximize learning, growth and challenge?

- *Can career paths lead down, as well as up?* Rather than the cliff-shaped career paths of the past century in which individuals ascended on an ever-upward path toward ever-greater "success," 21st-century careers need to become bellshaped. We need to create a career deceleration phase for employees in their 50s through 80s that parallels the career development phase of the 20s through 40s.

- *Do we need titles and, if so, for what purpose?* Titles serve two purposes. One is to identify to others (customers, colleagues within the organization) to whom they should look for specific actions or decisions. The other is to reflect our status in the organization. The first purpose will remain vitally important in the future of work—actually increasingly so. Collaboration occurs when responsibilities and roles are clearly defined. Titles that clarify the function the person performs are more essential than ever. But titles that recognize our progress "up" an organization need to be re-thought; chances are they cement us into a hierarchical structure that no longer serves our needs or, in some cases, even exists.

- *Do we all need to retire at the same time?* Extended life expectancies also will augur the end of "retirement" as we have known it—an abrupt end to work that occurs at a specific, common age for most individuals. Over this century, companies need to retire the concept, replacing it with a more flexible view of the second half of our lives.

- *Does a career need to be continuous and linear?* Why not retire at age 40 and go back to work at 60?[1] More companies are now looking at ways to provide employees with the opportunity to leave and re-enter the workforce. Sylvia Ann Hewlett and Carolyn Buck Luce have identified a growing need for what they call "off-ramping" and "on-ramping."[2] In surveys, a substantial proportion of individuals of all ages say that they would prefer "cyclic" work arrangements over any other option—periods of intense hard work for some amount of time (say, several months), followed by periods of leisure or learning, even if that "downtime" is only a week or so long.[3]

- *How long should we expect people to stay in one job or even in one company?* It is likely that average tenures will continue to be shorter than was common in the 20th century. Realistically, this means that jobs need to be redesigned to accommodate frequent movement and short tenures per role. The time required to get "up to speed" to perform a specific function needs to be shortened, perhaps through the use of just-in-time learning, easily interchangeable systems and well-structured and effective mentoring.

- *How many "employees" do we need?* Going forward, it is likely that much of the work necessary for any business will no longer be done exclusively or even (in many instances) primarily with "employees." The types of relationships that the corporation will have with the people who perform work on its behalf will encompass a wide range—contractors, freelancers, small company specialists, outsourcers and many others.

- *Should we redefine work in terms of tasks, not time?* Increasingly, roles need to be scoped and compensated according to the task performed—rather than by the time invested. In this approach, employees are assigned specific tasks and required to put in only as much time as it actually takes to get the work done, removing the need to keep regular hours or show up at the office each day, allowing people to work asynchronously, instead of in standard 9-to-5 routines, and from virtually any location. The distinction between "full" or "part-time" positions would give way to differentiation in the complexity of the task assigned.[4]

- *What will performance management look like in the new economy?* How can we do a quantum re-think of the pace of work? Young workers today want and expect fast and frequent feedback—daily interaction, ongoing input, "instant" response. As it becomes more important for companies to operate in a collaborative way, how can we incorporate peer-based feedback mechanisms and measures of intra-group activity? And how can we evaluate and constructively coach workers that we rarely see?

- *What is the role of corporations in education? How and where will businesses interface with academic institutions in preparing talent?* Corporations already are in the education business—and they need to be prepared to play an increasingly active role in creating a workforce with the skills and capabilities required for the evolving economy. The current educational patterns are not geared to produce a

> Realistically, this means that jobs need to be redesigned to accommodate frequent movement and short tenures per role.

workforce matched to today's business needs. Whether through formal in-company training, sponsored attendance at external programs, apprenticeships and/or increased mentoring, companies will need to help workers gain the necessary knowledge and abilities.

- *How can you insure that employees are choosing you?* When Zappos, the online shoe retailer, hires new customer-service employees, it provides a four-week training period that immerses them in the company's strategy, culture and obsession with customers. After a week or so in this immersive experience, the company offers the newest employees a $1,000 bonus if they agree to quit that day. Why? The logic is that if you're willing to take the company up on the offer, you don't have the sense of

1. Semler, R. (2004). *The Seven-Day Weekend: Changing the Way Work Works*, Portfolio, a member of Penguin Group (USA), New York, New York.
2. Hewlett, S.A. & C. Buck Luce (2005). "Off-Ramps and On-Ramps: Keeping Talented Women on the Road to Success," *Harvard Business Review*, pp. 43-54.
3. "The New Employee/ Employer Equation," The Concours Group (now nGenera) and Age Wave, 2004. This research project included a nationwide survey of more than 7,700 employees conducted in June 2004 by Harris Interactive for The Concours Group and Age Wave.
4. For further discussion, see Tamara J. Erickson, "Breakthrough Ideas for 2008: Task, Not Time," *Harvard Business Review*, February 2008.

commitment Zappos is looking for.[5] Zappos wants to learn if there's a bad fit between what makes the organization tick and what makes individual employees tick—and it's willing to pay to learn sooner rather than later. Increasingly we're learning that companies need to find ways to let employees understand for themselves what it's like to work there, and then encourage the prospective employee to evaluate the fit. Practices inside the company should be "Signature Experiences," deliberately chosen and specific to the needs of the organization.[6]

- *Who will "manage" the workforce of the future?* As the need to juggle a wide variety of individuals with diverse preferences and needs grows, and as a dizzying array of relationships increases, traditional line managers may find themselves happy to pass on the challenge of keeping track of such a complicated talent pool to another function. In many organizations, the responsibility for managing talent will come to rest with some type of staffing function—the next evolution of HR. In this new role, HR would be judged on the quality, engagement and "readiness" of the talent the businesses needs.

The Transformation Challenge: A New Human Resource Capability

The challenge of rethinking organizations for the future requires HR leaders with capabilities that include a willingness to bring fresh perspectives to old assumptions and specific capabilities:

- strategic thinking, particularly scenario development and options analysis to address uncertainty;

- finance and business acumen, including a sophisticated understanding of return-on-investment analysis;

- process design capabilities and skill with metrics;

- marketing and branding savvy; and

- ability to create environments supporting collaboration and innovation.

The changing context of work shaped by recent developments in demographics and technology will be profound. These changes will uproot traditional organizational designs and HR practices.

The changes will give forward-thinking HR leaders an opportunity to demonstrate the contributions they can make to the prosperity of the entire firm, ensuring that they will be key participants in the flattened, dynamic, networked and global corporations of the future.

Tamara J. Erickson is president of nGenera Innovation Network. She also is an author of many books including *Retire Retirement: Career Strategies for the Boomer Generation.*

5. Taylor, B. "Why We Went Zany for Zappos—And What It Says About Us," *Game Changer*, Harvard Business Online, May 27, 2008.

6. For further discussion, see Tamara J. Erickson and Lynda Gratton, "What It Means to Work Here," *Harvard Business Review*, March 2007.

counterpoints

The Systems We Build... The Conversations We Hold

Beverly Kaye, Founder and CEO
Career Systems International

Has the time finally come? In the early 1980s I published the results of my doctoral dissertation in a book that I called *Up Is Not the Only Way*. I talked about the need to develop career development systems within organizations. One of the concepts (the one that really "caught") was embedded in the title. I remember the nods from my HR colleagues back then. Clearly, not every deserving individual, even our talented and earmarked

hi-potentials, can be promised anything of the sort. We could not promise it then and we cannot now.

We've always known this, and yet we still haven't designed the systems and structures to suggest that there are other definitions of success that are, in fact, as sound, strategic, relevant and, at the same time, rewarding (in status and in compensation). We still nod, but we don't make the changes that are necessary.

Why hasn't this shifted? We all seem to be in violent agreement that the pyramid shape of organizations has morphed into, as the author suggests, a diamond or perhaps a rectangle.

Yet our reward systems still do not recognize this. Maybe the pain we feel in this current economy will be the hard driver for change.

We've been taught that structure drives behavior. While we could suggest a plethora of possible career moves, if our systems still point to vertical mobility as the brass ring, then nothing will change. Or, perhaps the change will finally occur because behavior will drive structure.

We're all familiar with the research on the Millennial generation. These workers want flexibility; they are not "sold" on the traditional hierarchical moves. They want choices nd options and they won't stand for any-thing less. So we must produce the new structure that the author seems to call for. We do not have a choice if we are to hang on to the talent we currently have and continue to attract the youngest generation. It is indeed a role for HR, and one where we must take the lead.

A new success structure and reward system also is needed for Boomers. Current events strongly suggest that Boomers will postpone retirement. Many will not have the choice. If organizations are in need of talent, we must be ready to offer the elders of our workforce different options, choices and the new directions they want. Clearly, for this group, *out* is no longer the "only" way. They are looking at their organizations to offer viable ways to stay "in," but stay "in" differently.

I would add one more critical component to the author's questions that call us to action: Have we equipped managers to have the critical conversations about mobility options with their direct reports? It is time to rede-sign the powerful conversation, the all-important critical one-on-one conversa-tion that is the message of the organization to the employee. We must imbue it with the attention it deserves.

Perhaps, along with everything else the author suggests, it is also time to re-invent the indi-vidual development plan. This tool was meant to be a conversation stimulus for considering the future. If taken seriously, it requires commitment, attention, preparation and accountability from all leaders and their direct reports—stronger commitment than we currently give it. I worry about the author's suggestions that the responsibility for talent management may be removed from the line and given to a staffing function. If we harness a tool we already have, educate managers and employees about the new mobility possibili-ties, and require that these conversations take place, it will bring us closer to acting on the options that are demanded. The future of work will be changed by the systems we build and the conversations we hold.

The Future of Work: It's Already Here, Just Not Evenly Distributed[1]

James Ware and Charles Grantham
Work Design Collaborative

Tammy Erickson has painted a provocative, if incomplete, picture of the future of work. In many ways it is a compelling image, for both organizations and individuals. It is a world of much greater fluidity, more attuned to individual differences and needs. But we are actually more interested in a slightly dif-ferent aspect of organizational and individual fluidity—what we like to call "cor-porate agility."[2]

For us, "agility" is about an organization's ability to move quickly, to grow and shrink at the same time in different parts of the world and to respond to local market conditions and opportunities faster than its competitors. Agil-ity is about paring fixed costs down to almost zero; it's about leveraging new technologies, facing new competitors and exploiting new business opportunities. And it's about under-standing and leveraging human talent, which—as Tammy rightly suggests—thrives on variety, challenging problems and creativ-ity. But most of all, agility is about designing work, and its surrounding business processes, around people, not around fixed assets like buildings and IT data centers.

In our experience, the benefits of fundamen-tally rethinking the very nature of work (and how, where and when it gets conducted) are simply astounding. We have seen companies achieve reductions in the cost of workforce support on the order of 40 percent or more—while at the same time attracting and retaining better talent and realizing higher lev-els of productivity and employee engagement.

What's the secret that enables that kind of performance improvement? For us, it is inte-grating the management of your people, your technology and your facilities/real estate assets. And *that* means actively embracing the notion that the most effective way to deter-mine where, when and how your work gets done is to leave those decisions up to the people actually doing the work.

But let's be clear: We're not advocating the end of hierarchy, the way Tammy seems to be. Hierarchy has its place—when it's based on merit and *relevant* experience. We can't stand industrial bureaucracies that create a hierar-chy of power and authority based on little more than time in grade. But we do recognize the value of task-based authority determined by knowledge and the ability to achieve results in the here and now. We want to see more organizations that encourage *multiple but temporary* hierarchies—each of them task-specific and accepted as legitimate *for the task at hand*.

In essence we're advocating what many people call "flexible work" or "mobile work." In short, stop requiring people to commute regu-larly to a central corporate office facility just for the sake of being there. Offer them the mobile tools they need to work any time, any place, and give them remote access to your corporate network, applications and data.

The reality of knowledge work is that it can't be scheduled like a factory assembly line, and it requires not *a* workplace, but access to *many* places. We need to move around as our moods and our activities change. To paraphrase the futurist Alvin Toffler, one workplace misfits all.

The beauty of these flexible/mobile work arrangements is that they enable individuals to choose where and when to do their best work, based on their personal work styles and the tasks they need to accomplish. Some people actually can get more work done sit-ting in a Starbucks than they can in a corporate office where they're constantly

---

1. We've borrowed and paraphrased that line from science fiction writer William Gibson.
2. See Charles Grantham, James Ware, and Cory Williamson, (2007) *Corporate Agility*, American Management Association.

being interrupted. You get higher productivity—and higher employee engagement—when you **trust** your staff to make those kinds of decisions on their own.

Certainly mobile work programs are not a simple panacea. They only work when your corporate culture and mission are clear and explicit, when your so-called "managers" are skilled at setting clear task goals and coordinating a dispersed workforce. And they work when you provide effective technology support along with HR policies and practices that achieve that elusive balance of individual accountability and collaboration that's essential to corporate success in the dynamic world we live in today – and will live in for the rest of our careers.

Of course, this vision of the future of work is easier to talk about than it is to implement. But we really don't think you have any choice. When you combine the emerging values and expectations of today's workers with the growing shortage of talent, you're a buyer of a very scarce resource, and you know full well that when the resources you need are in short supply, those folks you're attempting to recruit are in the driver's seat. Give them what they're looking for, or they'll be working for your competitors.

Moving from Despair to Directed

Sherry Benjamins, President
S. Benjamins & Company, Inc.

I agree with Tamara Erickson that changing the place of work and how work gets done is clearly in front of us if we want to hold on to the best and brightest and prepare for talent shortages. Tamara speaks as though it is our future. I think it is here now, and managers are not sure what to do about it.

Those of us working in the human capital space see how tough it is for managers to change, when many leaders have a "we've done it this way and it worked" mindset. There seems to be such reluctance to break molds. It

puzzles me how slow management has been in creating new ways to get work done. We have been talking about this for a long time.

I like the questions that Tamara poses. Who will manage this workforce of the future? Who is stepping up to this challenge? There clearly are world-class leaders stepping up, but not enough. I know the line manager would be happy to pass the talent baton over to HR, and I appreciate the weight on the shoulders of clients. However, they must own this agenda. They must lead talent planning and engagement, for it directly impacts them. So, what can we offer as a solution to our managers rather than a list of overwhelming questions?

Let's move our managers from a mounting sense of despair to a directed, actionable talent plan. We will not see change until we offer tools to help them run their businesses.

All of us, including our managers, have been set adrift in a sea of issues that need to be addressed. As HR leaders, we can begin with business conversations that bring the people discussion into everyday operational life and demonstrate our understanding of market principles and talent realities.

As I have found in my work during the past several years, and as Peter Cappelli[1] has recently pointed out, supply-chain management concepts are one place to start. Let's give managers a tool that simply and clearly shows the key challenges around talent today based on these concepts. The talent funnel shows the steps required and resulting data in identifying and hiring top talent. This includes ratios of candidates sourced, contacted, screened, signed off, presented and then hired. We factor in market data, realities of the company's brand, candidate experiences and overall reputation to create a real supply picture.

Why do this business conversation and the data about talent make a difference? Our experience shows the following benefits:

- **Education**—Many times this is the first time a hiring manager understands the broader picture of the talent supply market and realities of sourcing for specific skills.

- **Supply**—Real facts about how many (internal and external) candidates there are and how they proceed through the process of screen affects fall-out, interview, offer and hire. This is an eye-opening experience for line managers, especially if there isn't clarity

Exhibit: Talent Pipeline

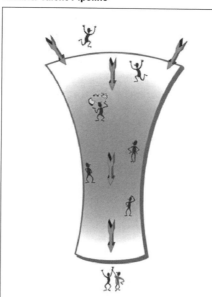

1. Sourcing Methods
   a. _____
   b. _____
   c. _____
   d. _____

2. Number Scored _____

3. Number Qualified/ Phone Screened _____

4. Number Interviewed _____

5. Number Offers _____

6. Number Hires _____

on requirements or issues about relocation or tailoring a work arrangement.

Process – Develop an understanding of the work required for HR and line managers to find and convert passive candidates in a highly competitive market supports reality-based planning.

Brand – Gather direct feedback from candidates that supports or detracts from the company's intended brand image: How do candidates see and experience your company? A strong positive brand supports you in tough times; a weak brand severely limits you. Candidates will share the truth about how they are treated.

Roles – Ensure managers understand the role they must play in planning, sourcing, selling and closing candidates. Every line manager is a talent manager today.

Communication – Conduct monthly people-supply-and-demand discussions and results. These keep the team on track and adapting as necessary.

Celebration – Enjoying success and celebrating the hiring or retention of great talent is worth recognition. When line managers celebrate and thank the team, this solidifies the support of everyone and announces this work is not going away.

There simply are not enough people to go around in the hot skill areas that many are seeking. Tamara is right to ask the tough questions about the future. The change starts with accepting the reality of your own company's track record. Now, we have increasingly complex arrangements given the Baby Boomers and Millennials renegotiating and creating new deals. As HR leaders we can start with business conversations that demonstrate our understanding of market principles and talent realities. We can be that strategic partner to our clients and introduce the business language of talent so we move the conversation from despair to directed. Let's not wait.

1. Cappelli, Peter (2008). Talent on Demand: Managing Talent in an Age of Uncertainty. Harvard Business School Press.

Wanted: Fully Engaged, Learning-Agile People

Lawrence P. Clark, Ph.D., Director
The Korn/Ferry Institute

In the article "Redesigning Your Organization for the Future of Work," Tamara Erickson makes some very provocative suggestions:

- Are position titles necessary? And, if so, for what purpose?

- Can career paths lead down, as well as up? Does career deceleration have a place in corporations?

- Who will "manage" the workforce of the future? Apparently not the line managers.

I will be the first to admit that when looking at different future possibilities, my track record for picking the winners from the losers is not that good. I still remember reading in the popular press that everyone would be driving personal helicopters in the near future. Experts assured us that the world of George Jetson would soon be a reality…and I believed them.

While the specifics concerning the future of work no doubt will offer interesting surprises, two factors will not change:

- First, the key personal characteristics of the people who will succeed in the "Future of Work" will not change.

- And, second, what organizations need to do with their employees regardless of their title, seniority or tenure with the company to compete in marketplace will not change.

Today, most organizations operate their business around the world via trade, flow of information technology, finance, manufacturing and migration. It has been estimated that global trade in goods and services will rise more than threefold to $27 trillion by 2030 (The World Bank, 2007). As organizations become truly global and operate in the evolving "Future of Work," it will be essential to move beyond simplistic, traditional staff-

ing approaches. Thus it is imperative to align staffing practices with critical business strategies. The demand for competent and experienced leaders is growing rapidly, and to succeed, organizations will need to identify and hire that talent wherever it exists.

Learning agility is one factor that has received much attention as a predictor of success. McCall, Lombardo and Morrison (1988) conducted the seminal research in this area two decades ago. In their book, *Lessons of Experience*, the authors discovered that many managers who produced positive results based on their current technical skills did not perform well when promoted. They found that numerous managers and executives derailed because rather than evolving by learning new skills, they tended to rely heavily on their current skills or to apply them incorrectly. The strengths that once made them "successful" had now become weaknesses. In contrast, those who thrived seemed far more comfortable with new, different and challenging situations and were willing to learn and develop from their "lessons of experience."

Two decades later Eichinger & Lombardo (2000) and McCall & Hollenbeck (2008) found that employees and executives who succeed have strong and active learning patterns. They are not more intelligent, but because they have more effective learning skills and strategies, they are "learning agile." In contrast, the ineffective employees and executives (many of whom had once experienced great success) failed because they did not learn from their jobs. They underestimated the new challenges their advancement brought and performed as they always had. The ability to learn from experience is what makes and develops expert leaders.

Organizations today, more than ever, need employees who are open, willing to learn and flexible enough to execute complex strategies. They need leaders who are curious about the world, quick to learn, thrive on new challenges and experiences. In addition, those leaders also must possess a high tolerance for ambiguity, great people skills, a vision and innovation. In other words, employees and ➤

part II: organizational effectiveness

leaders with "learning agility" will be critical to success in the work world described by the "Future of Work."

Once these "learning-agile" people have been identified, then what? Tamara Erickson asks, "How long should we expect people to stay in one job or even in one company?" How does an organization retain and maximize the amount of effort from these key people?

The answer is engagement. Engaged employees are far more productive because their work behavior is energized, focused and more aligned to the organization's needs. They believe in the mission, vision and leadership of their organization. Engaged employees are more likely to rise to challenges and remain with the company in supportive environments with caring, encouraging and empowering bosses. There is a direct correlation to productivity when these individuals feel appreciated, listened to and supported by the organization.

Engaged employees increase an organization's return on investment by an average of 11.4 percent. (Schneider, 2006). The Corporate Leadership Council also reported that highly engaged employees were 87 percent less likely to leave their organizations ("Driving Performance," 2004).

However, it has been reported that only about 25 percent of workers appear to be engaged truly in their jobs (Bates, 2004; Kabachnick, 2006). And, due in part to this low level engagement, Bates concluded that the U.S. economy is running at only 30 percent capacity. This issue is not limited to the United States. A study conducted by The Conference Board found the level of engagement across five regions of the world (Asia, Eastern Europe, Western Europe, Latin America and the United States) to be largely the same (Gibbons, 2006). The potential, therefore, is huge.

As Tamara Erickson indicates "the changes underway, including demand for skilled talent, will provide the catalyst required to create a new way of working and challenge many of the fundamental assumptions that underlie the

structure and design of today's organizations." What will not change in "The Future of Work" is the need for "learning-agile" people who are fully engaged in their work regardless of their career path or tenure at the organization—or who manages them.

References

Bates, S. (2004). "Getting Engaged." *HR Magazine*, 49 (2), 44-51.

"Driving Performance and Retention Through Employee Engagement." (2004). Washington, DC: Corporate Leadership Council.

Gibbons, J. (2006). *Employee Engagement: A Review of Current Research and Its Implications*. New York: The Conference Board.

Kabachnick, T. (2006). *I Quit, But Forgot to Tell You: Attacking the Spreading Virus of Disengagement*. Largo, FL: Kabachnick Group.

Lombardo, M.M., & R.W. Eichinger (2000). "High Potentials as High Learners." *Human Resource Management*, 39(4), 321-329.

McCall, M.W., Jr., & G.P. Hollenbeck (2008). "Developing the Expert Leader." *People & Strategy, 31*(1), 20-29.

McCall, M.W., Jr., M.M. Lombardo & A.M. Morrison (1988). *The Lessons of Experience: How Successful Executives Develop on the Job*. New York: Free Press.

Schneider, B. (2006). "Customer Satisfaction." *Leadership Excellence*, 23(8), 13.

The World Bank. (2007). *Global Economic Prospects: Managing the Next Wave of Globalization*. Retrieved August 25, 2008, from http://www-wds.worldbank.org/external/default/WDSContentServer/IW3P/IB/2006/12/06/000112742_20061206155022/Rendered/PDF/381400GEP2007.pdf.

HR's Next Evolutions

W. Warner Burke, Ph.D.
Teachers College, Columbia University

Tamara Erickson's article is organized in two sections: "Redesigning Your Organization for the Future of Work" which comprises by far the majority of the writing, and the much shorter section at the end, "The Transformation Challenge: A New Human Resource Capability." I am much more interested in the latter than the former. Erickson's questions about the future of work are provocative and

appropriate. Thus, no counterpoint from me although I have two quick observations about this section:

- First, when it comes to redesigning your organization in such a way that Erickson's questions are addressed, I have found the Lawler, Worley and Porras book[1] to be very helpful. Their Chapter 4 on "Structuring for Effectiveness and Change" is a direct response to Erickson's questions.

- Second, with her last question, "Who will manage the workforce of the future?" Erickson suggests that the next evolution of HR is talent management. I think there are two HR evolutions. I will address the second shortly. I make sure these days that our organizational psychology students understand that TM no longer stands for transcendental meditation; but it now signifies talent management. These students have a significant role to play in this next evolution.

In Erickson's short, final section, "The Transformation Challenge: A New HR Capacity," I was especially interested in her five capabilities for HR now and in the future. The reason for my interest is that I am program coordinator for our graduate programs in social-organizational psychology, which include a PhD program and an MA program of 45 credits in organizational psychology. Most of our MA graduates, about 75 percent of whom are women, enter the HR function (if they are not in HR already) of some large organization—corporations for the most part but nonprofits and government agencies as well. A smaller proportion, but sizable group nevertheless, joins consulting firms.

So, first of all, how are we doing with respect to Erickson's five capabilities? And second, what is missing from her list?

Our students are required to take a course in business functions so they learn to read financial and income statements; and they learn some of the basics of marketing. They also learn process design and measurement. So, we address three out of Erickson's five. We are not strong on strategic thinking nor on the ability to create environments that support innovation. We are OK on collaboration, however. I think these two areas (strategic thinking and innovation) that Erickson mentions are important capabilities for HR folks, and we here at the college need to work harder on them for our students.

I have two final points, one that Erickson touches on and one that she doesn't.

The first point concerns an elaboration on Erickson's question about who will "manage" the workforce of the future. As noted earlier, this concerns talent management. While the management process should address all kinds of talent that are important to the organization, I believe that we should concentrate on leader development.

More than 50 percent of people in leadership positions fail ("failure" meaning not accomplishing established goals). Why such a high failure rate? There is no single cause, of course. Primary reasons include circumstances—people in leadership positions cannot control everything, and selection criteria—we cling to the notion that people who are highly technically and professionally competent also will be competent in leadership. The correlation is zero. An outstanding accountant is unlikely to become an outstanding manager of the accounting function. The best way to ruin a good classroom teacher is to make her a principal. An outstanding engineer is not necessarily going to be an outstanding supervisor. We know this, the research is clear, but we continue to believe.

We also select people for leadership based on our beliefs (which differ greatly among us) about what a leader should "look like"—tall, for example, or "with presence." So, it is difficult for a search group to agree on who will make the best leader.

A third reason for leader failure concerns the person. People who are low in emotional intelligence are not exactly good leaders. I could go on, but let me stop by stating my belief that we need to concentrate more on leader selection and development in more

effective ways than we have in the past; and HR must provide leadership in this area.

Finally, what is missing in Erickson's list? Change management—organization change and development. Our students get a dose of this complex capability in at least one of their required courses. To highlight the need for this capability: 60 to 75 percent of organization change efforts fail. As much as they see the need, managers and executives do not know much about organization change. Most of them will even admit it. So, to whom do they turn to for help? Many turn to their HR people, and, unfortunately, do not receive adequate guidance. I would, therefore, add this capability to Erickson's list.

1.Lawler, E.E. III, C.G. Worley and J. Porras (2006). *Built to Change: How to Achieve Sustained Organizational Effectiveness*. San Francisco: Jossey-Bass.

The Future of Work— Cubed

Kevin Rubens, Senior Vice President Aon Consulting

The economic miracle of the last 25 years produced a worldwide boom in the numbers of scientists, engineers and other professionals. This development, along with advances in computing and telecommunications, fostered the beginnings of a global market for "knowledge workers." This trend will continue to evolve in sync with long-term economic development and population growth. Looking ahead, there is a fresh set of convergent technologies that will enable knowledge workers to collaborate in new ways. To capitalize on the opportunities that these advances present, companies will require innovative human resource strategies and sophisticated organizational models.

During the next two decades, technologies like 3D-TV, interest-driven social networking sites (with capabilities well beyond Facebook or LinkedIn) and virtual environments like Second Life will become ever more prevalent and advanced. In the words of one industry spokesman: "These technologies will blend the

interactive networking capabilities of the Internet with the sensory impact of television."

Other important breakthroughs are coming. Economists credit the exponential increase in silicon-based computing power as a major contributor to the productivity gains we have seen during the last generation. Many scientists believe that quantum-based computers are the next step. Quantum computers will reduce the time to solve some complex problems from years to seconds, and quantum algorithms will lead to radical improvements in the efficiency of data search.

The World Wide Web, coupled with ever more powerful search algorithms, will provide access to an expanding universe of data. Google's Larry Page and Sergey Brin aspire to nothing less than organizing all of the information in the world within 20 years. Add in speech recognition and translation software, and this world of information will be accessible to everyone.

The confluence of these three dynamic factors—a growing global market of knowledge workers; technological advances that further enable networked problem solving; and universal access to information—already has begun to transform how people work and how value is created.

Today's computer, Internet and telecommunications technologies offer only a glimpse of what is coming. Within a decade, geographically disbursed, multilingual, multicultural teams will be able to come together in virtual 3-dimensional environments to share ideas, solve problems and make decisions with instant access to information and experts located anywhere in the world.

These emergent technologies not only will facilitate greater communication among the pool of knowledge workers, they will become the world's primary educational media and repositories of original sources. As the arrival of Wikipedia demonstrates, in a networked economy, information grows as it is shared. Soon, people will be able to explore ideas, develop new concepts and learn in ways that will be revolutionary.

➤

part II: organizational effectiveness

Companies like IBM already are building and operating virtual training facilities and project team "war rooms." Corporate headquarters that exist within the virtual space will follow. Historians, archeologists, cultural anthropologists, designers, architects, multimedia specialists and linguists may be at work building three-dimensional re-creations of first-century Rome or 21st-century Shanghai—settings that can be used for virtual company retreats as well as for primary school field trips.

If this seems far-fetched, recall that only 25 years ago the first laptops appeared, cell phones weighed 8.5 pounds and were carried in a bag, and the Internet was in its infancy. Networking meant meeting people for cocktails.

The future landscape has profound implications for human resources and organization design. Workforce segmentation will be at the core of human capital strategy. The approach may be based on individualized considerations related to role, geography, generation, skills, value or other characteristics. For example, strategies related to talent acquisition and remuneration will be much more tailored to the different roles within a firm than they are today. Companies will have to be tuned-in to which jobs are tied to the local labor market and which are globally competitive.

It will be critical to interpret current market intelligence and monitor internal trends. For many workers, company affiliation will be less important than their professional or network affiliations. This means that firms will have to find ever more creative ways to secure and retain committed talent.

Successful organizations will be network-oriented and informally structured. Greater adaptability will be required to accommodate rapidly changing business models and gain access to required skills. It will be key to quickly assemble flexible internal and external teams to work on product design, solve customer problems or take advantage of emerging market. Future organizations will redefine their core staff requirements and seek ad hoc partnerships and alliances

to supply non-core skills. Social Network Analysis and Dynamic Network Analysis will become an integrated part of Organizational Analysis. In time, new ways of assessing the value produced by formal and informal "Value Nets" will drive investment decisions, much as predicted return on capital does today.

For many workers, company affiliation will be less important than their professional or network affiliations. This means that firms will have to find ever more creative ways to secure and retain committed talent.

As this unfolds, a new type of leader will emerge. If the author Eamonn Kelly is correct in his prediction that "the future economy is about knowledge and relationships," it follows that organizations will need leaders who are able to build and sustain networks, manage diverse teams and lead across cultures. Tomorrow's leaders also will need the capacity to process ever-greater amounts of information and formulate sound decisions based on a more complex set of inputs. Finally, the next generation of leaders will have to be as comfortable operating in virtual space as they are within the confines of bricks and mortar.

References

Boudreau, J.W. (2005) "Talentship and the New Paradigm for Human Resource Management: From Professional Practices to Strategic Talent Decision Science." *Human Resource Planning*, June 2005. www.hrps.org.

The Emerging Global Labor Market (2007). McKinsey Publication. April 2007. http://www.mckinsey.com/mgi/publications/emerginggloballabormarket/index.asp.

Global Labor Market Database 2008. Global Policy Network (GBN). Labor Market Statistics and Indicators. www.gpn.org/data.html.

Kelly, E. (2005) *Powerful Times: Rising to the Challenge of Our Uncertain World*. Wharton School Publishing.

Stross, R. (2008) *Planet Google: One Companies Audacious Plan to Organize Everything We Know*. Free Press.

Taylor, K.S. (1998) "The Brief Reign of the Knowledge Worker: Information Technology and Technological Unemployment." (Paper presented at the International Conference on the Social Impact of Information Technologies in St. Louis Missouri, Oct. 1998). http://bellevuecollege.edu/distance/econ/kst/Briefreign/BRwebversion.htm.

Thomas, D. and J.S. Brown (2007) "Why Virtual Worlds Can Matter: Working Paper" (October, 2007) University of Southern California - Institute for Network Culture. www.johnseelybrown.com.

"University of Michigan Develops Scaleable and Mass Produceable Quantum Computer Chip" (2005). University of Michigan News Service, Dec. 12, 2005. www.umich.edu/news/index.html?releases.

"Where Engineers Are: Seeing Through Perceptions, A Deeper look at China and India. Issues in Science and Technology Online." University of Texas at Dallas. 2007. http://www.issues.org/23.3/wadhwa.html.

"Virtual Worlds News: Business, Strategy, Insights and Analysis. Updates on the companies and community of professionals involved in the metaverse and virtual worlds industry." www.virtualworlds.com.

The Chinese Context

Arthur Yeung, *Associate Dean and Philips Chair Professor*
China Europe International Business School

I must say Erickson's ideas and questions are truly provocative and futuristic. Erickson challenges our conventional wisdom of how employees should be managed, selected, developed, promoted, assessed, rewarded, retired and even defined in the face of pervasive technology capabilities, prevalence of nowledge-based jobs and changing demographics/needs of talent. In some senses, such changes are similar to "disruptive technologies" to an entrenched management model: they bring a major paradigm shift in how talent is managed. While I intuitively agree that such powerful trends will inevitably redefine how our jobs will be performed and talent "managed," the questions that deserve pondering are "when," "how much" and "how" much changes will happen, especially in the context of the Chinese business environment.

Anticipating the timing and extent of disruptive changes is never easy. Popularized by the book *Future Shock*, written by Alvin Toffler in 1970, people started to hypothesize in the last few decades of the 20th century how work would be done differently by the year 2000. Given the radical improvements in productivity and connectivity created by technology, people started to fantasize about the ability of employees to work three or four days per week, anywhere, anytime. While parts of the prediction happened (e.g., improved work mobility due to connectivity), the dream of working three or four days per week did not materialize. On the contrary, people work at least as hard as before, if not more, as the boundary between work and life further blurs.

Will the potential work changes posed by Erickson's questions happen in China in the next several decades? Maybe. But one thing is for sure: These changes will take longer and may not be as sweeping as predicted. As Chinese workforces are still predominantly populated by blue collar workers working in the labor-intensive manufacturing sector (and with an abundant supply and reserve of *more than 100 million* urban migrants from rural areas to be absorbed in the manufacturing/service sector *every year*), the overall shift to the kind of work and employee arrangement described by Erickson will be very slow.

Nevertheless, I believe these changes may occur sooner in specific functions, firms or industries where work is knowledge based and competition for talent is fierce, such as the R&D function, Internet service firms,

professional service firms, creativity or design industries, etc. Also, among the 12 possible changes raised by Erickson, I anticipate some work and HR changes (e.g., shorter tenure and loyalty, the variety of employment relationships, the role of corporations in education and competition for talent) will be more readily acceptable than others in China.

For example, due to the disconnect between educational curriculum (which is largely theoretical in nature) and corporate needs, many Chinese firms already have played important roles in educating employees to work productively in corporations. Starting from month-long orientation programs that help the "single-child" generation transition smoothly from family/school to work settings in terms of basic work ethic, interpersonal styles, conflict resolution, etc., many Chinese firms are investing another two or three years to help fresh graduates unlearn and relearn basic knowledge, skills and behaviors that are important in business settings through systematic on-the-job training and mentoring. Some corporations even run their own technical schools to ensure a steady supply of qualified workers that are more ready to contribute. Therefore, playing a major role in education is nothing new to many Chinese firms.

Others changes (like titles and career deceleration) will be much more challenging and will not happen without much resistance, partly because they will affect the vested interest of current power holders, and partly because these changes are counter-cultural as Chinese (and other Asian) culture tends to value hierarchy and respect older people. Other changes (like managing career paths laterally) are something many Chinese firms would love to do but don't know how to do without the right HR infrastructure in place and the buy-in of employees (tied to ingrained cultural values of hierarchy).

Having mentioned these challenges does not mean innovation in work and talent management is not possible in China. Given the scale and magnitude of its workforce, any major change in China takes time. However, the

good news is Chinese entrepreneurs are open to learning and can embrace changes quite quickly once such work and HR innovation prove successful. The tipping point will be the appearance of a few successful role models among Chinese firms (not Western firms) that demonstrate the competitive advantages resulting from such work and HR innovations. While HR professionals can play a role in facilitating such radical transformation, the ultimate success relies on CEOs who are willing to take risks to drive change. At least this is the most likely and pragmatic scenario in China. Influencing CEOs, not HR professionals, is the key to success.

The Singapore Context

Dr. Alison Eyring, CEO
Organisation Solutions

"Redesigning Your Organization for the Future of Work" raises excellent questions; but my perspective is that to understand ways to redesign our organizations for the future of work, HR leaders would benefit by taking a more macro view of the future and of organization design. To do this, HR leaders might consider the following:

- *There is no such thing as a "future of work." There are many possible futures of work.* The author concludes that the context for work in the future will be shaped by recent developments in demographics and technology. No one can argue with these points. However, HR leaders should not fall into the trap of thinking that past (or even recent) trends will predict the future, nor that we can accurately predict that future. Scenario planning draws out key forces shaping the future and then defines a number of alternative worlds that may unfold. Understanding these worlds and their implications allows policy and other decision makers to develop robust business, organization and people strategies to prepare for success across potential worlds.

In our work, we've seen that scenario planning isn't just an exercise in theory. It can help make practical organization ➤

part II: organizational effectiveness

design decisions, such as determining whether to structure functional groups along country or business lines or where to accelerate development.

- *Organization design encompasses far more than talent management processes.* The useful questions posed by the author relate primarily to attracting, developing, managing and retaining people. In addition, HR leaders must help shape the design of the future organization more broadly. For example, global supply-chain-management practices rose in a world of low energy/ transportation prices. If cheap energy were to go away, would global organizations need to rethink where they source products? Would manufacturing return to local plants and not global manufacturing systems? Such decisions are core to designing future organizations; and HR should be part of this conversation as well.

- *Demographic trends and workforce values in the United States are not necessarily true for the rest of the world.* HR leaders cannot assume that workforce trends in terms of shape and values can be generalized across different markets. Each country has a workforce with its own characteristics; and each country will be impacted differently as the global economy ebbs and flows during the coming decades. Understanding how the future will play out for different countries is important for most businesses – regardless of their own HQ nationality. In turn, this can drive decisions around structure, HR policy and practice, choices to outsource or offshore and where and how to innovate.

- *The impact of technology and the ability to drive down the cost of collaboration are impacted by culture.* Technology has revolutionized the way we work and will continue to do so. Most recently, "Web 2.0" and the promise of virtual collaboration across companies and communities have gained great popularity. Our experience and research in Asia on geographically distributed workgroups indicate that the promise of collaborative technologies is greater than the delivery. Too often trust is destroyed and

relationships damaged when tools are used inappropriately. Seldom is the quality of the ideas shared as rich and effective as when the sharing takes place face-to-face or following the development of a relationship. We'll need to see significant changes in how organizations actually design work and work groups to be effective remotely before cost reductions are achieved.

Taking Action

The author calls on HR leaders to develop general capabilities (such as a willingness to bring fresh perspectives to old assumptions) and specific capabilities (such as strategic thinking, particularly scenario development). To develop these capabilities, HR leaders might try the following:

1. Challenge spoken and unspoken assumptions about what is "true" in the world that determines where the company operates, what work is done where and what types of people are needed to get the work done.

2. Spend less time extrapolating past trends into the future and more time thinking about what we don't know that could have a radical impact on how we organize ourselves.

3. Include more voices in discussions on the future. The design of organizations in the United States and the future of U.S. work are inextricably connected to what happens in the rest of the world.

The Indian Context

Geetanjalli Parmar, Management Associate AIG

Tamara Erickson's article, "Redesigning Your Organization for the Future of Work," is inspiring and provides good foresight into what may be termed as a "non-traditional work environment." Her principles and trends challenge the design and practices of most modern-day organizations. As a Millennial, I fully support the ideology behind

Erickson's recommendations. The changing business and economic landscape stipulate such revitalization and rejuvenation of organizational structures, roles and processes.

Would these fundamental talent management approaches work in the Indian business environment? No easy answers here. Would the Indian workforce welcome these structures and processes? Within certain industries and certain generations, of course! Although India has borrowed technology, organization structures and management practices from countries of the West, it's usually not enough to take practices that work in one culture and apply them in another.

Therefore, institutionalizing practices like lateral moves and titles will challenge the age-old belief of maintaining status quo within the Indian society. Nothing can replace a "promotion" for an employee, not even a raise, let alone a lateral move. Promotion for an employee is considered to be an uplifting of the individual in the society, which plays a major role in his motivation. The challenge and variety in the job takes a back seat if the employee is not considered as "growing." A manager in a large organization will still be looked down upon when compared to a General Manager in a small organization. So the "name" or "title" does play a major role in our country.

Does a career need to be continuous and linear? This would really not work in the Indian scenario. Unlike the West, once Indian employees get out of the job, whether in their "forties or after retirement," it is very difficult for them to come back and work. The majority of individuals will not be able to manage a break in service/employment. Whatever advancement in technology, process automation or outsourcing happens, you will not be able to limit the employment opportunities in India. Thus contrary to what Erickson states, the need for permanent staff is never going to come down, and all organizations are ready to invest in it.

Teamwork is the rule of the day in India. A manager with effective leadership and team working skills is preferred over the subject matter expert. Here Erickson is predicting the future, but in India it's a reality for the last decade. A team headed by a defined leader is usually more permanent in nature and is accountable for the achievement of defined areas of performance. It is indeed teamwork where "purposefully interacting, vigilant, agile and resilient individuals" lend support to the achievement of the larger visions and goals of the organization.

The decade of the nineties for Indian business organizations was both dramatic and traumatic. India borrowed technology, organization structures and management practices from Japan and Western countries. The underlying assumptions of how technology and management practices ought to work are anchored in their respective cultures. The internalization of borrowed technologies and organization structures in India has been accomplished with the critical input from human resources. HR professionals rose to the challenge and have played a key role in facilitating and building high performing, synergized teams, whose core competencies were in handling ambiguity in a rapidly changing work environment.

The European Context

Pam Hurley, Managing Director,
Tosca Consulting Group, UK

As I write this, newspaper headlines continue to be dominated by the global economic meltdown. Each day the news treats us to the latest moves by Paulson, Merkel, Sarkozy, Brown and others to stave off the devastating implications of a deep and prolonged world recession. Meanwhile, Iceland is looking to both Russia and the IMF to cover some big bets that have gone wrong, and the screens of the Asian stock markets are following their Western counterparts in turning red. Of course, 2008 will go down in history as a remarkable year for the markets and several household name institutions, and as a ruinous year for many who were employed by

them. But is it really the end of the world, as we know it?

The world as we know it is what we see through our own particular lens. That lens is coloured by our personal experiences, upbringing, national culture and a myriad of other factors. The world viewed through the lens of a 50-year-old American citizen working in, say, Michigan looks very different from that of a young miner in Botswana or an entrepreneur in Chennai. I was struck in reading the article "Redesigning Your Organization for the Future of Work" by the strength of the lens through which it views the world. The article seeks to explore the **world** of work of the **next several decades** and yet it reads to me very much as work in North America in 2008.

Here are a few factors that seem to be missing from the equation:

- Of the 470 million or so new jobs that will be created in the world between 2005 and 2020, just 2.6 percent or 12.5 million of them will be located in the United States. More than 200 million of the new jobs—over 40 percent—will be in India and China.

- The 25 percent of China's population with the highest IQs and the 28 percent of India's population with the highest IQs are each greater than the total population of North America today.

- A U.S. student today will have had 10-14 jobs by the age of 38.

- The population of Europe, especially Spain, Italy and Germany, is getting smaller – as well as older.

- Between 2000 and 2005, the BRIC countries – Brazil and Russia along with India and China – contributed almost 30 percent of global growth in U.S. dollar terms; the Chinese economy is growing at 11 percent per annum.

- Roughly one of every 35 persons in the world is a migrant, and their number is growing at almost 3 percent annually.

I could go on but I hope you already get the picture. I'm not brave enough to try to look several decades out; 2018 is far enough for me. So what can HR do to contribute to business success over the next decade? First and fundamentally, understand the business you're operating in. This issue has itself been around for at least a decade and yet survey after survey shows that most line managers – and many in HR – still do not think HR understands the business well enough to deliver what's required.

Second, become a true expert in a specific area that is key to business success. For example, if Generation Y (those born since 1980) will be a really important part of your workforce, develop genuine expertise in what will attract, retain and fully engage them and design programmes that will enable them to move on and out when they want to—and back in again, bringing you their extra skills and experience.

Third, focus hard on what is known as talent management. We all know that the capabilities of our workforce are going to be more critical than ever to business success as the only real differentiator. For Gen Y high-fliers the concept of talent *management* is an oxymoron—they just need an environment where they can see clearly what assignments are on offer and go for those that are a good fit. For experienced or aspiring international managers, the need may be more to provide access to cultural awareness programmes, to prevent them being trapped in one location, or to ensure that life as well career aspirations are recognised. And for those who don't aspire to global high-flying—often the majority—recognise that they too have valuable talent.

Above all, keep your head up and keep looking around you. Be prepared to raise—and answer—questions about the opportunities and threats of doing business with new partners, in new regions, of collaborating with colleges, of adopting new technology to ease team communication and so on. Make sure your binoculars are powerful and trained on the world.

➤

On the Future of Work – and HR

Yochanan Altman, Professor of International HRM, London Metropolitan University and the University of Paris (Pantheon-Assas), and Founding Editor of the Journal of Management, Spirituality & Religion

"It is the best of times; it is the worst of times." I can't resist paraphrasing Dickens' unforgettable opening line to *A Tale of Two Cities*, as the grimmest economic climate for 80 years has descended upon us. In Europe, the end of the "Anglo-Saxon Century" is lamented/celebrated (tick your choice); the BRIC countries are jostling to reposition the pecking order of the global economy; and on a dull autumnal London morning, writing this piece, the future looks particularly glum. Well, you will say, that may account for "the worst of all times," but what about the other half of the quote? My answer is that these testing times may also accord an opportunity to the HR profession to change direction. The collapse of financial markets has brought to the attention of the public and policy makers the risks of the relentless drive to maximise profit, or "the bottom line," at all **costs** (sic); a drive in which the HR profession has acted as a willing agent in the pursuit of the much coveted mantle of a "business partner" (as elusive as the golden fleece, I may add). So here is the silver lining in the current storm. But let me come to that later.

I was asked to comment on Tamara Erickson's discourse on the Future of Work. Peering into the looking glass, she sees a dynamic global economy with a demand for highly skilled talent. I like very much the questions/challenges she poses for us to ponder:

- how to enable career progression in flatter organizational structures;

- how to minimise formalization (e.g., roles, titles);

- how to prevent rigid age categorization (retirement age as a fixed chronology); and

- how to flexibly manage a career over a life span (with interim sabbaticals and life-work balancing).

Erickson convincingly argues that the very notions of "employee" and "job" may need to be redefined, with boundaries between work and non-work, home and office, increasingly

> The collapse of financial markets has brought to the attention of the public and policy makers the risks of the relentless drive to maximise profit, or 'the bottom line,' at all costs (sic); a drive in which the HR profession has acted as a willing agent in the pursuit of the much coveted mantle of a 'business partner' (as elusive as the golden fleece, I may add).

becoming blurred; and with the facilities of information technology making working time configuration obsolete. Consequently, issues such as performance (short-term, intermediate and long-term), management (of virtual non-standard employees), reporting (organizations without fixed structures) and formal and informal learning (corporate universities) should to be re-thought from scratch.

I fully concur with her on all of these. However, I take a different trajectory on two fundamental issues: the shape of the demographics of the future, and the challenge facing the HR function.

It is conventional wisdom that historical, pyramidal demographics have long gone. No more a wide younger generation base supporting older generations with the elderly at the (narrow) top. This indeed is so, but only if one counts the official numbers of the legal labour force. What official statistics do not reveal is the unaccounted for clandestine armies of illegal and semi-legal hotel maids, bar attendants, nannies, construction workers, taxi drivers, hospital auxiliaries, office

cleaners, rubbish collectors – that keep the megalopolises of New York, Los Angeles, London, going; as well as Riyadh, Hong Kong, Buenos Aires, Cape Town – facilitating the said "talent" to pursue their middle-class careers and life styles. The pyramidal demographics actually stay intact, except that, iceberg like, their base seems invisible. The challenge in the decades to come would be to bring these unaccounted millions into the realm of legality and human rights, into the formal economy and civic society. Perhaps this is a mission for the HR profession? Which brings me to my second point of contention.

Erickson wants to see HR leaders endowed with business leadership skills: strategic thinking, finance and business acumen, and proficiency with metrics, marketing and branding savvy. Noble competences and important too, except that they have little to do with the essence of HR, which ought to be to work with, service and help **people** in organizations (of all kinds, not just top management). The future of HR will not lie in pursuing business partnership status by applying the balanced scorecard to anything on two legs that moves. The future of HR is in championing the rights, needs, aspirations and dreams of **all** the talent that comes under their organizational umbrella. That way HR may make a contribution to the future of work too. **P&S**

Redesigning Your Organization for the Future of Work

Discovery Questions

- Do you agree with Tamara Erickson's statement that the *Work World* of the next two decades will be fundamentally different from the past in three areas: 1) Efficient technologies of collaboration, 2) Economic activity focused on knowledge and co-creation and 3) New talent demands based on individualized work arrangements?

- Why does the assumption that organizations are shaped like pyramids no longer apply?

- What are the new organizational "shapes" that are coming into existence? Illustrate how a "diamond" is different from a "rectangle" shaped organization.

- Why are organization design parameters around time and specific job descriptions becoming obsolete?

- What is the role of HR in leading organization design work?

- What are the twelve questions that Tammy Erickson asks HR to reflect on?

- Choose two or three cases that illustrate Tammy Erickson's point of view which you personally observed as playing a role in your organization.

Selected Facts

- What new facts that were presented got your attention?

- Does the assumption "structure drives behavior" hold? (Review facts from Beverly Kaye's response.)

- Organizational efficiencies, higher productivity and employee engagement are only possible if management of people, technology and real estate assets are integrated. (Comment on James Ware and Charles Grantham's response.)

- What are specific global contexts in which Erickson's thesis resonates? (Review European, Chinese, Singapore, and Indian contexts.)

- What are the true HR skills required to accomplish organizational transformation? (Review arguments presented by Yochanan Altman.)

- Review the value of internal and external partnerships as cited by Kevin Rubens.

Key Discussion Points

- What were the key points being made in this Point Counterpoint presentation?

- What trends will define the future of work?

- Discuss the implications of these trends on organizational design and on the world of jobs and careers.

- Present and illustrate the key questions arising from the challenge of redesigning our current organizations to keep up with the pace of change.

- Why do the majority of respondents insist that the "future of work" is already here?

- Is it individuals or teams that most greatly determine organizational performance?

- Discuss the role of HR in organizational transformation:
  a) Is HR leading the transformation?
  b) What skills are required of HR to lead the transformation?
  c) What are the barriers to change?

- Review the counterpoint presented by Yochanan Altman in his argument for HR returning to its roots.

Review of Solutions

- Identify 2-3 Big Ideas that are worthy of implementing in your organization.

- Name all possible approaches to organization redesign as recommended by all participants in this Point Counterpoint.

Recommendations Summary

- Identify one thing that we will do differently based on what we learned.

Learning Outcomes

- What one new piece of information did you learn that will be important to you?

Perspectives—Point/Counterpoint

Anna Tavis, Perspectives Editor

Note: It has been a little more than a year now since we first published the Point/Counterpoint format in our Perspectives section. We were excited then about beginning each journal with a conversation on leading-edge ideas by thought leaders, practitioners, consultants and authors. The idea of having a diverse group of people discuss a topic of interest to our readers seems even more relevant to us this year, when our challenging economy forces us to rethink everything about the ways we do business.

So, in 2009, our Point/Counterpoints will revisit many of our fundamental HR and business assumptions and models.

- In this issue, together with Karen Stephenson, we question traditional organizational structures.

- In our second issue, we will review David Ulrich and Wayne Brockbank's Model of HR as a business partner.

- In issue three, our point article will be Peter Cappelli's revision of talent management.

- We will conclude the year with our last issue dedicated to Peter Drucker's global legacy about management and leadership.

We invite all of you who would like to participate in these conversations to contact us and suggest the topics about which you might like to comment. Counterpoint contributions usually run from 500 to 750 words. You will receive the Point article and have a few months to create your response.

Contact us at **jstrother@hrps.org** if you'd like to join the conversation and be part of *People & Strategy*. We look forward to your involvement.

Neither Hierarchy nor Network: An Argument for Heterarchy

Karen Stephenson, NetForm, Inc.

Long ago, when the world was local, trust enabled our primordial ancestors to cooperate and overcome overwhelming odds. As our world became more globally interconnected, technology trumped trust. But as the world continued to shrink, a strange thing happened: Interdependencies began to grow and trust was again recognized as the missing link in free-trade agreements, civic-engagement initiatives and financial markets. Trust has been missing in action because we haven't been able to build meaningful, collaborative structures and performance metrics to ensure its sustainability. That's our job today.

No one disputes that the world is shrinking, as more and more people connect with each other through technology. As every connection is made, interdependencies extend from local to global, and so the social fabric or "network" is rewoven. A network is the nonrandom aggregation of these human connections and is both nuanced and nuclear in its collective power. Until September 11, 2001, organizational theorists largely ignored networks.[1] But networks are ancient tribal structures and permeate even the most familiar organizational forms we embrace as markets and hierarchies.

Networks do more than just connect us as individuals to each other. They connect our different institutions together in organic organizational sprawl. This mega-state of networked or connected hierarchies is known as heterarchy. There is no archeological precedent for heterarchy that we know of, largely because the world and our institutions have never been this interconnected.

"I'm a Prisoner of War in My Own Organization."

A three-star admiral told me, "I can lead men and women into battle, but I am a prisoner of war in my own organization." How does this happen? Governance is a morphing process that incrementally builds on the skeletal remains of past mistakes and policies such that the organizational structure becomes a great barrier reef.

The resulting labyrinths of processes can be difficult to thoroughly chart and, if not monitored, will alter the ecosystem in which the organization thrives. These "bureaucracies," as we have come to know them, inspire both anxiety and awe. Anxiety comes because they

---

1. With the exception of the seminal article by Powell, W. (1990) "Neither Market nor Hierarchy: Network Forms of Organization," *Organizational Behavior*, 12:295-336.

demand constant tending and feeding to be sustained; awe arises because they are mercurial, magically summoning power from unknowable depths to kill an innovation or destroy a career with aplomb.

The long list of quiet failures that beset would-be leaders as they attempt to win support for new initiatives is due to these bureaucracies and to the prevailing presumption that the key positional "power" people—and the status quo—eventually win out. But what is really going on is that bureaucratic status quo is just a map of favors curried by generations of people and cured over time into resistance to change. Has the reader ever tried to change a bureaucracy? I rest my case!

With the exception of lobbyists, most of us bemoan the existence of sprawling bureaucracies and resign ourselves to co-existing with bureaucratic compromise. But in 1955, the French anthropologist Levi-Strauss[2] made a bold assertion, largely ignored, that structure trumps scale. His insight has implications for bureaucracies. He goes on to explain that politics has more to do with a two-person household becoming a three-person household than the implications resulting from a 10 percent increase in a 300 million population. What he meant is that a network consisting of three or more people, and similarly a heterarchy consisting of three or more institutions, is essentially an "atom of organization." If you think this sounds simplistic, wait a minute and think it through with me.

- Take the example of a three-person network: you, your spouse and your spouse's mother. When you have had an argument with your spouse and your spouse tells his/her mother and the mother-in-law becomes angry with you, well then, that's a power squeeze most of us can identify with. In graph theoretical terminology, this is called a "signed graph." The tightening grip of a nuclear family on *your* degrees of freedom can have far-reaching implications. See Figure 1b.

The good news is that these triads of connections within our circle of families and friends

may be part of the solution for solving mega-organizational structures in the 21st century. Let me explain with a provocative example using Figure 2 as illustration.

- My elderly father had both Type II diabetes and Alzheimer's and was moved from his home to an assisted-living apartment (Organization A). On his arrival, an open sore was discovered on the heel of his foot and he was rushed to the hospital for immediate treatment (Organization B). After a close call with a diabetic coma, the antibodies cleared the infection on this foot. However, he had forgotten how to walk in the interim. So he was summarily shipped off to a physical therapy institute (Organization C) for treatment. The resulting increased activity awakened his curiosity and he was discovered wandering the streets outside the institute at night. He was then transferred to an Alzheimer's physical therapy unit (Organization D) where he was more confined but by this time completely demoralized. Having lost the will to walk, he remained confined in a wheel chair and was transferred to a fully operational Alzheimer's institute (Organization E) where he remained until he died shortly thereafter.

Figure 1a: Simple partnership or marriage held in place with simple contracts.

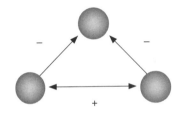

Figure 1b: A triad or signed graph of a nuclear family: You are at the top; your spouse is to the left; and your mother-in-law to the right. This structure can create interesting politics and not consistently positive relations.

Figure 1c: A triad or signed graph of public private partnerships in the United Kingdom consisting of the victim, the police and the health agency.

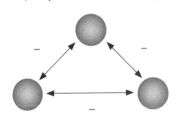

Figure 2: Heterarchies are collaborative endeavors whereby organizations are networked together. Organizations are depicted as yellow, layered silos and the collective and the combined activity is the blue network shown in the middle.

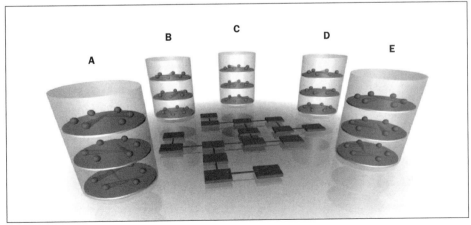

2.Levi-Strauss, "The Mathematics of Man," *International Social Science Bulletin*: Vol. 6, pp. 581-90.

part II: organizational effectiveness

TABLE 1: HETERARCHY IS GREATER THAN THE SUM OF ITS PARTS

Features	Market	Hierarchy	Network	Heterarchy
Relationship	Transaction	Authority	Trust	Collaborative
Exchange	Non-repetitive	Routine	Repetitive	Intermittent
Focus	Disinterested	Vested Interest	Personal Interest	Collective Good
Rate of Change	Dramatic but not Radical	Slow and Incremental	Rapid and Radical	Sense and Respond
Knowledge Management	Contracts	Policies	Conventions	Agreements

Anyone who has had an elderly parent, grandparent or a family friend may read in this story common threads of despair. When I interviewed the doctors, nurses and physical therapists about what had happened, everyone concurred that they had individually done their jobs within the local confines of their own organizational policies and protocols. Because no one was thinking globally or more collaboratively, the resulting multiple transfers of this elderly man were traumatic: They impacted his quality of life. This outcome is, of course, the exact opposite of stated healthcare goals and is referred to as a perverse outcome to policy.

Heterarchy is Not for the Faint of Heart

The concept of heterarchy is essential in understanding bureaucracies, so that they can be aligned and fit for purpose. Heterarchy (Figure 2 and Table 1) consists of at least three (or more) separate hierarchies, each with its own raison d'être, but which, in turn, must collaborate with each other to accomplish a collective good more complex than any one hierarchy can manage on its own. It is an organizational form somewhere between hierarchy and network that provides horizontal links permitting different elements of an organization to cooperate, while they individually optimize different success criteria. Its beauty is the way in which it permits the legitimate valuation of multiple skills, types

of knowledge or working styles without privileging one over the other.

Heterarchy is a good idea, but very difficult to implement compared to more familiar forms of hierarchies and networks. It requires a well-designed and coordinated network, ensuring alignment and common connections, largely through performance measures. Heterarchies can be seedbeds of contagion—of ineptness, of disease and of fraud as we have witnessed in the unintended consequences of ENRON, AIDS and the radioactive diffusion of distrust in the 2008 global financial meltdown. Or, heterarchies can link

Heterarchies are magnificently complex, linking together people and institutions to solve a complex task and or achieve a grand design.

together people and institutions to solve a complex task and/or achieve a grand design. Heterarchy could portend a premier form of 21st-century governance. Or it could be a harbinger of unimaginable perversity.

When We Don't Go Far Enough

In October 1998, Great Britain's Blair administration authorized agglomeration of several

smaller departments into the giant Department for the Environment, Transport and the Regions, or DETR. This directive failed because simply putting people in the same building, in the same hierarchy and changing the name of the organization is only a first step in a hierarchical process and does not automatically lead to or guarantee integrated working in a heterarchy.

Similarly in 2003, the U.S. Bush Administration created the Department of Homeland Security (DHS) by combining three separate government functions: intelligence (e.g., NSA, NRO and CIA); policing (e.g., Customs, FBI); and emergency and disaster response (e.g., FEMA, Coast Guard). Built up from approximately 60-plus pre-existing departments, DHS consolidated these departments and agencies in an effort to engage the agencies in meaningful collaboration. Unfortunately, because there were no shared processes, the move only deepened the competition among the constituencies.

Remember: In bureaucratic sprawl, one team jockeys for position with another; one directorate attacks another to protect its budget; and departments as a whole fight one

another to defend their turf. There is no infrastructure to join these systems into one integrated whole. As such, they are never more than (and often much less than) the sum of their parts. These competing segments calculate power by comparing and contrasting their stock or status with that of their peers. Competition, not collaboration, is the watchword. What is needed is a multi-organizational network to support the seamless exchange of information laterally in a heterarchy among hierarchies.

Collaboration, Not Competition

Philadelphia took a fresh approach to urban renewal in 2005. The city highlighted hidden connectors: It uncovered and heralded people doing good deeds. The resulting public revelation inspired a renewed fervor in civic engagement. Leaders revealed these unsung heroes by modifying a form of social network analysis. They mapped networks and identified the pivotal combinatorial points. The efforts led to a renaissance in civic engagement

and they are being copied in many major metropolitan cities in the United States.[3]

Also in 2005, a U.K. initiative sponsored by the Home Office, The Government Office of East Midlands, and the Office of the Deputy Prime Minister began to develop new performance measures using a modified form of social network analysis for local strategic partnerships. Although partnerships between two organizations may begin by "shaking hands" at the executive level, smarter measures are needed to sustain multi-agency collaboration throughout and not just at the top.

In both cases, "hidden" strategic connections revealed a *"virtual organization"* or heterarchy such as the one shown below. Connectors are hidden because they are not visible to a hierarchy that looks out, but not down. These connectors are critical for sustainability and they are essential collaborators in governing.

Trust and Technology

We are increasingly interconnected due to technology but that doesn't make us any wiser or closer to each other. Instead, the deep connection I am alluding to arises from sustaining trust across multiple agencies, hierarchies and countries. This is the 21st-century challenge for leaders and managers of heterarchy—the DETRs, the DHSs, the EUs and the United Nations of the world.

Connection by technology without trust is merely traffic. Trusted connection without technology is an opportunity lost. To survive as a species we need both, but not at the expense of the other. Trust and technology help humans connect across geographical distances or reach across a continental divide of cultural differences. It is self-evident and it is a social imperative: We must connect, but we must connect in ways that are meaningful and sustainable. That is why understanding, measuring and implementing heterarchical interconnection should be a top priority for policymakers everywhere.

Editor's Note: Stephenson's work was the subject of a feature article in The New Yorker *by Malcolm Gladwell (2000), and* Strategy + Business *by Art Kleiner (2003).*

> Connection by technology without trust is merely traffic. Trusted connection without technology is an opportunity lost. To survive as a species we need both, but not at the expense of the other.

Karen Stephenson, Ph.D., is CEO of NetForm, Inc., and is associate professor of management at the Rotterdam School of Management at Erasmus University.

Figure 2: Hidden collaborators in the heterarchy.

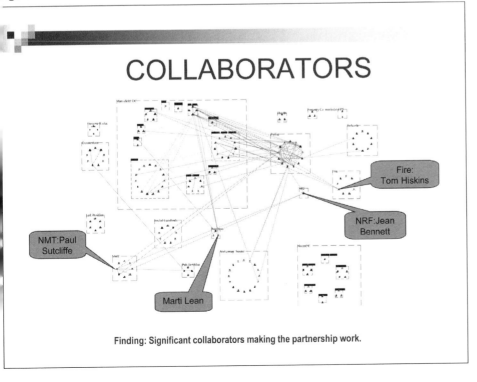

Finding: Significant collaborators making the partnership work.

3. Stephenson, K. (2007). "The Community Network Solution," *Strategy and Business*, Issue 49, Winter, 2007.

part II: organizational effectiveness

Concrete Examples Needed

Edgar Schein, MIT Sloan School of Management

Karen Stephenson's argument for heterarchy is valid in principle, but it is lacking in the details of how one would create effective heterarchies. As she correctly points out, trust between members of a network, whether those are individuals, groups or entire organizations, is the key to whether or not they can collaborate. We now have the technology that would enable large organizations to share information and coordinate their activities—and we may even have the will to collaborate—but do we know how to build the level of trust that may be necessary for valid information exchange.

The biggest barrier I see is that with globalism has come occupational multi-culturalism. Organizations reflect their national origins and build their own corporate cultures out of their own experiences.

Furthermore, as technologies become more complex, the members of task forces and teams also come from different occupational cultures (Schein, 2009). In fact, coordination and cooperation between different occupational groups may be a more difficult problem than even between national groups, as exemplified in the difficulty that surgical teams have in implementing technologies that require real teamwork between the surgeon, the anesthetist, and the nurses (Edmondson).

For a heterarchy to function, therefore, requires that in each link there is a common language and common cultural understand-ing. Once that common understanding has been achieved, building trust becomes possible: But it must be built, it cannot be assumed.

In my recent book, *Helping* (2009), I have argued that the building of trust is itself a very complex communication process in which we gradually test how much the "other" is willing to accept us for what we are and not take advantage of us for personal gain. The motive to want to collaborate has to be there for this process to work. And from this point of view, collaboration can be viewed as a mutual helping process. For the members of a heterarchy to function effectively requires a motivation to be mutually helpful. That is precisely what I find missing in so many organizational situations, in part because our larger capitalist frame of reference reifies competition as the basic motivator.

I believe that networking leading to functioning heterarchies is probably inevitable in today's world, but which organizations and institutions will effectively coordinate and/or collaborate is very much a mystery, given all of the structural and cultural barriers in the way of effective inter-organizational communication. What would be enormously helpful would be some concrete examples of how such heterarchies were created and what enabled them to function.

Edgar Schein is professor emeritus at the MIT Sloan School of Management.

References

Edmondson, A.C., R.M. Bohmer, & G.P. Pisano (2001). "Disrupted Routines: Team Learning and New Technology Implementation in Hospitals." Administrative Quarterly, 46, 685-716.

> I believe that networking leading to functioning heterarchies is probably inevitable in today's world, but which organizations and institutions will effectively coordinate and/or collaborate is very much a mystery.

Early Stages of a Journey

Robert G. Eccles, Harvard Business School

Karen Stephenson's "argument for heterarchy" is a provocative idea, yet an incomplete one. Before elaborating on why I think it is incomplete, let me elaborate a bit on three reasons why I like it.

- First, the implied anthropological approach is a refreshing one. The fact that institutions and the ways people work together are deeply embedded in past structures that have been adapted to present circumstances is largely ignored.

- Second, Stephenson is pointing out an important issue in today's globally interconnected world, which is the need for greater collaboration to ensure the required collective action for solving some of the pressing problems facing our country and the world today.

- Finally, the examples she uses to illustrate her argument are compelling ones. I also like the fact that they range from the small and the personal to the large and the institutional.

Let me now suggest some areas where I think her argument needs further elaboration. These should be considered as constructive suggestions for her future work and longer articles or even a book she might write on this topic—and I would be pleased if she did.

- **The implied duality needs to be made explicit.** Stephenson appears to be arguing that heterarchies are bad ("heterarchies are seedbeds of contagion—of ineptness, of disease and of fraud") and that "heterarchy is a good idea." Of course, any organizational form could be effective or ineffective, but Stephenson needs to more clearly articulate what makes for good and bad heterarchies.

- **The relationships between organizational forms need to be clarified.** Stephenson defines heterarchies as a "mega-state of networked or connected hierarchies," which begs such questions as:

(1) What is a network of networks? (2) What is the role of markets in heterarchies? and (3) Can there be a heterarchy of heterarchies? And, if not, what defines the boundaries of a given heterarchy? What is needed here is a kind of meta-table on Table 2 in her piece.

The role of information technology needs to be explained.
Technology appears in the very first sentence of her piece and it is in the first sentence of the last paragraph. Yet the reader, at least this one, is never clear on just what the role of technology (or what is exactly meant by this—IT?) is here. Nor is it clear whether technology is a prime reason for the emergence of heterarchies; a way to enable them to work better; or a negative factor if it is not combined with trust.

The importance of heterarchy to understanding the collapse of the financial markets needs to be demonstrated.
Stephenson briefly mentions this example, in an almost teasing way. Understanding why this happened is enormously important and I think her concept of heterarchy could provide some powerful insights.

- **The ways in which heterarchies can be made forces for good need to be identified.**
While examples of effective heterarchies are given, there is no framework that explicates how to make heterarchies forces for good. This is particularly important given the implied duality I have already mentioned.

While I think Stephenson is in the early stages of her journey on arguing for the existence of and the need for heterarchies, I like the direction in which she is going and wish her the best of luck. Her contribution to theory and practice has the potential to be a very important one.

Robert G. Eccles is a senior lecturer at Harvard Business School.

Of Hidden Connectors and a Violin Quartet

Charles Handy, London Business School and the Royal Society of Arts

Karen Stephenson has highlighted an increasingly important challenge to our organizations. She has focused on the need for institutions of all types to work collaboratively, but through a virtual network of hidden connectors rather than some cumbersome structural arrangement. She is right but, sadly, labelling the problem does not solve it: It may even make it worse.

Organizations, and even groups of organizations, are very prone to the practice of "boxing the problem." That is, having identified a continuing issue, they create a box somewhere on the organization chart, give it the name of the problem and put some people in it in the hope that they will deal with it. Unfortunately, this only adds to the bureaucratic tangle that Karen Stephenson wants to avoid. My concern is this: Bringing the hidden connectors into the light by, for instance, labelling them as the heterarchy might result in them being herded into just another box, and told to sort it out – to end up as just another committee.

The answer must be to keep them hidden, but this requires, from those hidden connectors, a willingness to downplay their own significance to create something bigger together. They are only likely to do this if they feel that they can be a part, however unrecognized, of some greater cause. This, then, is the new leadership challenge: to inspire people to want to reach beyond the bounds of their own organization to create something special, and to find the other connectors who will help them

to do this. This means that the leaders themselves need to have horizons beyond their own organizations, rather than concentrating on their purely local priorities – a quality that, I fear, is all too rare. However, Julia Middleton, of Common Purpose, in her recent book Beyond Authority has some nice examples of leaders who have done just that.

I am worried, too, by Karen Stephenson's all-too-accurate comment that technology without trust is merely traffic. My worry, to use a modification of another of her neat observations, is that technology trumps trust: that just because we can communicate we

> This, then, is the new leadership challenge: to inspire people to want to reach beyond the bounds of their own organization to create something special, and to find the other connectors who will help them to do this.

believe we can collaborate. After watching a violin quartet the other night, I asked one of the performers if they could play the same quartet virtually, if they were connected by some videoconferencing facility that linked them while being physically in different countries. She said that it might be technically possible but only if they had previously worked together and rehearsed in the same space. "The empathy and trust wouldn't be there otherwise," she said. Too true, I fear, and the same applies to any working group, be they playing violins or not.

The new heterarchies won't work unless those hidden connectors can, in a sense, become the equivalent of that violin quartet, where leadership is so subtle as to be almost invisible; where empathy is the favored way of communicating; and where personal rivalry is subsumed in the cause of their joint creation. That won't happen by e-mailing alone, just one more challenge thrown up by this new organizational form of heterarchy. Karen Stephenson is right to have drawn our attention to it.

➤

Charles Handy is professor emeritus at the London Business School and is chairman of the Royal Society of Arts in London. Among his 18 books are *The Age of Unreason* (Harvard Business School, 1989) and *Myself and Other More Important Matters* (AMA – 2008).

References

Middleton, Julia (2007). *Beyond Authority: Leadership in a Changing World*. New York: Palgrave MacMillan.

Neither Hierarchy nor Heterarchy: An Argument for Network?

Tracy Cox, Raytheon Professional Services LLC

As I read Karen Stephenson's article, I first appreciated her title selection to include the word "argument." This invites debate—and that is exactly what continues to advance the field and study of informal networks in business. Secondly, she begins the article with the words, "No one would argue that…" Thus, as is often the case, I will now play the role of "No one."

As we discuss a network relationship, it typically comes with two active ingredients: trust and reputation. As Ron Burt (2005) most eloquently discusses, trust is a **relationship** with someone in which contractual terms are incompletely specified. The more unspecified and taken for granted the terms, the more trust is involved. Without trust, I doubt that a relationship exists. This would seem to make it difficult to conduct meaningful business transactions across this "connection." So comes the question, from a business value perspective: Does the fact that we have more "connections" really matter?

As for the argument that heterarchy seems to be trumping hierarchy and network as we become more connected, I must first begin with the definition of heterarchy. From Wikipedia, a **heterarchy** is a system of organization replete with overlap, multiplicity, mixed ascendancy and/or divergent-but-coexistent patterns of relation. In social and information sciences, heterarchies are networks of elements in which each element shares the same "horizontal" position of power and authority, each playing a theoretically equal role.

My struggle begins with making applicable business sense out of theory. While heterarchies might exist in social settings, I'm just

possible that this phenomenon is reasonabl to expect in a purely social setting, but in th domain of business and markets, I believe to be just theoretical.

Finally, in Table 2 of Stephenson's article, sh does a very nice job of differentiating severa structures including Markets, Hierarchy Network and Heterarchy. My problem her is that the attributes under a heterarchy (Co laborative, Intermittent, Collective Good Sense & Respond, Agreements) easily describ several networks that I have studied an documented. I don't believe that a network focus is one of personal interest. In fact, ther are many situations where very cohesive net works take on such a strong identit associated with the team that the interests o the individuals take a back seat to the goal and objectives of the collective.

In fact, per Burt (2005), strong cohesion in network can lead to phenomenal gains i efficiency and productivity by ramping dow learning curves. It may also have negative side effects such as groupthink, gossip and char acter assassination. But these characteristic are a result of the "greater good" being fa more important than the individual's per sonal interests.

I agree wholeheartedly with the Stephenson' concluding remarks. The increased interconnections due to technology do not make us any wiser or closer to each other. Neither do they facilitate trust leading to economic gain, new markets, business partnerships or better performance.

I love the line that "Connection by technology without trust is merely traffic." But, the concluding remarks are such a strong argument for networks and our continued pursuit to understand them and leverage them—not for social studies, but for the purpose of increasing innovation and growth, improving profit margins through efficiency and productivity and creating economic prosperity for future generations. So maybe I am pushing for a changed title to the article. How about, "Neither Hierarchy nor Heterarchy: An Argument for Network"?

> My struggle begins with making applicable business sense out of theory. While heterarchies might exist in social settings, I'm just not sure I've seen one in business practice.

My first inclination, as I continue to study informal network structures across the world in a wide range of markets and cultures, is to challenge the notion of the world becoming smaller as more and more people connect. I am becoming more and more perplexed by the 21st-century definition of a relationship, given that we seem to be using the word " connection" far more in business as opposed to "relationship."

not sure I've seen one in business practice. The problem lies in the "theoretically equal role" of the players or entities in a heterarchy. In practical application, I don't know that this exists. While I have seen many instances of politically or structurally equivalent entities in networks, there always exists this element of informal power and influence inherent in any informal network that prevents "theoretically equal roles." It's quite

perspectives – counterpoints

Tracy Cox is director of performance consulting with Raytheon Professional Services, LLC.

References

Burt, Ron (2005). *Brokerage and Closure: An Introduction to Social Capital.* Oxford University Press.

What Happens Next?

Patti Anklam, Network Consultant

Karen Stephenson articulates the need for organizations to think across boundaries and suggests a new meta-organizational form, the *heterarchy*. Her article provides a good set of descriptors for what these networks look like. I am personally invested in understanding how to create and sustain networks, and would have liked to see in this article some guidance on working with these new forms.

Networks come about in several ways. There are those that are intentionally designed by (1) clarifying the network's *purpose*; (2) establishing a model for its *structure* and governance; (3) paying attention to the *style* of how the network is operated and led; and (4) ensuring that the network produces *value* to those who are in it as well as to the ecosystem in which it operates. Professional association networks, cooperatives and communities of practice are examples of designed networks.

Other networks are truly emergent in that they self organize around markets and ideas or in response to opportunities, threats or crises. Small groups of volunteers provide whatever they are capable of to assist survivors in the wake of a hurricane, and then connect with other small groups until a larger network is perceived and the ecosystem becomes tangible. Consider also the growth of the Linux open-source community that began with an individual's desire to create a free computer operating system and to tap into any and all available talent to develop and maintain it.

We can think of these two approaches as the top-down and bottom-up, with most failed examples being those imposed from the top down (the U.S. intelligence agencies example that Stephenson cites). The idea of heterarchy suggests that there is a third possibility: An external actor (or agent) provides a framework within which a network or networks find fertile ground for connecting and building relationships. A company may use a so-called "shaping strategy" (Hagel et al., 2008) to influence the composition of an industry and its role in it (think of Microsoft).

In complexity terms, an attractor is at work. The more well designed the attractor (or strategy), the more likely a rich and diverse network will form around it. Stephenson's own example of the renaissance of civic engagement in Philadelphia following the identification of unsung heroes is a useful example. The project itself was an attractor that fed awareness of a common purpose.

One of the big questions for a heterarchy remains: "What happens next?" What sustains a heterarchy once it is defined, however it has come about? How is trust created? What are the characteristics of its leadership? How is it renewed? How can we track the multiple, overlapping networks that emerge inside of the heterarchy (as will surely be the case)? Or do we need to?

If we trust our ability to approach complex systems in ways that do not shoehorn rules and measurements into a structure, but which honor adaptability and stewardship, then we may develop the tools we need to make our way across and within a new kind of sprawl.

Patti Anklam is a Network Consultant and author of *Net Work: A Practical Guide to Creating and Sustaining Networks at Work and in the World.*

References

Hagel, J. III, S. Brown & L. Davison. "Shaping Strategy in a World of Constant Disruption," *Harvard Business Review* (October 2008).

Miura, S. "Heterarchy in World Politics: Circularity, Distributed Authority, and Networks." Paper presented at the annual meeting of the International Studies Association, LeCentre Sheraton Hotel, Montreal, Quebec Canada.

Ogilvy, J. and P. Schwartz (2002). *Creating Better Futures: Scenario Planning as a Tool for a Better Tomorrow.* New York: Oxford University Press.

Valuing Heterarchy in the Public Sector

Barry Frew, Frew and Associates and the Center for Executive Education

I think Karen Stephenson's observation that the social networks that glue people together have been underestimated and undermanaged is particularly insightful. I agree with her notion that gluing this social organizational network to hierarchies provides leaders and managers a more complete picture of their organizations and their organizational relationships.

My work inside the Defense Department has introduced me to many great leaders who attempt to improve, and in some cases radically change, bureaucratic organizations. The services and the Department of Defense have good stories about changing deep-seated thinking, culture or status quo as the nature of threats shifts rapidly and unpredictably.

In her 2006 book, *Quantum Theory of Trust*, Stephenson talks about the building blocks of the network structure that forms the heterarchy by linking hierarchies. It is the roles of hubs, gatekeepers and pulse-takers, she says, that result in a small but powerful group of people and relationships that drive a culture. This makes sense to me and helps explain why some people are effective at change and some are not. I believe that effective and sustainable change requires different thinking at its core.

There are essentially two parts (poles) to any heterarchy: network relationships and organizational hierarchy structures. These are interdependent pairs. You need informal relationships and formal structures to produce effective work. Focusing on one pole at the exclusion of the other results in producing the negative side of that pole. It may be counter- ➤

intuitive, but visiting Barry Johnson's work (1992, 1996) on polarity management will support Stephenson's assertion of heterarchy from a different perspective.

The rigor with which she attacks her discipline and in innovating a way to identify the key operatives of hub, gatekeeper and pulse taker within an organization is impressive. But the operatives can be effectively used to create large-scale, sustainable, cultural and transformational change.

By identifying hubs, gatekeepers and pulse-takers, you have essentially identified those who "own" the culture. They are the thought leaders others reference and follow. By focusing learning events on this group, you can create tipping points. Whether learning is intended to improve some skill set or generate a new level of thought, using learning to change the thinking is key. A learning event intended to shape the desired attitudes, beliefs, thinking and the resulting behavioral changes that occur in that group can much more rapidly and efficiently affect needed cultural change within an organization. Trust lies in the relationships, not in the structure.

Private sector competition enables better products at lower cost: It doesn't work that

structure, rules, processes and standards for the combined good of that "market" are difficult to justify and even more difficult to implement. Civil servants steeped in the culture don't think that way and they are not rewarded for that behavior. Political appointees may think that way, but they cannot move quickly enough to "unlearn and reset" thinking before they are replaced. Using serious learning initiatives involving mixed-hierarchy participants to alter the thinking and behavior with new values, attitudes, beliefs and thinking about linking the organizations together can be an effective use of the heterarchy concept.

Barry Frew is president and CEO of Frew and Associates. He is also professor emeritus and founder of Center for Executive Education at the Naval Postgraduate School.

References

Johnson, Barry (1992, 1996). *Polarity Management*. Amherst: HRD Press.

Stephenson, Karen (2006). *Quantum Theory of Trust*. UK: Financial Times/Pearson.

Stephenson, who is a uniquely accomplishe scholar of network dynamics, does us all service by identifying a vehicle that may mak it easier to live there. The triad, a group o three people, operating across hierarchica boundaries, will become the driver of chang in a highly networked world.

But in this article Stephenson doesn't addres the most critical question: How explicitl must leaders track and follow what the triad are doing? And how much can we assume without actually talking about it, that al of us in our triads all aligned and oper ating together?

Consider three organizations, three hier archies that might be networked together i the heterarchical fashion that Stephenso posits.

- One might be a regulatory agency of a city government.

- Another might be a local non-profit, operating a group of street-front services, dependent on donations.

- And a third might be a multinationa business with both headquarters an factories in that city, recognizing that it future depends on attracting talented employees.

Together, these three organizations might decide to develop a new initiative around (say) school improvement. Before the project is over, hundreds of people from these three organizations will be involved, in probably dozens of triads.

In the end, success or failure will depend on the quality of conversations among people who recognize, know and trust each other: triad upon triad upon triad. Each group will be dealing with a separate part of the problem; each will face the problem of working in concert with others.

How much will they have to understand explicitly? And how much will pass, as if by osmosis, simply through the culture?

Trust lies in the relationships, not in the structure.

---

way in the public sector. When two agencies or organizations are in the same "market" (imagine homeland defense, health services or education, for example) the result often is inefficiency, duplicity and gaps between organizations. Shifting thinking from bureaucratic positioning to valuing heterarchy is powerful. The real seeds of excellence and completeness lie in the heterarchy garden.

One impediment to application in the public sector is that the "blue" network piece of the heterarchy depicted in Stephenson's figure 2 model is no organization's "responsibility." Investments in generating the common infra-

Heterarchies: Human Nature Transformed?

Art Kleiner, Booz & Company

Karen Stephenson's article provides a great start for understanding the dynamics of an increasingly non-hierarchical world: a world where there are fewer bosses and more colleagues, in which more people have to live as free agents, brokering their work and lives among a variety of organizations. We may or may not be approaching this type of society; and if we do approach it, we may or may not be ready to live there.

Now imagine the same type of problem at the scale of a country, or a region, with thous-ands of such triads at work on some critical problem.

One aspect of hierarchies that bureaucrats (and lobbyists) appreciate is scale. The only messages that travel up a hierarchy are quantified or quantifiable: estimates, allocations, quotas, budgets and similar types of information. Those can be aggregated and used to compare activity across a large multinational operation. One division of a company may make refrigerators; another may broadcast television programs; and a third may service nuclear power plants, but they can all be judged in context of each other by comparing profitability statistics.

But scale only goes so far. Knowledge, information, gossip, trust and personal connection—the kinds of information needed to start a new venture or communitywide project—do not easily travel en masse. They need time and conscious attention; they spread through one-on-one awareness. And it's not quite clear how much capacity people will have for this, especially when they have many commitments and calls on their time and attention; when they have families, friends, "day jobs," and the minutiae of daily life to attend to.

Will a networked society make it easier to manage these competing demands on peoples' attention? What kinds of personal disciplines will be required to make a heterarchy work? And what kind of moral or cultural support and guidance will people be given to develop and exercise that discipline?

I think Karen Stephenson, and other leading network researchers, already know the answers to some of these questions. But some of the questions have to do with the nature of the human condition. As Stephenson points out, heterarchies—multi-connected networks of hierarchies—have never existed before. Humans will adapt to them, but at some level, living in this new type of society will have to become second nature. And is there a precedent for that kind of transformation?

Art Kleiner is editor-in-chief, *strategy +business*, for Booz & Company. He also is the author of *The Age of Heretics* (2nd edition, 2008, Jossey-Bass).

Heterarchy: Technology, Trust and Culture

Ross Dawson, Advanced Human Technologies

Karen Stephenson is absolutely right to emphasize the rapid rise in *interconnection* that individuals, organizations and societies are currently experiencing, and the resulting *interdependence* that stems from that. Relatively few have yet grasped that the degree of interdependence generated in a globally connected economy significantly changes the drivers of individual and collective success. Central to these drivers are the organizational structures that coalesce value from disparate participants.

Certainly understanding that heterarchy is a better organizational form than current alternatives is an important first step. But for that, it is important that "heterarchy" is a term that can be used with clarity and common understanding. Unfortunately there appears to be no consistent definition of heterarchy available from standard dictionaries; and the term is in fact used differently in social sciences and biology.

The definition for heterarchy offered by Stephenson in her footnotes is "an organizational form somewhere between hierarchy and network that provides horizontal links that permit different elements of an organization to cooperate whilst individually optimizing different success criteria." While this is a useful definition, this needs to be understood and accepted by others before the argument for heterarchy can proceed to action. A more commonly used definition is that used by Carole Crumley, who states that heterarchy is "the relation of elements to one another when they are unranked or when they possess the potential for being ranked in a number of different ways."[1] This evokes both the reality of multiple levels, and the communication between levels that is critical in transcending the dysfunctions of pure hierarchies.

It is valuable to remember that organizations are intrinsically systemic. Systems theory and its progeny have helped us understand how some characteristics of systems and organizations can be self-sustaining. As such, shifting from hierarchies to heterarchies can only be done effectively by viewing the interrelated entities as elements in a system, which very likely will incorporate mechanisms that make structural change difficult.

In this context, Ashby-Ross's law of requisite variety[2] suggests that organizations (or sets of organizations) cannot be controlled or managed if they do not have as much flexibility as their environment. In an intensely connected world, this degree of organizational flexibility is very difficult to achieve. However the shift to a heterarchical structure will create many additional dimensions of flexibility, as information flows become less constrained. As such, heterarchical structures are extraordinarily relevant today.

The challenge is both in "understanding, measuring and implementing heterarchy," as Stephenson describes, and even more pointedly, in understanding the interventions that facilitate the creation of effective heterarchical structures. Organizational network analysis is by far the most relevant tool to uncover these patterns. Yet we have far to travel in effectively working at the intersection of technology, trust and culture that is required to succeed in this transition. **P&S**

Ross Dawson is CEO of Australian-based consulting firm Advanced Human Technologies, and is chairman of Future Exploration Network, a global events and strategy company.

1.Crumley, C.L. (1995). "Heterarchy and the Analysis of Complex Societies," *Archaeological Papers of the American Anthropological Association*, Volume 6. Issue 1.
2 Ross, W.A. (1956). *An Introduction to Cybernetics*. Chapman & Hall.

learning guide

People & Strategy 32.1 Point Counterpoint:

Neither Hierarchy nor Network: An Argument for Heterarchy

Discovery Questions

- What is the significance of the leading quote in Karen Stephenson's article on Heterarchies ("I am the Prisoner of War in my own Organization")?

- There are three organizational structures that Karen Stephenson refers to in her article. What are they? Give examples from your own experience where you have seen those three types of organization.

- The centerpiece of Karen Stephenson's article is the discussion of "Heterarchies." Find the definition of Heterarchy as Karen Stephenson proposes it to be. Discuss responses offered in the Counterpoint articles.

- Contrast and compare "heterarchies" with hierarchies and networks. What is different and what remains the same in all three organizational structures?

- Please, comment on the growing importance of trust networks. What are they? How do they operate?

- Reflect on the following quote from the lead article citing your own experience: "Connection by technology without trust is merely traffic. Trusted connections without technology is opportunity lost. To survive as a species we need both, but not at the expense of the other."

- What is the key message in Karen Stephenson's article? Summarize your findings.

- Review all the Counterpoint responses to the ideas offered by Karen Stephenson. Which ones do you find particularly relevant to your own point of view. Explain.

Selected Facts

- What new facts that were presented got your attention?

- Review comparative Table 1–Heterarchy is greater than the sum of its parts.

- The key differentiating factors between –Market, Hierarchy, Network and Heterarchy include: relationship/exchange/focus/ rate of change/knowledge management.

- Globalization and the continuing growing differentiation between different professional groups (according to Edgar Schein) contribute to the complexity of such phenomena as networks and heterarchies.

- The best illustration of how heterarchies work come from Healthcare, financial services, and government institutions, as well as global conglomerates.

Key Discussion Points

- To best understand the emergence of "Heterarchies" show its evolution as a form of social organization from hierarchies to networks.

- The current market reality is such that all three forms of organizations co-exist at the same time. This multiplicity of social forms of organizations will continue to grow. Illustrate this.

- What are the change management steps required to operate successfully in complex heterarchical environments (Art Klein, Patty Anklam)?

- Based on Barry Frew's response from his work at the Department of Defense, illustrate the key operating principles for Heterarchical organizations.

- Based on Tracy Cox's response, illustrate why there could be some challenges in applying the "heterarchy" argument inside a particular business. Do you think this argument may apply to your organization?

- What is the future of multiple organizational forms as they evolve in the global economic and social life of an organization.

Review of Solutions

- Identify 2-3 Big Ideas that are worthy of exploring for your organization.

- Review (hypothetically) the ratios between structural and trust networks in your organization.

- Even though the article does not recommend a specific step by step implementation plan, where do you need to start focusing in order to facilitate a successful functioning of a heterarchy?

- How will the role of HR change when we have all become aware that companies by and large operate as heterarchies?

- Why will the role of HR become pivotal in the functioning of a heterarchical organization, including private, public, and non-profit?

Recommendations Summary

- Identify one thing that we will do differently based on what we learned.

Learning Outcomes

- What one new piece of information did you learn that will be important to you?

part II: organizational effectiveness

From the Perspectives Editor

Anna Tavis, Perspectives Editor

In this issue of *Perspectives*, we assess whether the growing popularity of social networking in the workplace is inevitable and, if so, why. Jeanne Meister and Karie Willyard, co-authors of *The Workplace 2020*, lead the discussion, and their viewpoint is clear: "Social networking is here to stay, resisting the groundswell will hurt the business and may carry high talent costs."

We are not surprised that our discussants, coming from vastly different organizations, side with the lead authors in their support for bringing electronic networking to the job. What differentiates their responses is how much they question such unabashed enthusiasm and the cautions and pragmatism they offer.

Rob Quish of JWT is a most enthusiastic practitioner of social networking. Rob puts on his branding hat and proposes an easy workaround to the resistance he often encounters advising companies. He argues that changing the name to "Utility Media" would make it more palatable to blue chip companies and reflect its true value.

Jim Bowles, now of BTS and formerly with AT&T, suggests that business processes be wrapped around social media to ensure alignment with business needs. Standalone social networking has little place in business and should be left to personal time.

Mathew Breitfelder does not have to sell social media at MasterCard Worldwide. He is blogging, twittering and friending through his day in the office, all in the service of the business. And Anne Berkowitch, CEO of SelectMinds, was among the earliest adopters. She offers a very pragmatic, step-by-step approach to thinking about social media when you are starting to experiment with it.

Chris Hoyt, whose role at PepsiCo is to push the traditional boundaries of recruitment, sums up the discussion by stating that companies should embrace what employees clearly value. Because they value social media, you should move past your anxiety to achieve a significant advantage in the Talent Marketplace.

This rich dialogue in *Perspectives* tells us that heavy use of social media is here to stay and highlights how you can best adopt it.

Five Myths and Realities About Using Social Media in Your Company

By Jeanne C. Meister and Karie Willyerd, co-authors of The 2020 Workplace: How Innovative Companies Attract, Develop & Keep Tomorrow's Employees Today *(Harper Business, 2010)*

With Facebook now at 500 million users, it's pretty clear that social media has moved beyond a fad of a few insiders and into the mainstream. What does the future hold for social media inside your organization? Here are a few myths that should provide some clues as to how social media will soon become mainstream inside most companies.

#1 MYTH: Social media is a time waster at work and should be banned.

REALITY: Millennials have grown up searching out and connecting to their tribe to ask questions, network with colleagues and look for new career opportunities. Some forward-thinking companies, with large and growing Millennial workforces, have recognized this and are using Facebook to source, network and recruit new talent. Professional service firm Ernst & Young was the first to create a Facebook page and now has more than 43,000 *friends* who routinely query the firm about possible internships, recommended courses to take while still in college and descriptions of job profiles.

#2 MYTH: Social media is a fad and will fade away in a few years.

REALITY: This couldn't be farther from the truth. While the face of social media will certainly evolve, using social networks will only grow in importance as the Millennial generation becomes 50 percent of the workplace by 2020. In the past year, Facebook has grown from the eleventh to the fourth most trafficked Internet site, according to ComScore (www.comscore.com). It now accounts for seven percent of all time spent online in the United States. We call companies that have

A company's approach to using social media can fall into one of three areas: proactive, prohibitive or neutral.

---

ntegrated social media tools internally "uber-connected," and they are experiencing ncreases in internal collaboration, innova-on and employee engagement as a result of reating a corporate social network.

3 MYTH: If you build it, they will ome . . .

EALITY: Wrong, wrong, wrong. Social nedia is not an add-on or an accessory to ommunications or learning, but it is surpris-ng to see companies suggest they need to add ome social media to the mix. In other words, 's not a widget that can easily be plugged in vhen needed. To be successful, social media eeds to be part of and aligned with a com-any's strategic priorities, employer brand, nessaging and the workflow of each and very employee. Like any change, introducing ocial media requires a change management trategy that includes setting a vision, stating vhy the change is necessary, providing lead-rship and communicating ceaselessly. Until hange goes viral, implementing social media equires thoughtful planning.

4 MYTH: My employee population is oo old to deal with social media for earning.

EALITY: The fastest growing segment on acebook is people between the ages of 35-49 ears old. People are using social media in heir daily lives to stay in touch with old riends, monitor their children's and grand-hildren's activities, as well as play social ;ames. More than 100 million people in the Jnited States and the United Kingdom play ocial games such as Farmville and Mafia Vars, and their average age is 48. Using social nedia is fast becoming a way of life for mul-iple generations.

#5 MYTH: Social media is difficult to measure in terms of a return on investment.

REALITY: Start with specific business goals such as increases in new hire retention, employee engagement scores or employee productivity. One study Capital Analytics did for Sun Microsystems showed a 75:1 return on investment for peer-to-peer learning. The savings were attributed to decreases in devel-oping formal training programs to share best practices. Instead, Sun Microsystems accessed the company social collaboration platform as a training vehicle, often contributing content to share with peers.

The myths about social media illustrate how the market is still in the early stages of devel-opment and maturity. Over time, these myths will start to disappear as companies and people get a better appreciation of what's really involved and how social media can be integrated into the strategic priorities of the company.

As we connect, communicate and collaborate with friends on a social network, we bring these digital expectations to the workplace. And forward-thinking employers will lever-age social media to drive new business, communicate with customers and allow for greater innovation and problem solving

inside their organizations. However, compa-nies must provide clear guidelines and training for how to use social media respect-fully and responsibly. A place to benchmark is the 157 organizations that already have created detailed social media guidelines and see how these can be adapted to fit a com-pany's specific needs. These can be found at: www.compliancebuilding.com/about/publications/social-media-policies/

A company's approach to using social media can fall into one of three areas: proactive, prohibitive or neutral. As we move closer to the 2020 workplace, it's foolhardy to think one can prohibit usage of social media in the workplace. Rather, companies should use the next couple of years to be proactive, bench-mark what works and what their competitors are doing and create policies, guidelines and training for how to leverage social media for improved business results.

Jeanne Meister is a partner in Future Workplace. She is an internationally recognized workplace learning consul-tant dedicated to delivering competitive advantage, innovation and improved business results for organizations.

Karie Willyerd is the former chief learning officer at Sun Microsystems and currently a partner in Future Workplace.

Meister and Willyerd co-authored the book, "The 2020 Workplace." For more information, visit **www.the2020workplace.com**.

To be successful, social media needs to be part of and aligned with a company's strategic priorities, employer brand, messaging and the workflow of each and every employee.

part II: organizational effectiveness

Social Media: Creating Richer Relationships in the Workplace

Rob Quish, chief operating officer, JWT North America, and chief executive officer, JWT Inside, an employee marketing communications agency.

> Now we have sharing technologies, and yet we are reluctant to use them…. Leveraging social media is not about cut-and-paste sharing, but rather dynamic and SOCIAL learning, people-to-people, enabled and enhanced by technology.

Jeanne and Karie's mythbusters are great and well-intentioned to a segment of business leaders who secretly or openly challenge the rising tide of change brought on by social media. Perhaps social media's problem in the workplace is its name. Somehow 'social' sounds frivolous (a la 'I'll have a chardonnay to be social') or dangerous (e.g., 'be careful of social diseases!'). Let me first rebrand and redefine social media for the workplace. Then, I'll come back and defend why 'being social' is key to developing an engaged workforce and why that's all business.

Let's think of social media differently. Call it Utility Media— digital workforce platforms to drive engagement. Here are three ways you can make it useful:

1. **Recruitment Relationship Marketing** — A common practice for some companies is to blast mass reaching approaches to 'fish in the ocean' for talent when needs arise. Utility Media like Facebook, LinkedIn or Plaxo allow companies and recruiters to cultivate relationships with potential hires over time. These deeper relationships before hiring logically lead to more of the right people coming onboard. These platforms allow companies to manage relationships with whole segments of your candidate pool (think of it as group intimacy) as one might have had in the days of rolodexes and phone calls with individuals (kind of like the executive search world today). Remember, though, if you want to build a relationship it has to be two-way: You'll need to give to get. To earn these folks' attention you'll need (technology-led) listening skills and a content-creation machine to attract their attention, encourage connectivity and build a vital relationship. More like dating and less like fishing!

2. **Enterprise Learning** — Every company with which I've worked since the 1980s has talked about sharing best practices. Now we have sharing technologies, and yet we still are reluctant to use them. Ironically, one popular use of technology in learning is recreating a classroom experience on the PC. I have very few fond memories of classroom learning. So the thought of trying to recreate an imperfect setting seems crazy. Rich experiences like online gaming should be the success criteria for formal training, while mobile applications should be explored for quick-fix Q&A. Leveraging social media is not about cut-and-paste sharing, but rather dynamic and SOCIAL learning, people-to-people, enabled and enhanced by technology.

3. **Employee Engagement** — We like to say that in every company there is a string of connectedness between the CEO and every employee. And in strong companies that string is very short. When employees know the business purpose, why the goals are important and their vital role in making them happen, employees are well on their way to higher engagement. Getting people to participate in the company's communications through online techniques like storytelling, chat and video sharing allows them to both understand and OWN the company's aspirations. From there, engagement soars and businesses more profitably achieve outcomes. This shortens AND strengthens the string.

Okay, so why is 'social' important? TN Employee Insights, the global engagement study powerhouse inside research giant TNS tells me that relationships with co-workers are an essential element to the kind of productivity-driving engagement smart companies aim toward. TNS's studies (numbering in the millions of employee surveys per year) have shown that in the hierarchy of employee needs, collaboration and other relationship measures rank just after the basics around job satisfaction and relationship with manager/boss. Employees connecting with co-workers using social media are a huge boon to richer relationships in the workplace. Bringing a new aspect to communications opens new possibilities for building trust, loyalty, sharing ideas and developing a stronger culture.

Last, ask yourself, do you want social people in your company? I walked by the employee entrance to the W Hotel on Lexington Avenue yesterday and there was an awning over the entrance (I assure you it is not the norm in NYC to have an awning to protect employees from the elements.) Printed in bold white letters on the chic black awning was: **Stage Door.** Being social is a prerequisite at the W and they want employees to turn it on the moment they walk in the door. Quashing social media within their employee base, rather than embracing it, would be like stopping politicians from kissing babies. . . it's unnatural. Who knows, if you need social employees maybe your company should have a prerequisite for the number of Facebook friends for new hires.

Rob Quish is chief operating officer, JWT North America. He is directly responsible for JWT INSIDE, the employee marketing and communications agency.

NSFW? Shaping a Professional Approach to Social Media

Jim Bowles, Ed.D., BTS USA Leadership and Management Practice, and retired vice president Workforce Development AT&T Wireless

It may be a bit premature to suggest that doing anything but yielding to current trends in the evolution and proliferation of social media is prohibitive. In fact, at the risk of alienating friends, colleagues, my children and other power users of this technology, I would posit that as this technology movement continues to evolve, it will be ground down by the ever-present risk management/legal machine to a more controlled sustainable approach: a "business process aligned" model.

Business Process Alignment

The disciplined use and proliferation of social media applications certainly has broad and pervasive potential benefits to the business community. The fact that employees entering the workforce are skilled at using these tools will continue to enhance learning, efficiency, collaboration and innovation. Talent management professionals who recognize the strategic value of this technology can incorporate internal social media solutions that align clearly to the business. And through creating meaningful points of employee connectivity and alignment to the broader business strategy, they can positively influence inclusion efforts, employee engagement and all the related downstream business benefits that might naturally accrue from these.

The Continued Refinement of Social Networking

Unquestionably, there is a faddish element of the social networking movement. Now that many Boomers have experienced the thrill of finding old college buddies, they and their younger colleagues are finding that there are limits to the benefits this technology provides. Facebook recently has been cited as being No. 1 in customer service complaints, and has made the lists of companies that consumers loathe most. In addition, research continues to prove the downside of multi-tasking relative to productivity, as well as that humans can only manage so much information, or so many friends, in a truly meaningful way. More importantly, as privacy and exploitation concerns continue to surface, there will be a moderation effect, in which private use of these sites becomes more refined and to some extent, compartmentalized. This trend is already evident: In the world of professional networking, LinkedIn has become the go-to Web site for accumulating vast numbers of professional contacts. In business, expanding external, customer-centric use of social media/networking tools, likely will drive compartmentalization in contrast with more controlled and focused internal applications.

We also know, and will want to keep in mind, that the kiss of death for any movement like this is its adoption by the establishment.

When CNN is twittering and tweeting, it is a sure sign that a downturn in usage of that site, led by the young, is around the corner.

Fair and Balanced

In a more controlled, compartmentalized environment, companies taking a balanced or restrictive approach to on-the-job social networking should not be cast aside as reactionary Luddites. Given the yet to be understood (or litigated) legal, employee relations and competitive ramifications, abdication of rational controls appears to be a risky and costly business practice. Does this approach preclude some of the work/life balance benefits associated with the pursuit of ongoing connectivity? Absolutely not. For many (perhaps most) employees, much of this connectivity is occurring off network through wireless broadband access. Smart phones and PDAs are rapidly becoming the avenue of choice for those who want to stay in touch, yet there are certainly jobs/situations where even use of these tools should be restricted (public safety/public transportation, etc.).

Through aligning social media around business processes, the true wild card is the purely *social* social-networking element. Given the steep adoption curve of Facebook, it might seem that resistance to wide-open usage is futile. However, with an emphasis on leveraging aligned business processes, there are ample reasons businesses to approach the social networking issue with thoughtfulness and care. In the application of social media tools, a balanced approach to social networking—in which employees are encouraged to use their own time to maintain professional connectivity—is an appropriate business decision.

Jim Bowles, Ed.D., is managing director of BTS USA's Leadership and Management Practice. Previously vice president of workforce development in human resources for AT&T Mobility, Bowles led divisions of leadership, staffing, learning and organizational development at the company in a time of rapid industry growth and consolidation.

Talent management professionals who recognize the strategic value of this technology can incorporate internal social media solutions...to the business.

Myth #6: Social Media is a Technology Issue

Matthew Breitfelder, vice president, Global Talent Management and Organizational Development, MasterCard Worldwide

I completely agree with Jeanne Meister and Karie Willyerd that social media will help change the game on how companies are managed in the future. In their compelling article, Meister and Willyerd respond to five myths with concrete examples of what leading companies already are doing to dispel them. But a sixth myth lingers for me — that social media in organizations is still "framed" primarily as a technology issue.

Meister and Willyerd underline the importance of connecting social media with corporate business priorities and challenges. We should start framing social media this way: as a problem-solving tool to address persistent issues with which all companies struggle. This approach will help us move beyond the debates in companies about the risks of implementing social media toward more focus on the very real returns we can achieve to better serve customers, connect with stakeholders and execute strategy.

As with any new innovation, the early adopters do assume the most upfront risk, with fast followers benefiting from a clearer roadmap to success. Wise companies will connect the dots between early lessons in social media and longtime challenges in organizations to

> As practitioners, we know the problem needs solving, but we do not have many tools in our toolbox. Social media enables employees to quickly receive information about what these stakeholders care about and to engage with them in new ways.

reframe social media as a problem-solving tool. A few additional thoughts:

- Most research shows that more than 70 percent of corporate strategy and change initiatives fail to deliver expected results. Equally alarming, 80 percent of employees at Fortune 500 companies are not "highly engaged" in their work. Social media can help us solve both problems — by quickly aligning employee energies against strategic priorities and connecting untapped employee knowledge with the greatest customer needs. This flattens hierarchy, fosters employee pride and speeds decision making.

- As Meister and Willyerd mention, social media is a powerful tool for learning. Ninety percent of corporate learning occurs informally — either on-the-job or from colleagues at work — but most corporate learning resources are allocated to formal courses and eLearning. As practitioners, we know this problem needs solving, but we do not have many tools in our toolbox. Social media enables us to

capture, foster and leverage informal learning efficiently and effectively.

- Most CEOs tell us that a critical new skill for leaders is engaging with a range of new stakeholders globally. In many companies this is uncharted territory. Social media enables employees to quickly receive information about what these stakeholders care about and to engage with them in new ways. Pepsi's Project Refresh is one of the most innovative examples of this in action.

At our company, we are moving quickly to make the most of social media, both externally with customers, consumers and industry influencers, as well as internally with our employees. Across the company, we are tweeting, blogging, friending and YouTubing. In July, on his first day as the new CEO of our company, Ajay Banga launched the organization's first company-wide internal blog to engage employees in a dialogue about issues that matter to MasterCard. In just a few short weeks, more than 70 percent of employees have participated. If you listened carefully, you could hear a few myths fading away.

> Social media can help us solve both problems — by quickly aligning employee energies against strategic priorities and connecting untapped employee knowledge with the greatest customer needs. This flattens hierarchy, fosters employee pride and speeds decision making.

Matthew Breitfelder is vice president of Leadership Development at MasterCard Worldwide, where he is responsible for a range of programs to build a strong pipeline of leaders and drive culture change.

What Does Success Look Like for Your Company: Social Media Starting Points with Measurable Returns

Anne Berkowitch, chief executive officer, SelectMinds

We've all read conflicting reports about how to enact social media inside a company — the questions the discussion raises loom large. Do we ease into social media? How prepared do we need to be when we open up the floodgates? What platforms do we try first, second or third? Do we need to hire someone to manage social media? How do we measure the value of our efforts and demonstrate that value to executives?

The answer to all of these questions lies in what our business objectives are for social media activity. Social media is no longer separate from marketing, branding, public relations, human resources, lead generation, customer service or any other facet of a business. It has the potential to be an integral part of each of those departments' daily activities and play a critical role in their success.

The questions we should be asking before any others include:

- What do we hope to gain from engaging in social media?

- Does our business lend itself to being social intrinsically?

- What does success in social media look like for our business?

And most importantly:

- How will we measure social media ROI?

When it comes to HR, social media should not be tapped only as a way to identify future employees, but also as a driver for attracting them to our business, retaining them moving forward and leveraging their own networks for further growth. Let's consider for a moment an integrated social media plan for a company's HR department that would help practitioners find quality talent via the assets they already have on staff. Not only can a strong understanding and use of social media in business be an influential selling point for job seekers, but it also allows people to maximize their own personal networks to drive business growth. Growth generated via referrals is the best kind, especially when it comes to recruiting — referred candidates outperform job board candidates more than threefold in terms of retention and termination rates, not to mention that a referral candidate is 54 times more likely to result in a hire than a job board candidate.

- Decide on initial and projected social media goals that align with current, overall business goals.

- How can social media and referral networking be leveraged — for recruiting, business development, branding?

- Benchmark where competitors are in this process.

- What platforms have they adopted?

- What level of activity are they maintaining?

- What other technologies might they be using?

- Test the social media waters via internal-facing social media vehicles.

When it comes to HR, social media should not be tapped only as a way to identify future employees, but also as a driver for attracting them to our business.

While the solution to creating a social media strategy may not seem clear, it is necessary to be able to measure the success and engagement of the actions a company takes online so that future decisions can be made. Deciding on an initial goal that aligns with business aims first, tracking its impact on the bottom line, and expanding from there is a recipe for success. Also, when it comes to corporate networking online, understanding the viral power of those networks is integral to one's own success — referrals bring in 25 percent of recruits at 50 percent savings per employee. Thus the impact can be enormous.

So as we start to think about creating a social media plan, let's keep this outline in mind:

- Evaluate where the company is in terms of social media activity — even if it feels like square one, it might not be.

- Who in the company is involved personally?

- Do they identify as part of the organization?

- Internal chatting tools

- Private micro-blogging platforms

- Corporate referral networking solutions

A goal as simple as driving recruitment initially allows social media activity to be internally focused. By creating a channel for employees to leverage their personal networks, help their connections as well as their business, and potentially earn a bonus in the process engenders positive employee sentiment and will drive measurable returns for the organization as well.

> **Anne Berkowitch** co-founded Select-Minds in 2000. Since then, she has played a key role in developing Select-Minds' client relationships, and in helping the company evolve into a leading provider of Purpose-Driven Networking solutions and services.

part II: organizational effectiveness

Let's Concentrate on Managing the People

Chris Hoyt, talent engagement & marketing leader, PepsiCo

Ms. Meister and Ms. Willyerd write an interesting article with many great points related to the validity of social media taking a somewhat permanent residence within our various working generations. To be clear, however, the definition of "social media" is communication built upon a platform that allows for the contribution and exchange of user-generated content. While Facebook has risen to become a giant among social channels, it certainly does not stand alone when considering the ever-growing need of people to collaborate and communicate on topics ranging from weekend picnics to billion dollar projects.

There are other social communication tools and networks that should not be ignored and are considered social in nature. In fact, many of them have been around and in use for years. Tools and platforms like Lotus Notes released in 1989, allow for threaded discussions and the collaboration of any number of projects. Today Lotus Notes offers features very similar to other products, like Microsoft's SharePoint, that include blogs, Wikis and seamless calendar and e-mail integration and are being rapidly adopted around the

What is typically a mainstream social network can be surprising as well. Twitter, a micro-blogging service that allows for 140-character updates, rocketed into popularity throughout 2009. And while at a glance Twitter may seem to some as a silly collection of ramblings, many companies are seeing incredible success using it to offer service and/or sales options to their customers. Are employees venting about their noisy cubical neighbors? Sure. But they are also connecting with peers to work on various projects or even using advanced search features to connect with talent within their professions.

My role at PepsiCo is to push the boundaries related to how recruiters find and engage top talent internally and externally. I get to see the creation and evolution of countless social networks and how they impact people and business. One thing is always constant: No matter the name or the appearance of the network and regardless of its casual or professional adoption rate, ease of use drives its evolution or demise.

Smart and savvy companies have moved past anxiety over social media and network phenomenon and have embraced their use for more than just customer interaction.

> While Facebook has risen to become a giant among social channels, it certainly does not stand alone when considering the ever-growing need of people to collaborate and communicate on topics ranging from weekend picnics to billion dollar projects.

And it doesn't end with Facebook and Twitter. MySpace is still a contender for highly trafficked social sites, and so are more professionally driven social networks like LinkedIn. The broad range of networks isn't necessarily

Incredibly valuable organizations, such as the Social Media Business Council and Word of Mouth Marketing Association, move to help educate (via collaboration!) both large and small companies about social media for business. I'm of the opinion that the companies that adapt the demands of their employees to fit their business needs and that concentrate on managing the people, not restricting the media channels, will see increased productivity, quality and even employee retention in the long term.

> ...Twitter may seem to some as a silly collection of ramblings, many companies are seeing incredible success using it to offer service and/or sales options to their customers.

globe. These were never deemed "scary" or "time wasters," because they were typically limited to internal company use and did not include surveys to help you discover what type of Disney Princess or virtual Farmer you might be.

about niche topics either. We have an almost endless list of sites and forums from which to select because of a growing demand for constant communication in the formats that users desire.

Chris Hoyt is a mobile marketing/recruiting evangelist and self-proclaimed Social 'X' addict. As Talent Engagement & Marketing Leader at PepsiCo, Hoyt pushes the boundaries of each aspect of full-cycle recruiting.

Five Myths and Realities About Using Social Media In Your Company

Discovery Questions

- What are we dealing with in our organization today that relates to this content area?

- Learn how to develop strategies for integrating social media into the culture and business strategy of your organization.

- Learn how social media can facilitate collaboration and creativity.

- Understand the myths and realities of how social media shows up within organizations.

- Learn in-organization uses of tweeting, blogging, friending, and You-Tubing.

- Learn how to maximize the value of employee referrals for recruiting.

- Identify what business processes could benefit from user generated content.

- Check out Social Media Business Council and Word of Mouth Marketing Association.

Selected Facts

- What new facts that were presented got your attention?

- 50% of the workforce in 2020 will be from the Millenial generation.

- The average age of people playing social games online is 48.

- Facebook has more customer complaints than any other website.

- 70% of change initiatives fail.

- 80% of employees are not "highly engaged."

- 90% of corporate learning occurs informally on the job and from colleagues.

- Candidates referred by employees outperform job board candidates more than threefold in terms of retention and termination rates.

- Candidate referred by employees are fifty-four times more likely to result in a hire than a job board candidate.

Key Discussion Points

- What were the key points being made in this Point Counterpoint presentation?

- How does social media facilitate collaboration and creativity?

- What are the change management issues when introducing social media?

- What guidelines should exist for using social media respectfully and responsibly?

- Why should you consider renaming Social Media as Utility Media?

- How can social media be used to support recruitment relationship marketing?

- What are the implications for how best practices are shared and how learning occurs?

- How important do you think it is to have a "best friend at work"?

- "We don't hire anyone with less than 200 Facebook friends"—good idea or not?

- What legal, privacy and risk management concerns should an organization have?

- What business processes can we align to the effective use of social media?

- How can social media functionality be used to better serve the organization's customers?

- What have our competitors done in this area?

- How do people management practices need to evolve in order to get the most positive impacts from social media?

Review of Solutions

- Identify 2-3 Big Ideas that are worthy of exploring for our organization.

- Give to Get: Develop (technology-led) listening skills and a content creation machine to attract their attention, encourage connectivity and build a vital relationship.

- What restrictions on the use of social media sites should organizations require?

- Alignment of social media functionality and business strategies may help flatten hierarchy, foster employee pride, and speeds decision-making. How?

- Social media enables us to capture, foster, and leverage informal learning efficiently and effectively. How?

- Social media in marketing, branding, public relations, human resources, lead generation, customer service, or any other facet of a business can be an integral part of each of those departments' daily activities and play a critical role in their success.

- In HR, use social media to identify future employees, as a driver for attracting them to our business, retaining them moving forward, and leveraging their own networks for further growth.

Recommendations Summary

- Identify one thing that we will do differently based on what we learned.

Learning Outcomes

- What one new piece of information did you learn that will be important to you?

Perspectives

Anna Tavis, Perspectives Editor

In this special issue, *People & Strategy* has partnered with the International Peter Drucker Society and The Drucker Institute to celebrate the centennial of Peter Drucker's birth. Drucker is the 20th century's most prominent management thinker and one of its great social philosophers. We invited Drucker's disciples from around the world to contribute their personal reflections on Drucker's influence in the development of their countries' approach to studying management and their management cultures.

Richard Straub, President of the Peter Drucker Society of Austria, leads the discussion by focusing on the impact of Drucker's Viennese roots on the evolution of his thinking. Following Straub, the conversation broadens its geography to Europe, Japan, China and India. Drucker's global citizenship comes across strongly in the essay by Thomas Sattleberger, CHRO of Deutsche Telecom, who emphasizes Drucker's continuing relevance as a humanist. Danica Purg, president of IEDC-Bled School of Management, focuses on Drucker's aesthetics, his heightened awareness that management is an art form rather than a science. We conclude with an essay on Drucker's influence in the United States, contributed by Rick Wartzman, the executive director of The Drucker Institute at Claremont Graduate University.

For many of our readers, this selection of essays will provide a fresh insight into Drucker's sustaining contributions to global management thinking. For others, the historical perspective will be particularly interesting. We invite all of you to reflect with our wonderful contributors on the importance of Peter Drucker's legacy for 21st-century management.

What Drucker Means Around the World

A World Citizen of Austrian Origin: The Rediscovery of the European Roots of the Father of Modern Management

Richard Straub, Peter Drucker Society of Austria

November 19, 2009, marks the 100th anniversary of the birth in Vienna of the world-renowned thinker on management and society, Peter F. Drucker. Although Drucker spent the greater part of his life in the United States, his youth in Austria and his experiences in Germany and England strongly influenced his world view. He grew up in a home that served as a salon of sorts for the cultural and intellectual elite of the Danube Monarchy—hence his early acquaintance with eminent figures such as Joseph Schumpeter, Sigmund Freud, Othmar Spann and Friedrich von Hayek.

His origin in a cultural and intellectual hotbed left deep marks on Peter Drucker. We do not realize today that when we discuss the need for global mindsets, cosmopolitan attitudes, valuing cultural differences, multilingualism, a global business orientation and transdisciplinary thinking, it was all there at the beginning of the 20th century, in a world that another famous Viennese writer, Stefan Zweig (1881-1942), called "Yesterday's World." The Austro-Hungarian Empire crumbled in a cataclysmic tremor ultimately leading into the horrors of the Nazi regime. Its best and brightest were pushed into a global diaspora, impoverishing "old Europe" and bringing a wealth of inspiration and intellectual treasures to their new home countries.

Having been a witness of the ascent of totalitarian fascist and communist regimes in Europe, Drucker's intellectual journey became focused on the idea of a workable society based on freedom—where citizens are provided a meaningful existence, i.e., status and function, with an ethical foundation of mutual responsibility by the individual and his or her society. As the underlying economic theory, he adopted the thinking of a fellow ustrian, Joseph Schumpeter. He thought that Schumpeter had produced the only effective contemporary theory of capital-sm," which is centered on private initiative nd where the enterprising manager is both he justification and motivating power of he system.

t is via this route that Drucker discovered management as the "life-giving force of mod-rn capitalism." He concluded that in a pluralistic society of specialized institutions, management's task is to make organizations perform, beginning with the business enter-rise, for the community and for the ndividual alike. Management "organizes human beings for joint performance and hould make their strength effective and their weaknesses irrelevant." Thus, management is he most important "organ" of our modern society—a role deeply embedded in the real-ty of our social existence as human beings. Consequently, the contribution of manage-ment is a fundamental contribution to a functioning society and not just to the indi-vidual institution it serves. It is clear that thinking about management from this per-spective and understanding the consequences leads to different conclusions than those we have seen emerging during the last 20 years.

John Micklethwait, the editor-in-chief of *The Economist*, said in a BBC interview that Drucker was not only a great management thinker but he was one of the greatest thinkers of the 20th Century, given the sharpness of his mind and the breadth of his intellectual curiosity. With his inquiry into society and management, he takes a very European approach, rooted in a humanities-based general education and an open mind that made him a relentless lifelong learner in the best sense of the term.

Drucker's holistic and ecology-based approach brought him into marked contrast with the academic establishment. The latter tried to define management as a "science" while he saw management in its many dimensions and facets (and in particular in its fundamental social role) as a "Liberal Art." Management "deals with action and

application, and its test is its results," Druck-er wrote. "This makes it a technology. But management also deals with people, their values, their growth and development—and this makes it a humanity…Management is thus what tradition used to call a 'liberal art:' 'liberal' because it deals with the fundamen-tals of knowledge, self-knowledge, wisdom, and leadership; 'art' because it is practice and application."

him again and remind ourselves what the true responsibility of management is as a role within society. Certainly, it is not serv-ing the short-term interests of financial markets or other parochial stakeholders. Europe, like other continents, needs Peter Drucker's thinking to build a sustainable and functioning society. Europe, though, also has the privilege of calling Drucker a "great son."

Consequently, the contribution of management is a fundamental contribution to a functioning society and not just to the individual institution it serves.

Warren Bennis and James O'Toole observed in their May 2005 *Harvard Business Review* article, "How Business Schools Lost their Way," that the schools suffer from "an over-emphasis on rigor and an underemphasis on relevance. Business schools have forgotten that they are a professional school."

As a European and Austrian, I feel strongly that Peter Drucker has been denied the recognition that he deserves on the European continent. This is in stark contrast to the reception Drucker has experienced in Japan.

In the United States his earlier books, like the *Concept of the Corporation* and *The Practice of Management*, had enormous influence on the way large U.S. corporations organized and developed their management methods. However, in the 1970s and 1980s his influence on actual practice started to wane. He raised his voice against the excess-es and misdirected behaviors in financial engineering that ultimately destroyed long-term value. His voice was heard, given his fame and reputation at the time as the "father of modern management," but he was not listened to.

Peter Drucker's centenary provides us with a unique opportunity: to start listening to

Richard Straub is president of the Peter Drucker Society of Austria.

Peter Drucker's Early Works—Austria and Germany: The Foundations of His Weltanschauung

Guido Stein, IESE Business School

Peter Ferdinand Drucker, Viennese, was born in 1909 to a cultured family that fostered both his literary vocation and his restless intellect. He combined law studies in Hamburg and Frankfurt with a job in an export company, and later as a journalist with the *Frankfurter General Anzeiger*. His doctoral thesis in law dealt with the so-called forms of quasi-government (*quasi-Regierun-gen*) such as revolutionary governments, governments in exile or colonies in the pro-cess of becoming independent.

His first book was a study of Friedrich Julius Stahl, a mid-19th-century legal philosopher, and an outstanding political traditionalist and parliamentarian, in Berlin and Erfurt. ➤

Entitled *Friedrich Julius Stahl, Political Conservationist and His Historical Evolution*, the book was published in 1933 by the prestigious German publisher J.C.B. Mohr und Siebeck of Tübingen.

Why should Peter Drucker, at the age of 34, have chosen to write about an unknown author who was practically ignored by German historians of political thought? Berthold Freyberg, a personal friend, provided a probable explanation for such a choice. Drucker's penchant for the innovative and creative syntheses of things, otherwise deemed incompatible, would seem to account for his intellectual fascination with the figure of Stahl, who could be described as the personification of paradox, notorious for his seemingly irreconcilable points of view.

Stahl, Jewish by birth, became the spokesman for Protestant political orthodoxy. Of Bavarian background, he worked earnestly for the Prussian crown. A committed conservative, he resisted absolutism in favor of constitutional monarchy. In short, he was a person difficult to categorize, like Drucker himself. It might well be ventured that there did exist a personal

is viewed as a succession of contingent events and behaviors; that is, events and behaviors that might have never occurred, and always under the watchful care of Divine Providence (*Die Augen Gottes*). This confers upon such events and behaviors a specific dignity. (Later, he would see this tendency combined and emphasized in his readings of Burke, de Tocqueville, Bertrand de Jouvenelle, Calhoun, in *The Federalist Papers*, and in North American history and politics.)

Drucker saw this Jewish thinker not as a portent of characteristic features that would shape future political and social reality, but as one who examined the discontinuity facing the present; someone who was not asking the question "What will the future be like?" but rather, "What can we learn about today in order to build the future?" Like Bergson, he preferred to "draw out tendencies rather than to prophesize about what will happen." This was Drucker's approach to the profound cultural changes (discontinuities) that, because often hidden, cannot easily be perceived on the horizon, accustomed as we are to our expectation of continuity. [See, for example, Drucker's books *Landmarks of*

an assessor for various British financial institutions. Some years later he was to become a professor and consultant, activities he would alternate with his work as a writer and that would continue right to the end making him the most influential management philosopher to date.

Guido Stein is assistant professor of Managing People in Organizations at the IESE Business School in Spain.

Is Peter Drucker Still Relevant Today?

Thomas Sattelberger, Deutsche Telekom AG Board of Management

Who listens today in continental Europe when Tom Peters, Ken Blanchard and/or Noel Tichy are mentioned – all of them celebrated management luminaries of the last 25 years? Instead, the superlatives pile up when a conversation ends with the name of Peter F. Drucker. He was assured the top spot in the global ranking of business leaders as recently as 2001 and again in 2003. Three years after his death, and in his centenary year, we wonder what is left of Peter Drucker. To put it another way: Is Peter Drucker—is his thinking—still relevant today? To answer this question I first set out the main features of Drucker's way of thinking. Second, I present Drucker's insights in detail and apply these findings to the present day. Finally, draw some conclusions post-Drucker.

What characterizes Drucker's way of thinking?

Peter Drucker tried to understand the world in all its complexity. Together with most other Austrian thinkers of his time, he shared an aversion to oversimplified explanations without reference to the highest system: society. However, Drucker's thinking is driven by an overwhelming desire to extract universal guidelines from practical experience. Reading

> This was Drucker's approach to the profound cultural changes (discontinuities) that, because often hidden, cannot easily be perceived on the horizon, accustomed as we are to our expectation of continuity.

affinity that influenced Drucker's choosing Stahl, which shows quite tangibly that Drucker adopted a certain conservative frame of mind during those years that, along with his inveterate tendency toward iconoclasm, accompanied him throughout his life.

In his reflections on Stahl, Drucker goes on to describe a lively, dynamic conservativism (*lebendiger konservatismus*) in which history

Tomorrow (1957), *The Age of Discontinuity* (1969) or *The New Realities* (1989).]

After publishing his study of Stahl, Drucker left Germany and established himself in London, where he worked for a financial firm and attended classes given by John Maynard Keynes. In 1937, he moved to the United States to serve as a correspondent for several English and Scottish newspapers, and as is work carefully, one is struck by three characteristic features of his way of thinking:

1. Drucker analyzed things from a bird's-eye view of society. Therefore, the starting point for any thought or action is society and community. His yardstick for "management" was always its effect on the common good.

2. The Drucker method combines fundamental skills and knowledge into a highly predictive analytical tool. His motto was, "Learn from practice for practice." Grounding his work on inner independence, deep historical knowledge and common sense, he minimized the academic success but maximized its practical relevance.

3. Insight is nothing without clear language and easily understandable presentation. As such, he wrapped his findings up in common-sense principles, understandable to everyone.

What insights did Drucker gain?

Going right back to Drucker's great works (*Concept of the Corporation* (1946); *The New Society: the Anatomy of Industrial Order* (1950); and, above all, *The Practice of Management* (1954)), we can identify three central insights.

First and foremost, Drucker elevates the pluralism of organizations into their defining feature. He proposed that organizations are effective because "each is autonomous and specialized, informed only by its own narrow mission and vision." The crux is that all earlier pluralist societies destroyed themselves because no one took care of the common good, as Drucker states. Due to advanced specialization, the common good is increasingly lost from sight and the foundations of society start to crumble. Drucker has a ready answer: "If our modern pluralist society is to escape the same fate, the leaders of all institutions will have to learn to be leaders beyond the walls."

Companies are social organizations in the sense that their fate is inexorably linked to that of society. Ducker's resulting maxim leaves no room for misunderstanding: "Value and service first, profit later." What turns the company into a social and political system is its most valuable resource and therefore the focus of management: its people. Therefore, "every enterprise is a learning and teaching institution," and "training and development must be built into it on all levels." Following Drucker, what really counts for a company are its goals and values. If an organization is not goal oriented, it simply confuses its employees.

Drucker defined management as a social function enabling people to achieve their best performance. For him, the main problem of management was crystal clear: Many people fail to see that companies are a "social phenomenon," in which a very small number of decisions are behind 90 percent of all results. As such, Drucker appeals: "Always ask yourself if you are doing the right thing before doing things right." And the right things in management are mostly connected with developing people. For Drucker, the social function of management goes hand-in-hand with the question of legitimate power. To be legitimate, management must become a true profession like medicine.

What guidelines does Drucker give us to shape today and tomorrow?

Today's world is marked by the worst economic crisis in 80 years. Alongside the real economy, its moral foundations are in a deep crisis of legitimacy. In 2009, Drucker's original concerns are more topical and cutting-edge than anyone could have imagined.

According to Drucker, the most important lesson from the failure of socialism is the collapse of belief in an all-encompassing, all-powerful state. Unfortunately, the moral failure of management has cleared the way for its return. For us, the most important lesson from history should be that all social organizations are essentially fallible and none should stand above the others. Instead of creating a new state monstrosity, we should reinforce the relationship between the community and the company as a social organization.

Although Drucker was principally an advocate of "the market" as an instrument of

> He proposed that organizations are effective because "each is autonomous and specialized, informed only by its own narrow mission and vision."

control, he retained "serious reservations" about capitalism, which adores the economy itself as "the be-all and end-all of life." If we are to take from Drucker only one guiding principle it is that we should overcome the limitations of the pure capitalist world view and turn our attention to the major questions of society:

- Which value system should form the base of our society?

- What should the relationship between the individual and society look like?

- How are responsibilities divided among state, business and civil society?

Ultimately, the only way for us as managers to reconnect with society is to face the moral allegations in public and ground our actions on a solid moral basis. Whereas doctors take a professional oath and sit rigid public examinations, any charlatan is free to call himself a "manager."

Inversely, management's moral yardstick must be its own Hippocratic Oath, which Drucker defines as: "Above all, not knowingly to do any social harm." We now must regain ➤

our voice, saying two things: First, there is no doubt about our profession's moral standards. Second, we will speak out against any violation of our professional standards, whoever is responsible. Finally, to turn management into a true profession, we also must radically rethink our entry, promotion and recognition policies.

Until the economic crisis, the Anglo-Saxon MBA was the main route into management. Spin-offs of Harvard and its like have exported their model worldwide according to the mantra "one size fits all." Exaggerating the case, one could say that traditional, lemming-like MBAs often are hotbeds of soulless, purely economistic learning. Neither are they better in terms of content: functional silos remain intact; students are not taught systematic, interdisciplinary thinking; leadership is reduced to hero-worship.

Instead, management education must return to its European roots, meaning that training puts the evolution of the self back ahead of social masquerading. Questioning the existence of any certainty is essential for character building. Thus, the main pillars of Drucker's method must stand at the center of reformed management education: unbounded thinking, moral resolution, inner independence and a sound knowledge of history.

for society, the economy and the individual as well.

> **Thomas Sattelberger** is chief human resources officer, Deutsche Telekom AG Board of Management.

Peter Drucker's Influence in Japan

Chuck Ueno, The Drucker Workshop (the Drucker Society of Japan)

There are a great number of Japanese company executives who devote themselves to the thought of Drucker as the person who invented management. The classic *The Practice of Management* sold 1 million copies in Japan, out of 5 million copies in the world. Drucker's books are always listed as best-sellers.

After the war, many Japanese company executives were influenced by Drucker's thoughts and his practical management, and these principles came into play in developing the postwar Japanese economy. Drucker wrote about his expectation that Japan

learned the main point of corporate management and the directionality of politics from Drucker's writings.

Lucky Encounters

In June 1934, at 24 years of age, Drucker by chance encountered Japanese traditional painting at an art gallery in London and became captivated by this art form. This interest triggered Drucker's attraction to Japanese culture and spurred his lifelong interest in Japan.

By the mid 1950s in Japan, the urgent demand caused by the postwar reconstruction after World War II was almost satisfied. This economic situation led to a growing interest in improved management techniques. The Japan Productivity Center (JPC), established in the spring of 1955, organized seminars, continuously dispatched overseas inspection teams and worked diligently to close the management gap between Japan and the United States relative to productivity improvement.

Taizo Ishizaka, Chairman of the Japan Business Federation, who visited various places in the United States as the head of the top management team dispatched by the JPC, wrote this recommendation for *The Practice of Management* (1956, Japanese edition): "This book was provided for the executive suite of any company which I visited during an inspection trip." This made a big ripple, and Drucker's *The Practice of Management* suddenly was accepted in Japanese industry. Whereas before practitioners were having a difficult time with business administration, they finally recovered from their uncertainty and were prepared to move the country forward.

Visiting Japan

Drucker visited Japan for the first time in 1959. After that, he traveled to Japan every other year, staying for several weeks and bringing his family. These visits continued until 1996 when he was 86 years old.

After his first trip to Japan, Drucker said: "My Japan visit was undertaken with pleasure. I wanted to watch Japanese traditional painting

> There were enormous numbers of people (Japanese statesmen, corporate executives and businessmen) who learned the main point of corporate management and the directionality of politics from Drucker's writings.

Is Peter Drucker still relevant today? In my opinion, the answer has to be "yes." Today's answers may be different, but the central questions are still the same. Moreover, most of Drucker's principles cut to the core of all being and, therefore, are timeless. That goes

would reach a turning point and develop into a new society. Drucker always looked at "new society" and was trying to ascertain the future of management. There were enormous numbers of people (Japanese statesmen, corporate executives and businessmen) who tell the truth." However, after the first trip Drucker became passionate not only about Japanese traditional painting but about the country itself. Drucker met corporate executives who had vision and courage; and he was convinced of Japan's potential. He discussed the implications of Japanese-style management for Westerners for the first time in the 1971 *Harvard Business Review* article, "What We Can Learn from Japanese Management."

Diamond Inc., which translated many of Drucker's books, has published 80 of his titles in Japan (including collections of his writings) since *Automation and the New Society* (1956). A total of 4 million copies have been sold by Diamond Inc. alone as of November 2005 (Memo, 14 Nov. 2005, Diamond, Inc.). This sales volume is possible for a literary book in our country, but for business books, even by a non-Japanese, we have never seen

Peter Drucker's Contribution to Indian Management Thought and Practice

Vaibhav Manek, KNAV and PRISM Center of Learning

Note: KNAV is an international accounting, tax and business advisory firm. The PRISM Center of Learning offers the Drucker Curriculum in the Indian subcontinent, in partnership with the Drucker Institute, Claremont Graduate University.

Among the scores of nations that have been influenced by Peter Drucker, India is a prominent one. Drucker is a name that invigorates many minds and businesses in India. In terms of his contribution to management studies, right from undergraduate courses on commerce and economics, to professional courses such as chartered accountancy, to management degree courses at India's business schools, the work of Peter Drucker is widely read and acknowledged.

Most students in India's colleges and universities studying various disciplines of management, law, commerce, social sciences, organizational behavior and finance would have grown up having read Drucker.

> Drucker is one of three Americans whose concepts of management helped raise the Japanese economy after World War II, the others being William Edwards Deming and Joseph Moses Juran.

Contribution and Influence on Japan

Drucker wrote in the preface to the Japanese edition of *Innovation and Entrepreneurship* (1980), "Great time passed since I started minute observation for Japan. I visited Japan regularly for more than 25 years, and the most were considerably long-term stays. In both the economic world and the government, there are many extremely close friends...However, I did not work very much in Japan." Drucker also said, "Corporate executives whom I got to know in Japan are my friends, not my clients. I don't think I got any consulting charges from them."

Drucker is one of three Americans whose concepts of management helped raise the Japanese economy after World War II, the others being William Edwards Deming (1900-1993) and Joseph Moses Juran (1904-2008). In June 1966, Drucker's contributions to the modernization of Japanese industrial management and Japan-U.S. friendship were recognized, and the Japanese government conferred on him the Order of the Sacred Treasure (Zuihousho), an honor established on January 4, 1888, by Emperor Meiji of Japan as the Order of Meiji.

an equal to Drucker's books. His popularity remains a deep-rooted factor in Japan.

In his book, *Management Challenges for the 21st Century* (1999), Drucker wrote: "I very much hope that Japan will find a solution that preserves the social stability, the community and the social harmony that lifetime employment provided, and yet creates the mobility that knowledge work and knowledge workers must have. Far more is at stake than Japan's own society and civic

harmony. A Japanese solution would provide a model — "for in every country a functioning society does require cohesion."

> **Chuck Ueno** is director of The Drucker Workshop at the Drucker Society of Japan.

> Most academicians, professors, researchers and doctoral students of management have read Drucker's books and articles.

Likewise, most academicians, professors, researchers and doctoral students of management have read Drucker's books and articles. Some have even acknowledged references to Drucker's thoughts and ideas in their work, and have built upon his thoughts.

Drucker's seminal work on "organization," his thoughts on the concepts of "knowledge ➤

worker" and "innovation and entrepreneurship," and his work on the "effective executive" have found a tremendous following in India. Many corporations use Drucker's thoughts in their training programs and imbue these thoughts in their executives' work.

Infosys Technologies, one of India's and the world's most respected companies, is built on the foundations of ethical management and integrity in leadership, ideals that Peter Drucker stood for all his life. Says Kris Gopalakrishnan, CEO and co-founder of Infosys, "Drucker is an essential. Others have only picked up on his thoughts."

Drucker in, *Landmarks of Tomorrow*, writes with reference to India: "I am convinced of Gandhi's lasting impact—unless indeed, Independent India collapses into anarchy, civil war, totalitarianism, or before a new conquest by a foreign invader. But it is unlikely that there will ever be an attempt to realize Gandhi's society, that post-mortem dream that was to be more truly a fulfillment of the basic values of the West than any other Western country has ever been, and which yet was to rest on the non-Western foundations of India's own spiritual heritage. That attempt—despite its nobility and popular appeal—has failed."

entrepreneurship can be found manifested in many of India's current booming economic scenarios. As a prominent example, the Indian population of more than 1 billion, once considered a liability, is now considered a meaningful contributory asset—both in terms of gross domestic output and a large market, which no serious global corporation can afford to ignore. This has led to large foreign direct investments and has unleashed a new breed of Indian entrepreneurs ready to conquer the world, which ultimately has resulted in more disposable income in the hands of the average Indian.

From mobile phones to Internet technology to consumer goods to high-end services, one can also see the luxury segment of high-end brands coexisting and thriving. Information technology application is an area where India has gained an undisputed global leadership position, with many corporations outsourcing their non-core business and knowledge processes to Indian BPOs and KPOs, and having their software written by sophisticated Indian companies.

In 2004, Peter Drucker in an interview in an issue of Fortune said: "The medical school in New Delhi, All India Institute of Medical Sciences, is perhaps one of the best in the world.

Vaibhav Manek is the hon. vice president of the Drucker Society, Mumbai, India. He is also a partner in the KNAV, Mumbai Office and cofounder of PRISM Center of Learning.

A Thinker Beyond His Time

Shuming Zhao, School of Business, Nanjing University

After attending the Academy of Management Conference in Hawaii in August 2005, my wife and daughter accompanied me on a much-anticipated trip to Claremont Graduate University (CGU) to visit with Professor Peter Drucker. It turned out to be our last meeting as he passed away in November 2005. The news was difficult to accept. Just as his thoughts and ideas were always new and provocative, I imagined that Drucker would stay young forever. Seeing the collected work of Drucker on my bookshelf is comforting. Although he is gone, his works, his spirit and his thoughts will endure, making his life memorable to those who admired and learned from him.

The First Meeting

My first encounter with Drucker was in the summer of 1981, when I was attending his lectures at CGU. At that time, very little was known about Drucker in China. China followed a highly centralized planned economic system and managerial model. Because there was little emphasis placed on the importance of learning management theory and practice, I chose linguistics and education as my graduate major, rather than management. I did not regret that choice until I returned to China to work at Nanjing University in 1983. By then, many aspects of life in China were changing. China had adopted an economic reform and opening-up policy. The changes became increasingly significant over time.

By 1984 China had embarked on a semi-commodity economy, which made me realize

> Although he is gone, his works, his spirit and his thoughts will endure, making his life memorable to those who admired and learned from him.

It is important to note that Gandhi's ideals have never been fully realized in India, although many institutions were founded on those principles. Today, it is the free market and the knowledge worker that are driving the economy, with full freedom for citizens to set up entrepreneurial ventures in an environment that fosters business.

Similarly, the thought that it is incongruity that ultimately leads to innovation and

And the technical graduates of Indian Institute of Information Technology in Bangalore are as good as any in the world. Also India has 150 million people for whom English is the main language. So India is indeed becoming a knowledge centre."

Drucker's belief that we are driving towards an era of knowledge workers is amply proven in this part of the world.

the growing importance of management principles and practices. I became determined to study for a Ph.D. in management at CGU. My return to Claremont provided a number of learning opportunities to interact with Drucker and enhance my knowledge of management.

effective and rewarding. Managers lead employees not only through knowledge, ability and skills but also through vision, encouragement, responsibility and integrity. Drucker explored the importance of individual humans to an organization, how to build harmonious relationships between

sion to talk with Drucker about China's economic reform and enterprise management. He agreed that China's economic reform and enterprise management have achieved substantial success. Drucker emphasized that management practice always precedes management theories. He recalled that in those years when he was learning the Japanese management experience, he traveled to Japan many times to understand the practice of management.

He suggests that we must understand and appreciate individual characteristics if we are to treat employees as human beings who contribute to the organization through their talent.

Although he was an accomplished wellknown thinker and communicator, Drucker was human. In conversations with students, he would take the time to emphasize and explain points. To his students, Peter Drucker the legend became Peter Drucker the teacher. In him, you found a knowledgeable senior mentor who was effective at giving systematic guidance and support.

The Pioneer of Modern Human Resources Management

Drucker, as the founder of modern management, has contributed a significant body of work in the field of human resource management. His writings convey the basic theme of "human-centered" management systems (Drucker, 2005). "Human beings are the most important resource of enterprises" is his central point.

In his 1954 seminal book, *The Practice of Management*, Drucker emphasizes the unique value of human resources for their individual contributions to an organization. He suggests that we must understand and appreciate individual characteristics if we are to treat employees as human beings who contribute to the organization through their talent.

Drucker's writing and consulting challenged managers to empower employees with a sense of accomplishment to make their jobs more

individuals and organizations, and how to create organizations that build responsibility and self-management.

As a "social ecologist" Drucker has become known as a thinker who integrates the spirit of "the unity of knowledge and practice" (Drucker 2006). His perspective draws attention to the importance of analyzing changes from both social and historical perspectives.

We discussed that technology and capital are merely tools for developing countries, which will produce sufficient effects only by the efficacy of competent managers. The core challenges facing China are to cultivate large numbers of effective managers who understand how to manage and how to lead. They must promote the development of enterprises, and also know how to motivate employees and reward their achievements. He emphasized that in today's China, and even all over the world, nothing is more important than this. Following this way of thinking, China should cultivate its own managers who are familiar with and understand the country and people, and also are

The core challenges facing China are to cultivate large numbers of effective managers who understand how to manage and how to lead.

This approach allows one to appreciate the influence of management and predict the direction of change. Leaders look at change as opportunity, and seek to find suitable effective responses both inside and outside of organizations. Managers must know how to shape future policy, create transformation, and at the same time balance between innovation and perpetuation.

Accurate and Profound Insight about China's Development

Visiting the last time in 2005, I had the occa-

deeply rooted in the Chinese culture, society and environment.

The change in China is dramatic. The change is not evolutionary change: It is revolutionary change. The development of Chinese production has evolved from "Made-in-China" to "Copy-in-China" to now "Innovate-in-China." This evolution is totally supported by human talent. With the increasing penetration of a knowledge economy worldwide, the importance of human resource management has gradually emerged as a critical theme. ➤

part III: leadership development

It is noteworthy that since the 1980s, scholars, managers and business leaders have come to appreciate the relevance of Drucker's management ideas in China. Evidence of his influence can be seen in the Drucker learning institutions that have been established in cities including Beijing, Shanghai, Nanjing and Xi'an. Simultaneously, a number of Chinese enterprises have gained great achievements through the application of modern management practices that are

His interest in art, and Japanese art in particular, can be seen as a spinoff of his admiration for Japanese management that inspired him to build a collection of Japanese art.

derived from Drucker. Zhang Ruimin of Haier Group of China illustrates one well-known example among others.

We honor Drucker's memory as a friend, mentor and teacher. Undoubtedly, he will be long remembered for his lasting unique contributions to the theory and practice of management—the founder of modern management.

Note: This article is excerpted from a longer article which is part of NSFC Research Project 70732002.

References

Drucker, P. F. (1954). *The Practice of Management* [M], New York: Harper & Row.

Drucker, P. F. (2005). *The Effective Executive* (in Chinese) [M], China Machine Press.

Drucker, P. F. (2006). *Management Challenges for the 21st Century* (in Chinese) [M], China Machine Press.

Shuming Zhao is a professor at and dean of the School of Business, Nanjing University, People's Republic of China.

Peter Drucker: More than a Management Thinker

Danica Purg, IEDC-Bled School of Management

Peter Drucker is perhaps the best example of a European who later in the United States became the most impressive management thinker of our times. In his personality the old and new times flowed together, and he has been as much a citizen of the world as an American. Without idealizing his youth in Austria, we can see that it certainly provided him the social, historical and cultural basis for development of his skills and talents. And as it counts the same for great artists, it is difficult to say what part of his extraordinary feeling for the "Zeitgeist," always including a view to the future, came from his talent of observation and understanding, or from his craftsmanship.

Being a lawyer by education, he increasingly believed that the main issues in business could not be resolved by legal or organizational solutions only. Increasingly, cultural, sociological and psychological analyses and associations filled his books. More and more he stressed the importance of self-knowledge and what he called the quality area of ethics.

Therefore, it has been a special but not a surprising experience that his home library has been filled with books about art. His interest in art, and Japanese art in particular, can be seen as a spinoff of his admiration for Japanese management that inspired him to build a collection of Japanese art. But it has been certainly more than that. How otherwise can we understand that he was for several years the sole teacher on Japanese art in Pomona College? Art helped him to understand better the Japanese culture, and particularly the business culture.

He saw also here—as everywhere else—the parallels. He defined Japanese paintings as "copying to perfection" and "creative imitation," and so he saw the Japanese industrial and managerial approach. His obsession with quality had a relation to art as well. He describes in one of his books how he attended a 1929 performance of Verdi's Falstaff at the Hamburg Opera. He was so much impressed by the composition that he wanted to carry out his own life's work in the spirit of Verdi, who once said: "All my life as a musician I have striven for perfection. It has always eluded me. I surely have an obligation to make one more try."

Willingly or unwillingly, Peter Drucker has inspired me not only to integrate ethics in management education at IEDC Bled School of Management, but also to develop the topic of "Art and Leadership" to enrich leadership development with lessons from art as a tool for reflection on organization, on oneself and on the meaning of life in general.

Professor Danica Purg is president of IEDC-Bled School of Management, Slovenia.

Managing Yourself

Bob Buford, The Drucker Institute

As Peter Drucker understood so well, we have a problem—a big problem, a 30-year problem.

At the beginning of the last century, life expectancy was around 50 years. If you are 50 years old today, you are in the period I've dubbed "halftime." It's a feeling of "Been there. Done that. Now what?" You

...ow can reasonably expect to live 30 more ...roductive years.

...uch of this special issue of *People & Strategy* ...focused on how Peter Drucker's deep ...nowledge of the globe has helped to make ...is teachings relevant to an amazing mix ...f countries and cultures. But Drucker, of ...ourse, was focused on generations as well as ...eography, on people as well as places.

...nd toward the end of his own long life—one ...hat saw him wear the multiple hats of ...niversity professor, management consultant ...nd writer—he began to explore how untra-...itional, serial careers were creating a ...uandary for the many who had expected ...felong stability.

...In a few hundred years," Drucker declared, ...when the history of our time is written from ...long-term perspective, I think it very prob-...ble that the most important event those ...istorians will remember is not technology, ...ot the Internet, not e-commerce—but the ...nprecedented change in the human condi-...ion. For the first time—and I mean that ...terally—substantial and rapidly growing ...umbers of people have choices. For the first ...ime, they will have to *manage themselves*."

...Managing oneself, however, is far easier said ...han done. As Drucker warned: "We are ...otally unprepared for it. Up until around ...900, even in the most highly developed ...ountries, the overwhelming majority of ...eople simply followed their father's foot-...teps—if they were lucky. If your father was ...peasant farmer, you were a peasant farmer. ...f he was a craftsman, you were a craftsman. ...here was no such thing as upward mobility. ...Now, suddenly, a very large number of people ...choose what they want to be. And what's ...nore, they will have more than one career. ...The average working life span is now close to ...0 years. In 1900, it was 20."

...Ready or not, we live in an age of self-...letermination. But with this marvelous ...pportunity has come tremendous anxiety. ...can say with certainty, based on hundreds ...f conversations and e-mails about midlife

issues that I have received, that most people don't know what to do with the second half of their lives.

"A pier is nothing other than a frustrated bridge," Shimon Peres has said, capturing this predicament both precisely and poetically. "It is connected to one shore only and does not have another shore to attach itself to."

We have a lot of "frustrated bridges"—pro-fessionally as well as personally. What's more, our angst has been exacerbated by a period of almost indescribable financial insecurity.

Among Drucker's greatest strengths was his ability to "look out the window and see what's visible but not yet seen." His contribution was to ask the right questions at the right time. In his last book, *Management: Revised* (with Joe Maciariello), Drucker wrote the following:

Knowledge workers . . . face drastically new demands:

- *They have to ask, "Who am I? What are my strengths? How do I work?"*
- *They have to ask, "Where do I belong?"*
- *They have to ask, "What is my contribution?"*

Can any of us afford not to be wrestling with the answers?

Peter Drucker, American

Rick Wartzman

Peter Drucker's core philosophy—that effec-tively managed, ethically led organizations are the key to a healthy society—was forged in Europe. It was there that the Vienna native devoured the works of Wilhelm von Hum-boldt, Joseph von Radowitz and Friedrich Julius Stahl. It was there that he was exposed to the economic theories of Joseph Schum-peter and John Maynard Keynes. And it was there, most significantly, that he witnessed the rise of Fascism.

Yet it was in the United States, where Drucker arrived in 1937, that his philosophy has been tested to the fullest—for better and for worse.

Although he retained a thick Austrian accent throughout his long life, Drucker became an American through and through. He was a keen observer of the national scene, leading some to liken him to a latter-day de Toc-queville. He loved baseball (and even advised the Cleveland Indians for a season). The White House sought his counsel.

But it was through his landmark books on how organizations should function, includ-ing 1946's *Concept of the Corporation* and

> Managing oneself, however, is far easier said than done. As Drucker warned: "We are totally unprepared for it. Up until around 1900, even in the most highly developed countries, the overwhelming majority of people simply followed their father's footsteps— if they were lucky."

Bob Buford is the chairman of the Board of Advisors at the Drucker Institute.

1954's *The Practice of Management*, that Drucker truly shaped his adopted home, helping to usher in what historian Alfred Chandler has called "the Golden Age of busi-ness" in America.

➤

part III: leadership development

Specifically, Drucker's ideas and ideals led countless executives in the decades after World War II to try to balance the needs of shareholders, employees and the community at large. And his principles helped create a work environment that provided dignity and a sense of fulfillment for millions of people.

Over time, however, Drucker would not only see his wisdom embraced; he would also watch it being woefully ignored.

By the 1980s, Drucker had grown tired of the naked greed exhibited by U.S. corporate leaders. (Partly as a result, he increasingly

Given his level of outrage, one can only imagine what Drucker would have made of the latest economic crisis, an extraordinarily costly mess triggered by everything he decried: an emphasis on short-term gain over long-term stewardship; the substitution of cleverness for genuine innovation; a widespread failure to heed the first responsibility of every professional: "Above all, do no harm."

Surely, Drucker would be angered and deeply saddened by what has transpired during the last year or so. But we can also assume that Drucker would not have given up completely on American business. Deep down, after all, Drucker's thinking always had "a hopeful cast," in the words of his biographer Jack Beatty.

> Specifically, Drucker's ideas and ideals led countless executives in the decades after World War II to try to balance the needs of shareholders, employees and the community at large. And his principles helped create a work environment that provided dignity and a sense of fulfillment for millions of people.

When Jim Collins and his coauthor Jerry Porras dug into the backgrounds of "visionary companies" such as General Electric, Johnson & Johnson, Procter & Gamble, Hewlett-Packard, Merck and Motorola, they found Drucker's "intellectual fingerprints" everywhere: "David Packard's notes and speeches from the foundation years at HP so mirrored Drucker's writings," Collins has remarked, "that I conjured an image of Packard giving management sermons with a classic Drucker text in hand. When we finished our research, Jerry and I struggled to name our book, rejecting more than 100 titles. Finally in frustration I blurted, 'Why don't we just name it *Drucker Was Right*, and we're done!'" (They eventually instead settled on *Built to Last*.)

turned his attention to the work of nonprofits.) He likened those on Wall Street to "Balkan peasants stealing each other's sheep." He spoke out against the obscene amounts of pay being pulled in by CEOs—a peculiarly American phenomenon.

Few top executives, Drucker said, can fathom "the hatred, contempt and fury that has been created" because of their king-sized compensation. "I don't know what form it will take, but the envy developing from their enormous wealth will cause trouble." He thought that pocketing millions while passing out pink slips was, in particular, "morally unforgiveable."

After the publication of *Post-Capitalist Society* in 1993, Drucker was asked by an interviewer whether he believed his books had been properly understood. "I would hope that American managers—indeed, managers worldwide—continue to appreciate what I have been saying almost from day one: that management is so much more than exercising rank and privilege, that it is about so much more than 'making deals,'" he replied. "Management affects people and their lives."

Can there be any doubt that America needs Drucker now more than ever? **P&S**

> **Rick Wartzman** is the executive director of the Drucker Institute.

What Drucker Means Around the World

Discovery Questions

- What are we dealing with in our organization today that relates to this content area?

- Heightened global awareness of the similarities and differences in management history and culture between the US, Europe, Japan, China and India.

- Ability to put management theory in the context of history and society.

- Understanding of how significantly work, careers and management has changed over the last hundred years.

- Greater appreciation for the societal impact of organizational practices.

- Recognition of the "art" part of management as well as the "science" part.

- Appreciation for a point of view that has lasted a hundred years and still has an important place in management practice.

Selected Facts

- What new facts that were presented got your attention?

- Drucker grew up in Austria amidst the cultured famous old world elite then experienced the rise of the Fascists and Nazis, shaping his belief in the freedom of the individual.

- The Austrian Economist Joseph Schumpeter's Theory of Capitalism stipulated that the individual and their initiative is the driving power of the economy.

- Drucker's doctoral thesis in Law focused on how alternative governments operated.

- Drucker's corollary to the Doctor's Hippocratic Oath is "Above all, not knowingly to do any social harm."

- The main pillars of Drucker's method should define how management education occurs: Unbounded thinking, moral resolution, inner independence and a sound knowledge of history.

- Drucker taught that managers lead employees not only through knowledge, ability and skills but also through vision, encouragement, responsibility and integrity.

- Drucker taught that technology and capital only achieve results through the efficacy of competent managers.

- Drucker's core philosophy is that effectively managed, ethically led organizations are the key to a healthy society.

Key Discussion Points

- What were the key points being made in this Point Counterpoint presentation?

- Describe how Drucker saw Management as the most important "organ" of our society.

- Did Drucker see Management as a Science or an Art? Why?

- Drucker had an overwhelming desire to extract universal guidelines from practical experience. Give an example.

- Drucker believed in "Value and Service first, Profit later"—how does this fit with his view of the role of Management in Society, not just in the organization?

- Drucker wrote that "every enterprise is a learning and teaching institution" which as a social function enables people to achieve their best performance. Are we living up to that?

- What role did Drucker see for organizational goals and values?

- What is Sattelberger's concern about the content of current MBA programs?

- Describe how Drucker both impacted and was impacted by Japan.

- What different needs do Knowledge Workers have (e.g. for mobility)?

- How is the worker of 1900 different than the worker of 2000?

- Discuss the insecurity and anxiety present in this description of the Knowledge Worker in Drucker's last book: "Knowledge workers face drastically new demands. They have to ask "Who am I? What are my Strengths? How do I work? Where do I belong? What is my contribution?"

Review of Solutions

- Identify 2-3 Big Ideas that are worthy of exploring for our organization.

Recommendations Summary

- Identify one thing that we will do differently based on what we learned.

Learning Outcomes

- What one new piece of information did you learn that will be important to you?

From the Perspectives Editor

Anna Tavis, Perspectives Editor

As the first decade of the 21st century draws to a close, we can look back confidently at the 20th century and call it the management century. Peter Drucker's centennial in 2009 became a testimonial to the success we have had in management development. The situation is quite different, however, when it comes to leadership "science." There are more than 60,000 books on leadership on our shelves, and we still have not "cracked the code" on what true leadership really means and how it can be achieved.

Twenty-first century neuroscience is now attempting to come to leadership's rescue. Brain research is entering leadership discussions center stage and may help to close the gap between our goals and our practices. *People & Strategy* invited David Rock, the pioneer of brain-based thinking about leadership and the founder of the NeuroLeadership Institute, to lead our discussion for this special issue. Rock's article "How Neuroscience will Impact Leadership" sets the stage for a breakthrough conversation among Paul Lawrence, a Harvard scholar, Marshall Goldsmith, the world's best-selling leadership author, and three practitioners: Terry Hogan of Citigroup, Christine Williams, of NASA and Tobias Kiefer of Booz and Co.

According to David Rock, we now are able to access those areas of the brain where important leadership brain functions take place. We can even pinpoint specific training and development activities to influence brain centers to drive more effective behavior in four key domains, including the leader's ability to: 1) solve problems and make decisions 2) regulate emotions, 3) collaborate, and 4) facilitate change.

The following exchange of ideas is a mere anticipation of the breakthroughs yet to come. Our selection is an invitation to all students of leadership to continue to follow the hard science that is radically changing the ways we train and develop 21st century leaders.

Impacting Leadership with Neuroscience

By David Rock, Founder of Neuroleadership Institute

While speaking at a conference recently, I asked a room full of HR and training professionals if they wanted to improve the quality of the leaders in their organizations. Everyone raised a hand. Then, I asked who was confident they knew how to develop their leaders. Not a single hand went up.

This situation is not an isolated occurence. A 2008 study showed that 'improving leadership' was the second most urgent human capital imperative for most companies' business strategies. Given how widespread the problem is, perhaps we need a breakthrough here, something so fundamental that would offer a new approach to the very foundations of leadership thinking.

Up until now, most of our leadership theories evolved out of behavioral observations, or through social psychology research. It appears that this approach has not delivered what it was supposed to do. Despite the fact there are now more than 60,000 books on leadership, there is no broad agreement on what exactly leaders do, or what it takes for them to do their jobs successfully.

Recent developments within neuroscience have given us the ability to shed some new light on how the brain functions in real time. This new brain research may provide the missing link between leadership behavior and leadership development. Since 2007, there has been an effort to gather relevant neuroscience findings into a new field called 'NeuroLeadership.' NeuroLeadership

explores the neuroscience underpinning four key leadership skills, called the four domains of NeuroLeadership. These domains include:

1. The ability to solve problems and make decisions;

2. The ability to regulate emotions;

3. The ability to collaborate with others; and

4. The ability to facilitate change.

While the NeuroLeadership field is still new, there already are identifiable benefits to applying neuroscience research findings to our understanding of leadership characteristics. Clearly, there are tangible benefits to improving leadership development techniques. Multiple studies show that the best

Neuroscience is offering more theoretical breakthroughs that already are making a big difference. Using neuroscience to explain leadership issues now is happening across major, corporate, government and non-profit organizations...

leaders have both strong business and inter-personal skills. Yet many leaders have focused on their business skills and let their interpersonal skills lag. Telling leaders to be more self aware, authentic or to create trust can be both a tough sell and mission impossible for the trainers and coaches.

How do you take someone who has become a hard-nosed executive and build his or her soft skills, after decades of being rewarded for driving results? To begin, you need to speak in a respectful language, which means a language based on hard data, like brain research. Drawing on the four domains of NeuroLeadership, program designers and facilitators are able to explain the theoretical foundations, in biological terms, of most aspects of self and social awareness. At our annual NeuroLeadership Summit, hundreds of leadership practitioners discuss the benefits of underpinning a leadership development intervention with neuroscience. In short, science gets leaders turning to programs they normally would not do. It has them switch off their BlackBerry devices while they are there, and helps them ease into ideas that otherwise could be personally threatening.

Several other benefits to drawing on neuroscience are just emerging. We are beginning to test leaders' brain functioning to gain clues about how they will operate in certain conditions. For a while we could test how well someone could solve linear and non-linear problems. Now, we also can test for how well people regulate their emotions, how well they connect emotionally with others, and how well they focus their attention, all based on

brain tests rather than questionnaires. We even have a way to measure overall neural integration, a marker for adaptability. As these technologies become more widely available, we can get better at putting the right people into the right jobs, as well as target development needs to the individual.

Another emerging area of research involves the ability to predict directly a leaders' effectiveness. In a lab at MIT, scientist Alexander Pentland is able to accurately predict who will succeed in an influencing task, without needing to hear what the leader says. The approach draws on biological signals like body movements and tone of voice, based on research called 'Honest Signals.'

Finally, with a more accurate understanding of what leaders do and an ability to quantify a leader's abilities, we can begin to measure and therefore improve leadership programs more successfully. Currently, billions of dollars a year are spent on leadership development, with very little

understanding of what we are trying to achieve, and minimal capacity to measure outcomes with hard data.

Improving the quality of our leaders has never been more important. Neuroscience is offering some theoretical breakthroughs that already are making a big difference. Using neuroscience to explain leadership issues now is happening across major corporate, government and non-profit organizations, including NASA, the National Defense University, Citibank, Microsoft and other firms around the globe. While the research is still new, the benefits are available to change the way we lead.

David Rock is the founder and CEO of Results Coaching Systems (RCS), which has operations in 15 countries across the globe. He co-authored a feature article with neuroscientist Dr. Jeffrey Schwartz, called 'The Neuroscience of Leadership.' He also wrote, 'Managing with the Brain in Mind.' He is the author of several books including 'Coaching with the Brain in Mind' (Wiley & Sons, 2009), and 'Your Brain at Work,' (Oct. 2009). Rock founded the NeuroLeadership Institute and Summit, a global initiative bringing neuroscientists and leadership experts together to build a new science of leadership development.

Drawing on the four domains of NeuroLeadership, program designers and facilitators are able to explain the theoretical foundations, in biological terms, of most aspects of self and social awareness... and helps them ease into ideas that otherwise could be personally threatening.

How the Brain Enables Good Leadership

Paul R. Lawrence, author of Driven to Lead: Good, Bad, and Misguided Leadership *(Jossey-Bass, 2010).*

Leadership has yet to make the leap from art to science. I believe that recent research into how the human brain makes decisions, combined with recent discoveries in human evolution, now offer the building blocks of a useful science of leadership.

From Animal Instinct to Human Decision Making

Other animals have instincts and physical traits suited to their environments. Humans have instincts, but these only get the decision-making process started. We take a wide variety of information into account and only then figure out what to do. And while humans are not individually very strong, quick or deadly, they are very effective in groups because, unlike other animals, they can trust their companions to help them rather than opportunistically rob or abandon them. A human making a decision, unlike an animal obeying an instinct, has to consider others' survival as well as his or her own—even when those imperatives conflict. Such decision making is the foundation of complex human societies, organizations of all kinds and leadership.

The Four Drives

How does this apply to everyday leadership? Let's look inside the brain. Humans evolved four basic drives, each essential to both survival and good leadership.

- The drive to acquire—to get what we need or value, from food, shelter and offspring to expertise and promotion at work.

- The drive to defend—to protect what we need or value, including our company's market share and reputation.

- The drive to bond—to form long-term, trusting, caring relationships that go beyond mutual benefit, including relationships with coworkers, customers, suppliers and investors.

- The drive to comprehend—to make sense of the world and ourselves, which enables forecasting, inventing and problem solving.

Each of these drives monitors signals from our sense organs, adds its own evaluation, and sends the signals to other parts of the brain. Imagine a CEO whose company has just lost a key long-term contract because a competitor dropped its prices. The drive to acquire tells him to push sales harder. The drive to comprehend tells him to learn how his competitor cuts prices. The drive to defend tells him to downsize. The drive to bond tells him not to cast good employees overboard. Clearly, these last two imperatives conflict.

These four drives are not a metaphor. Researchers can now see them at work inside the brain. For example, brain-imaging studies have shown the *nucleus acumbens* "lighting up" with increased blood flow when people choose a generous rather than a selfish option—the drive to bond in action.

The Four-Drive Decision

Amazingly, the variety and even conflict of the drives is not the problem—it is the solution. It stimulates another part of our CEO's brain, the prefrontal cortex, to formulate possible responses that are sent back to the drives for review until a solution is "good enough" for all four.

> **Paul R. Lawrence** is the Wallace Brett Donham Professor of Organizational Behavior Emeritus at Harvard Business School. During his 44 years on the Harvard faculty, he taught in all the School's programs and served as chairman of the Organizational Behavior area and also of both the MBA and AMP programs. He did undergraduate work in sociology and economics at Albion College and did MBA and doctoral training at Harvard. His research, published in 26 books and numerous articles, has dealt with the human aspects of management.

Neuroscience Provides Tools to Navigate the New Business Reality

Terry Hogan, Director, Executive Development, Citibank

The four domains of NeuroLeadership; problem solving, emotion regulation, collaborating and facilitating change provide an interesting lens through which to examine the field of global leadership development. Leaders today face greater challenges than ever before as they work across multiple geographies, functions, product lines and national cultures. Leaders in a globalized business world are often managing this multiplexity with the same toolkit they had previously, long before the tall technical silos and corporate hierarchies, which at one time helped to bring efficiency and productivity, gave way to a cross-border, matrixed, digital, virtual and protean workplace.

Problem formation, intercultural acuity, co-creation and the balance between change agentry and adaptation are the new cardinal points for global leaders, who must now charter new mental maps. The neuroscience of leadership juxtaposed on the global mindset suggests that there is no longer an option for teaching leaders business skills or soft skills, because there is no longer a difference between the two. A mechanistic view of leadership cannot apply to an unpredictable, global world. We need a holistic view of the leader, leadership competencies, and the models, frameworks and methods for development.

Neuorscience provides a useful framework for understanding how leaders gain insights while learning to work in new ways across traditional boundaries in a borderless world. Leadership, and especially global leadership, is a transformational learning experience, wherein new ways of thinking and behaving occur through fundamental paradigm shifts. Global leaders must be able to scan the environment for meaningful data points that allow them to formulate effective strategies and plot new courses of action. These data points often come from unexpected sources in another part of the company or the world, or come through combining products and services in a new way for an emerging market, or by being able to recognize and understand the cultural influences that make for differences in local business practices. Leaders, therefore, need to be able to see and process information in new ways, making connections between phenomena that have never been linked before in their minds. This is systems thinking, and it is the hallmark of resourceful and innovative leaders throughout history.

The dialogue between the science of the brain and the art of leadership demonstrates this kind of systems thinking. This missing link is actually one of many that will help us to develop people to lead in an interconnected world. Another such critical link is cultural neuroscience It looks at the mutual influences of biology, cognition and social psychology, and promises exciting implications for the development of global leaders.

Disparate academic disciplines are but a mirror image of the silos in corporations. The need for systems thinking in the development of leaders also calls for us to work across the functional support silos of learning and development, organizational development, expatriation, human resources, talent management, diversity and compensation. Reductionist thinking from academics or corporate HR practitioners cannot develop the skills required to perform effectively in a global world. The multiplexity of an interconnected world calls for our collaboration as well. As this continues to happen, we will finally have an opportunity to develop these skills in global leaders.

Terry Hogan is director of Citi's Executive Development where she is responsible for the design and delivery of senior leadership development programs, team training and other organizational support interventions. Her current research focuses on linking overarching business objectives and learning and organization development to global leadership and intercultural competency. She holds a master's degree in Intercultural Relations and Global Leadership from the School of International Studies at the University of the Pacific and the Intercultural Communication Institute and a Bachelor of Science degree from Oregon State University.

Applying Neuroscience to Leadership Development: Designing Learning with the Brain in Mind

Christine R. Williams, Director, Systems Engineering Leadership Development, NASA

As a science and technology organization, NASA has always had strong commitment to employee training and development. Technical learning involving the hard sciences aligned well with our culture and mission, and as a result was well-received by our employees and managers. This was not always true of the leadership-development activities that focused more on self-awareness and learning to improve employee and organizational performance. This learning was normally referred to as soft science or the more commonly used, and less complementary name "touchy feely."

In 2008, as part of NASA's efforts to enhance the critical skills of systems engineering, NASA leadership took a deeper look at the factors that contributed to mission success. By studying successful systems engineers,[1] it became clear that technical expertise was only a part of the equation. The defining factor between good and great systems engineers was indeed the effective implementation of the softer sciences, such as the ability to engage and motivate employees, build effective teams, communicate well at all levels and think systemically. Mission success depended on what was then defined as the "Art and Science" of systems engineering.[2] To build on this understanding, NASA initiated a new developmental program to accelerate the development of the Art and Science of systems engineering.

While an understanding of neuroscience already had been introduced into a few NASA leadership programs, with the creation of a new Systems Engineering Leadership Development Program we now had an opportunity to integrate what we learned about neuroscience into every part of our program design. From the start of the program, we taught participants about the brain and discussed how we intended the design of the program to work with human needs and our evolutionary preferences rather than against them.

We designed every aspect of the program with the brain in mind, from the length and flow of learning activities to how we introduced and built the learning community. Logistics was a major factor in creating the right environment for learning. We changed factors such as lighting and even the food we served for breaks. The design of stretch assignments was particularly challenging as it took these leaders completely out of their comfort zones. We had to make it safe for them to not only give up the usual control of selecting their ➤

> Leaders, therefore, need to be able to see and process information in new ways, making connections between phenomena that have never been linked before in their minds.

part III: leadership development

own assignment, but we also had to create an environment that made it safe for them to fail, recover and grow.

While creating a more effective learning environment was our first step, our ultimate goal was to have these developing leaders understand what we were doing and how we changed the program to meet their needs more effectively, and reduce, overwhelm, and mitigate the fight, flight or freeze response, so they could do the same when they returned to their organizations. This next step is still emerging as part of the program's design to help these leaders take their personal experience out of the classroom and back into their organizations where they can implement structures and processes that improve employee effectiveness and success.

Christine R. Williams serves as the head of the Systems Department within the NASA Academy of Program, Project and Engineering Leadership (APPEL). Her programs are considered world-class by both industry and government standards, and she has been invited to speak internationally on the topics of leadership development, executive coaching and the application of advances in neuroscience to improving employee learning. Williams received her BS in Oceanography, and later graduated Summa Cum Laude from The Johns Hopkins University with an MS in Organizational Development and Applied Behavioral Science.

[1] Williams, C. & Derro, M.E. (2008). *NASA Systems Engineering Behavior Study*. National Aeronautics and Space Administration. Retrieved September 19, 2010 from http://www.nasa.gov/news/reports/NASA_SE_Behavior_Study.html

[2] Ryschkewitsch, M., Schaible D., Larson, W. (2008). *The Art and Science of Systems Engineering**. The National Aeronautics and Space Administration, Retrieved September 19, 2010 from http://www.nasa.gov/pdf/311198main_Art_and_Sci_of_SE_LONG_1_20_09.pdf

> Neuroscience has started to impact leadership development and it will further shape it. NeuroLeadership is more than a framework. It influences entire training designs and approaches...

Neuroleadership—More Than Another Leadership Framework

Tobias Kiefer, Global Director Learning & Development, Booz & Company

It is a cold and rainy winter day. I am in the process of designing a new leadership program. I experience the frustration of more than 60,000 leadership books. I decide to go a different route: Design a change program with the "learner's brain in mind" – by combining deep emotional moments that require peak attention from participants and finally bring participants to generate their own insights and takeaways. No frameworks, no preselected leadership skills participants should memorize.

Neuroscience has started to impact leadership development and it will further shape it. NeuroLeadership is more than a framework. It influences entire training designs and approaches—on multiple levels:

1. The Value of Leadership Programs: The data neuroscience is providing is certainly the meat for rationalizing investments into people development. It helps to stop the myths around leadership development and adds data to the rumors about human behavior. It will help to sell the value of leadership programs. NeuroLeadership links changed behaviors to business results—with data and metrics.

2. Training Design and Investment: Remembering one of the key insights about the brain, that no two brains are alike, will help to shape training and coaching toward positive change. By considering

key factors like Attention, Generation, Emotions and Spacing (AGES-Model), we can design programs that will radically change the nature of training for both facilitators and participants. It offers chances to reduce costs for training. We already have first indicators that the average cost structure will change dramatically: From spending almost 50 percent of training costs on travel and accommodation towards spending more than 80 percent on real learning.

3. Understanding Fundamentals of How the Brain Works: Explaining the core functions of the brain to participants (and I am really talking about the core) will help drive the changes in people further.

Looking at the current environment, with cost pressures on the one hand, and more than ever the need for innovation, creativity and leadership, on the other, we need more effective change approaches than what we have today. We need more than training—we need real change. Change starts with understanding the current status, the system (the brain), and creation of insights.

NeuroLeadership—the conversion of the art and science of leadership development should be considered a great tool to make this happen. It is the tool that rationalizes the kinds of programs designed a few years ago—by coincidence and by trusting intuition and insights. It led, in our case, to a program full of deep emotional and experiential moments of silence and learning spread over two weeks. The program has become one of our flagship programs and serves as the framework for more AGES-based models. It is NeuroLeadership put into practice.

Dr. Tobias Kiefer is the Global Director Learning & Development at Booz & Company–a global management consultancy. Kiefer is known for his approach to tie highly experiential modules into high performance leadership programs. As coach, trainer and motivational keynote speaker he uses experiential and neuroscientific elements to enable smarter thinking and to achieve better results with his clients. His experience from extreme outdoor sports and his experience as consultant and leader of a global team create a variety of insights in his programs. Since March 2010, he is participating in the Postgraduate Certificate of Neuroleadership.

Removing Obstacles to Leadership Development when Leaders Are Already Successful

Marshall Goldsmith, best-selling author of MOJO and What Got You Here Won't Get You There.

NeuroLeadership is a fascinating field, which may uncover the key to helping leaders develop the soft skills they need to take themselves, their teams and their organizations to the next level. This can be a significant challenge when what these leaders have been doing has been met with success.

We tend to repeat behavior that is followed by positive reinforcement. The more successful we become, the more positive reinforcement we get, and the more likely we are to experience the success delusion. This forms our belief "**I behave this way. I am** successful. **Therefore, I must be successful because I behave this way.**"

The good news is that our positive beliefs about ourselves help us become successful. The bad news is that these same beliefs can make it tough for us to change.

Belief 1: I Have Succeeded

Successful people have one consistent idea coursing through their veins and brains: "I have succeeded. I have succeeded. I have succeeded." This strong belief in our past success gives us faith to take the risks needed for our future success. This positive belief can become a major obstacle when behavioral change is needed, as we all tend to reject or deny feedback from others that is inconsistent with the way we see ourselves. Thus, it is very hard to hear negative feedback and admit that we need to change.

Belief 2: I Can Succeed

Successful people believe that they have the capability to have a positive influence on the world—and to make desirable things happen. They believe that through the sheer force of their personality, talent and brainpower, they can steer situations in their direction. This unshakeable belief presents another obstacle to helping them change behavior. When we believe that our good fortune is directly and causally linked to our behavior, we can easily make a false assumption. "I am successful. I behave this way. Therefore, I must be successful because I behave this way. It can be especially challenging to help successful leaders realize that their success is happening in spite of some of their behavior.

Belief 3: I Will Succeed

Successful people are optimists. Optimists tend to chronically over-commit. It can be extremely difficult for an ambitious person, with an "I will succeed' attitude to say "no" to desirable opportunities. This 'I will succeed' belief can sabotage our chances for success when it is time for us to change behavior. When I ask people who attend my programs why they did not implement changes they said they would, the most common response is, "I meant to, but I didn't have time." They believed that they would get to it later, but 'later' never came. Our excessive optimism and resulting over-commitment can be as serious an obstacle to change as our denial of negative feedback or our belief that our flaws are actually the cause of our success.

Belief 4: I Choose to Succeed

Successful people believe that they are doing what they choose to do, because they choose to do it. They have a high need for self-determination. This usually works in favor of successful people when they apply it to achieving their mission. It can work against them when they should "change course." The old saying 'winners never quit' is often true.

These four success beliefs all filter through us and create in us something that we do not want to believe about ourselves. I call it the success delusion. Few of us are immune to the success delusion. Pick one of your own quirky or unattractive behaviors. Now ask yourself: Do I continue to do this because I think it is somehow associated with the good things that have happened to me? Does this behavior help me achieve results? Overcoming the success delusion requires vigilance and constantly asking yourself, "Is this behavior a legitimate reason for my success, or am I just kidding myself?"

Marshall Goldsmith is the million-selling author of *What Got You Here Won't Get You There* – a New York Times bestseller, Wall Street Journal No. 1 business book, and Harold Longman Award winner for Business Book of the Year. His newest book, *MOJO*, is a *New York Times* (advice), *Wall Street Journal* (business), *USAToday* (money) and *Publisher's Weekly* (non-fiction) best seller. It is now available online and at major bookstores.

Few of us are immune to the success delusion.

learning guide

How Neuroscience Will Impact Leadership

Discovery Questions

- Why will "improving leadership development" continue to be the most pressing Human Capital imperative in business today?

- Why have our efforts been largely unsuccessful as we have tried to find the "right" solutions for developing leaders? What worked and what did not work in the mainstream approaches to leadership development used in the late 20th century?

- When have we begun bringing relevant Neuroscientific insights into leadership development approaches?

- What are the four most critical leadership skills that neuroscience helped us identify and focus on in developing effective business leaders?

- Why do such leading companies as Microsoft and Citibank and governments agencies such as NASA turn to Neuroscience for the solutions of their leadership development challenges?

- Explain your point of view on the future of Neuroleadership research and its impact on leadership development approaches in business, government and non profit organizations.

Selected Facts

- A mechanistic view of leadership can no longer apply to an unpredictable, global world. We need a holistic view of the leader, leadership competencies, and the models, frameworks and methods for development. 21st century Leadership roles require a larger dose of self-awareness, emotional intelligence, personal resilience and change agility. The idea here is that as new scientific technologies become more widely available, we get better at putting the right people into the right jobs, as well as target development needs to the individual.

- Problem formation, intercultural acuity, co- creation and the balance between change agility and adaptation are the new cardinal points for global leaders, who now must charter new business territory. The neuroscience of leadership suggests that there is no longer an option for teaching leaders business skills or soft skills, because there is no longer a difference between the two.

- The need for systems thinking in the development of leaders calls for us to work across the functional support silos of learning and development, organizational development, expatriation, human resources, talent management, diversity and compensation.

Key Discussion Points

- Prior to Neuroscience, we were using assessment methods based on self reporting and external observations. What new testing methods are becoming available to the field of leadership development through Neuroscientific research?

- What do you believe will change in leadership development based on broader availability of reliable scientific measurement methods?

- What other sciences, beside neuroscience, will impact our approaches to leadership development?

- Review and compare examples of implementation of a few Neuroscientific insights as presented by Counterpoint authors.

Review of Solutions

- Do you believe that your organization is ready for the evolution of leadership development approaches based on 21st century science? Explain.

- Identify 2-3 Big Ideas that you believe may be easier to implement in your organization.

- Compare your company's readiness level with the companies described in the counterpoint articles.

Learning Outcomes

- How does the information presented in this Point Counterpoint exchange influence your own view on how Leadership Development needs to be conducted?

Recommendations Summary

- Identify one thing that we will do differently based on what you have learned in these Perspectives.

From the Perspectives Editor

Anna Tavis, Perspectives Editor

As the economy is slowly climbing its way out of the recession, the key questions that managers and their HR partners should ask themselves are about what could be done differently. One area ripe for improvement is onboarding, the practice of bringing new executives on board.

We invited George Bradt, a business executive, entrepreneur and the author of three books on onboarding, to lead our discussion. George Bradt takes the position that the onboarding process is an act of transformational leadership. The recruiting manager, in Bradt's version, takes the front seat in the onboarding drama. Bradt's hiring manager takes on the roles of producer, director and stage manager, each with complementary duties. The employee is the actor, busy with many tasks.

We invited a diverse group of authors to revisit the topic with Bradt's point of view in mind. We thank Charles Forgang, a New York City-based employment attorney; George Olcott, who writes from Oxford, UK; Robert Rigby-Hall, SVP of HR at Lexus-Nexus; Matthew Walter of Bank of America; and Sonja Weckström of Right Management, who is based in Helsinki, for their provocative contributions.

This timely and lively discussion opens up new choices for developing and implementing a pragmatic and aligned approach to setting up the new hire for success.

Onboarding: An Act of Transformational Leadership

George Bradt, principal, Prime Genesis Executive Onboarding and Transition Acceleration

Onboarding is an act of transformational leadership. This is true for both hiring managers and for the new employees themselves. New employees must assimilate into teams and organizations while, at the same time, improving those organizations. This is two-way transformational leadership as organizations transform new employees while new employees are transforming the organizations they are joining.

For their part, hiring managers (direct supervisors of new employees) must be important initiators, drivers and supporters of those transformations as part of their fundamental responsibility to inspire and enable others. For hiring managers, bringing new employees into their teams or organizations is one of the most important investments they make with

some of the highest potential impact. In my experience, it is unconscionable how many hiring managers do not take this as seriously as they should.

Exhibit: Hiring Managers' Roles in Onboarding

* **Producer** – Assemble resources. Align stakeholders. Pivot off Total Onboarding Plan.
* **Director** – Partner with new employee to map out Personal Onboarding Plan.
* **Stage Manager** – Announce, introduce, and support behind the scenes.

Digging into hiring managers' roles in acquiring, accommodating, assimilating and

accelerating new employees, it is useful to think about what they do across three phases. At first, hiring managers are producers, assembling resources for success. Then, they act as directors, working with new employees to map out onboarding plans. Finally, hiring managers become stage managers, working behind the scenes to support new employees' efforts.

Producer

"If I'd known then what I know now, I never would have accepted this job." In our work onboarding executives, we hear this when hiring managers fail in their role as producers. Sometimes hiring managers aren't clear on what their new employees' roles should be. Sometimes hiring manages fail to align other stakeholders around roles before ➤

part III: leadership development

starting to recruit. Sometimes hiring managers fail to help candidates fully understand roles before accepting offers. Any one of these is a recipe for disaster.

Job 1 is for hiring managers to clarify expectations of new employees, especially about deliverables and interdependencies. Out of this clarification comes the required strengths and a Total Onboarding Plan; mapping out the steps of acquisition; accommodation, assimilation and acceleration; responsibilities for the various efforts; and a timeline of when they are going to be completed.

because anything candidates can discover in a couple of days of due diligence, they would have discovered in their first couple of weeks on the job. Far better for them to decline the offer than to start and quit. Scenario No.2 is that candidates do their due diligence and then accept the offer. This starts manager/subordinate relationships off as partnerships instead of as buyers/sellers.

Director

No one hires people because of their strengths in onboarding. They hire people to deliver

happen around the actors on stage: setting the stage and providing resources and support for their new employees.

Hiring managers should be accountable for accommodating new employees by making sure they can do work on day one—even if there is a system in place to do this.

Managing the announcement cascade well can be particularly helpful. Who hears about new employees—from whom and when—can make a big impact on how they feel about new employees. In many ways, the first step for hiring managers to assimilate new employees is through proactively introducing key stakeholders to them.

If I could wave my magic wand, no one would ever let anyone start recruiting anyone ever until key stakeholders were aligned around all aspects of a cohesive Total Onboarding Plan.

Job 2 is to get others aligned around those expectations and the Total Onboarding Plan—before starting to recruit. This is often hard work. It almost always slows down the start of recruiting. But the payback in terms of reduced risk of failure for the new employee and the organization and acceleration of results is huge. If I could wave my magic wand, no one would ever let anyone start recruiting anyone ever until key stakeholders were aligned around all aspects of a cohesive Total Onboarding Plan.

Job 3 is partnering with candidates to make sure they know what they are getting into before accepting offers. We've seen too many Pyrrhic victories where hiring managers closed sales that they never should have closed. We strongly suggest that hiring managers actively help candidates do real due diligence between getting offered and accepting the job.

Either of two scenarios may occur. Scenario No.1 is that candidates do their due diligence and turn down offers. This is a good thing

results that organizations can't deliver without them. Why then would anyone take a sink or swim approach to onboarding a subordinate? It is in everyone's best interest for hiring managers to do what it takes to help their new employees succeed over the short and long term.

Co-creating Personal Onboarding Plans is how onboarding accountability is handed off from hiring managers to new employees. Hiring managers are best equipped to provide input and direction about stakeholders, messages and priorities for the Fuzzy Front End before day one, day one and new employees' first 100-days. New employees have to make things happen. This and getting alignment behind Total Onboarding Plans upfront are two essential points of inflection for successful onboarding.

Stage Manager

After handing off Personal Onboarding Plans, most hiring managers' work is behind-the-scenes. Like stage managers, hiring managers' main priorities are things that

Resources and support to help new employees accelerate progress often include mentors and coaches beyond hiring managers as well as outside transition accelerators as appropriate. However, new employees' most important relationships are always the ones with their hiring managers.

Onboarding Leadership

Onboarding is more successful when hiring managers and new employees each take leadership roles in the efforts. Leadership is about inspiring and enabling others to do their absolute best, together, to realize a meaningful and rewarding shared purpose. Onboarding is not about acquiring, accommodating, assimilating and accelerating new employees. Those are merely steps on the way to realizing a shared purpose. This is why onboarding is an act of transformational leadership for all.

Editor's note: This article is adapted from *Onboarding – How to Get Your New Employees Up to Speed in Half the Time* (Bradt and Vonnegut, Wiley 2009).

George Bradt is a principal with PrimeGenesis. In his consulting role, he focuses exclusively on executive onboarding and transition acceleration.

Curtain Up on the Two-Way Transformational Leader Model

Charles S. Forgang, Esq., founder and principal of the New York Law Offices of Charles S. Forgang

Working as a New York employment lawyer who, virtually every day, counsels executives and professionals in negotiating their seemingly well-thought-out entrances into companies, and both planned and (all too frequently) unplanned departures from companies, I found it refreshing to read George Bradt's insightful analysis.

It is my firm belief that if more hiring managers would affirmatively undertake the steps outlined by Bradt, a recognized authority in executive onboarding, by truly internalizing the process and related responsibilities (as opposed to merely "going through the motions"), I might become quite less busy in representing executives with respect to either their unfortunate terminations or their resignations for more enlightened pastures.

Bradt seems to hit the nail on the head when he suggests the two-way transformational leadership model. The responsibility is not merely that of the newly hired executive to assimilate and shine, but at least equally that of the company to provide the proper forum—meaning one where proper onboarding has enabled the new executive to commence work with the proper expectations in place and key stakeholders aligned.

Indeed, the business lawyer in me virtually always applauds due diligence as supporting an intelligent means of decision making, so that one may better weigh potential risks against rewards. In the job market, however, a prospective new hire may be all too nervous to ask all of those tough questions, especially in the current economy where there may be a long line (or at least a perceived long line) of candidates for any one position. Yes, candidates are often afraid that by asking the most difficult question they risk alienating a com-

> In the job market, however, a prospective new hire may be all too nervous to ask all of those tough questions, especially in the current economy where there may be a long line (or at least a perceived long line) of candidates for any one position.

pany, or in particular, the hiring manager, who might then shortly become his or her new boss. Yet without the proper sharing of information, mistakes can be made all too easily, frequently yielding mutually costly results.

I often describe the essence of my business representing executives as "scrambling and unscrambling eggs"—bringing executives and companies together (the fun part of my job), and helping them separate (not so much fun). Indeed, I find "scrambling" to be much easier than "unscrambling." I keep thinking of some of my clients' words over the years, something to the effect of "if only I knew then what I know now," or "if only I had been prepared for this," or "why didn't they tell me . . . none of this had to happen." Or, as Bradt suggests, certain "sales" should never have closed, at least it would sometimes seem, until more information was appropriately shared by (and even within) the company, so that both the incoming executive and the company are more fully on the same page.

If we were to reflect back nearly a half-century ago to the New York World's Fair, followed by Expo '67 in Canada and ensuing exposi-

tions (á la "The World of Tomorrow"), we would be reminded of how we were told that "communication" would facilitate the essence of so much of the future. Yet, at least in my view, companies have often missed the mark in communicating with and about their new hires, and effectively assimilating them by taking sufficient proactive steps. I concur with Bradt's position that the "sink or swim" model should not (or at least rarely) be a goal when intelligent onboarding more typically supports the success of the new executive. And by extension, it supports the company and its mission, even if only in the seeming microcosm of that executive's division. The most successful journey will often mirror that initial relationship between the new executive and his or her hiring manager, especially as Bradt suggests, when each of them takes leadership roles in the efforts.

Thus, I applaud Bradt's analogy to the theatre world, viewing the hiring manager's role in onboarding as that of producer, director and stage manager. Surely, a company enabling this to happen requires commitment, time and, above all, human capital. But it is not purely an altruistic act to help the new exec-

> The most successful journey will often mirror that initial relationship between the new executive and his or her hiring manager, especially as Bradt suggests, when each of them takes leadership roles in the efforts.

utive, because the ultimate benefit should, hopefully, redound in a similarly powerful way to the company. As Bradt opines, when steps are taken towards a "shared purpose," onboarding becomes "an act of transformational leadership for all."

When one of our brightest stars takes to the Broadway stage, that star has already spent much time working with a skilled director and creative team, is dressed by a professional dresser in a costume specially designed for the part, is surrounded by fellow actors supporting his or her entrance, is most typically bathed in flattering light by a professional lighting designer and "miked" for clear sound by a professional sound designer, all before the actor stands before an educated audience anticipating his or her big moment. Shouldn't we also want our companies to have properly onboarded its leaders?

Curtain up!

Charles S. Forgang the firm's founder and principal attorney, concentrates in Employment, Corporate and Business Law.

Onboarding: The International Dimension

George Olcott, Ph.D., senior fellow at the Judge Business School, University of Cambridge

George Bradt correctly highlights the important role the hiring manager plays in ensuring that the process of onboarding new employees is the act of "transformational leadership" that he or she intends. Rapid globalization, however, means that opportunities for long-term growth are likely to lie in increasingly distant markets, particularly in emerging economies, and hiring managers who are looking to fill leadership roles have to deal with higher levels of complexity than ever before.

As Bradt outlines, in playing the three key onboarding roles as producer, director and stage manager, the hiring manager needs to be aware that a host of factors beyond his or her control, not least of which is physical distance, will render the process of acquiring, accommodating, assimilating and accelerating new employees for overseas posts more difficult. In acting as "producer," for example, the hiring manager needs to align other stakeholders to the role prior to the recruitment process, and to help the candidate fully understand the role he or she is expected to play. The greater the distance from head office, the more difficult it is for the hiring manager to grasp the reality of stakeholder alignments, and therefore, the less able he or she is to give a clear and accurate account of how the new leader should approach the issue of stakeholder relations.

Recent academic literature highlights the particular difficulties of managers at multinational corporations (MNCs) who are operating in "institutionally distant" countries; that is, countries whose institutions (cultural, political and economic) are clearly different from those of the MNC's home country. Managers who are sent to such countries, for example, have to decide the extent to which he or she imposes values represented by home office "best practice" and accommodates local norms which may conflict with "best practice."

Whether the company appoints an internal or external candidate, there are a number of

extra factors to be taken into account whe the post to be filled is in "institutionally di tant" locations. One key decision is whethe to hire a local manager, or if not a loca national, then at least someone who has lon experience in that market and who ma speak the language. Such a person is clearl at an advantage in understanding the com plex web of local institutions and buildin relationships with local stakeholders, incluc ing customers, and is more likely to understan local norms and operate within them. Th drawback of such a candidate is that a he c she needs to make a large investment to buil up his or her relations with head office stake holder groups and in understanding th essential elements of the organization's cul ture. The internal candidate from head offic has the opposite attributes. He or she has keener understanding of what head offic

> The greater the distance from head office, the more difficult it is for the hiring manager to grasp the reality of stakeholder alignments and therefore the less able he or she is to give a clear and accurate account of how the new leader should approach the issue of stakeholder relations.

considers "global best practice," but not nec essarily how he or she can reconcile thes with local norms. The key investment i likely to be in the assimilation with local insti tutions and stakeholders.

During 15 years of working in Japan, I have seen countless examples of MNCs failing tc think through these basic issues, leading tc unnecessary expense and stalled careers. Bu far more damaging, are the long delays in the achievement of key business objectives, or in some cases, complete withdrawal from the market. Hiring managers operate with limited knowledge at the best of times. The farther away from home the leadership posi

The farther away from home the leadership position is, particularly in "institutional distance". . . the greater the need for thorough communication and preparation in enabling the new employee to exercise the kind of leadership the organization expects.

tion is, particularly in "institutional distance," the more constraining these limitations become and the greater the need for thorough communication and preparation in enabling the new employee to exercise the kind of leadership the organization expects.

Putting together an effective Total Onboarding Plan is far more complex when cross-border moves are involved; but given the stakes for many MNCs, it is unthinkable that they would proceed without one.

In 2006, LexisNexis started putting significant focus on onboarding. I fundamentally believe in starting things like this at the top. So, with the help of PrimeGenesis, we developed onboarding plans for all new hires at the VP level and above. Our success rate went through the roof. Don't think we didn't have failures though—there is only so much you can do to lead a horse to water. At the end of the day it's both the recruiting line manager and the new hire that have to work jointly on it.

So if you agree with the premise that onboarding is so important, why do so few recruiting managers do it well? Ask yourself, honestly, how good are you at it? The price of failure is significant: You've wasted all that time interviewing; work hasn't been done because there was nobody in the role; now the person you brought in isn't clear what he or she is doing; this person has become disengaged and unhappy, finally deciding that this isn't the place to be; and now you're back to square one—recruiting again! This whole process may have happened in a matter of weeks or more likely over several months.

I think the reasons are simple.

- New recruits are excited and don't know what is in store for them. They've done some research about the company and role, but probably spent most of their time "selling" themselves through the interview process, and at the same time, they convinced themselves that what you're offering is a great opportunity.

Dr. George Olcott is senior fellow at the Judge Business School, University of Cambridge, UK. In 2008, he joined PrimeGenesis, a U.S.-based consulting firm specializing in executive onboarding.

They need to walk in the door on day one confident in knowing what's expected of them and with the credibility to talk about the business and their own priorities. How many times can you say this is how you have started a new job?

Planning Ahead: The Critical Success Factor

Robert Rigby-Hall, chief HR officer for LexisNexis Group a leading global provider of content-enabled workflow solutions with 18,000 employees around the world.

"All the world's a stage, And all the men and women merely players: They have their exits and their entrances." – so said both William Shakespeare and George Bradt; at least that's my conclusion based on his analogy of hiring managers being producers, directors and stage managers!

As time has passed, we have found line managers wanting more and more assistance in developing onboarding plans—to the point that we have trained all our HR leaders. Now, the majority of new hires in management roles will have detailed 100-day plans developed ahead of their joining. Critical is the phrase "ahead of joining." They need to walk in the door on day one confident in knowing what's expected of them and with the credibility to talk about the business and their own priorities. How many times can you say this is how you have started a new job?

- Line managers are busy and just happy that they've got someone coming in that's a great hire who will really make a difference. They expect the person to come in and hit the ground running, the person to be a self-starter, someone who knows what needs to be done—all explanations for why they don't dedicate time to setting them up for success and supporting them in the critical first few months.

In my mind, this is not only about making sure the person is successful. It's also about making sure they can perform faster and at a ➤

part III: leadership development

In my mind this isn't just about making sure the person is successful. It's about making sure they can perform at a higher level and faster. We all want to be blown away by the new hire and be able to sit back after six months and say this was one of our best hires.

higher level. We all want to be blown away by the new hire and be able to sit back after six months and say this was one of our best hires. So investing early on in setting them up for success and making sure they, and other stakeholders, know what they're there to do is key. Invest in the first few weeks, and it will pay dividends over the following months and years.

One final point, make the onboarding a critical part of the overall integrated HR process (see Exhibit that follows). That way it's not a discrete exercise and everyone—managers and new recruits—understand how it fits in.

Robert Rigby-Hall serves as chief HR office for LexisNexis where he handles internal communications and corporate social responsibilities activities.

Even More Action Needed

Matthew R. Walter, Ph.D. is a vice president in Executive Development and Talent Management at Bank of America.

After leading an executive onboarding process across a global enterprise, I can appreciate Bradt's perspective on the importance of the role of the hiring manager. While it usually requires the coordination of a team of individuals including HR, staffing and leadership development, the hiring manager is without a doubt the key to a successful transition.

In his article, Bradt efficiently captures many of the basic responsibilities that a hiring manager is tasked with during the onboarding process and categorizes them into three phases. He also states that "it's unconscionable how many managers do not take this as seriously as they should." While I agree with this notion, I believe that hiring managers need to engage in the process even more than the article proposes, and the mentioned phases could be more serious as well.

The first several months of the transition for a new leader are some of the most significant for determining long-term success. The organization is evaluating its decision to hire the leader and will be monitoring performance progress closely. Meanwhile, individuals are evaluating their decisions by assessing their fit with the organization and their role. An uncorrected mistake early on can fester and remain with new leaders for extended periods of time, eventually derailing them. Because the hiring manager has the most invested, he or she should be the one held accountable for a successful transition. Therefore, I believe there are a few additional responsibilities that should be addressed.

1. **Coach/Mentor** – While the article does mention the need for a mentor outside of the hiring manager, it does not address the manager's direct responsibility as a coach. One such opportunity is for the manager to collect feedback from stakeholders about the new leader's progress. This provides the new leader with early feedback and an opportunity to course-correct before derailment occurs. A leader faces a host of challenges in a new environment, and who better to lead them through those than the hiring manager.

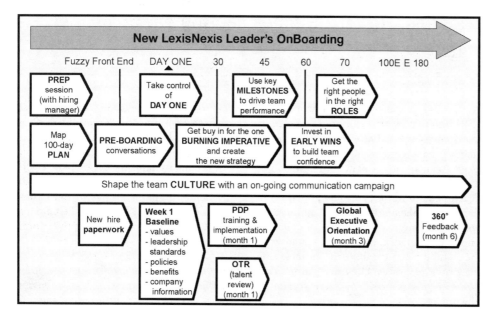

New LexisNexis Leader's OnBoarding

> Onboarding plans, no matter how well-mapped and detailed, should never result in a hand-off to the new leader. The onboarding plan should be a living document that both the new leader and the hiring manager regularly reference and update.

Onboarding: Process Plus a Broad Organizational Mindset

Sonja Weckström, principal consultant, Right Management

2. **Navigating the Organization** – In the third phase of onboarding, Stage Manager, it's suggested that "after Personal Onboarding Plan hand-offs, most of the hiring manager's work is behind the scenes." I believe this statement is inaccurate for two reasons. First, onboarding plans, no matter how well-mapped and detailed, should never result in a hand-off to the new leader. The onboarding plan should be a living document that the new leader and the hiring manager regularly reference and update. The transition process takes months to complete in a dynamic environment, which will require changes to the original plan. Secondly, the hiring manager should not be relegated to behind-the-scenes work. The manager needs to be out in front of the new leaders, helping them to navigate their new organization. This includes introducing them to the key stakeholders and helping them to align the greater resources of the organization to drive success.

3. **Culture Assimilation** – Every organization has a unique culture based on aspects of its history, industry and geographic location. New leaders are responsible for learning the culture and engaging it as part of their transition. If hiring managers have done an appropriate job during the selection process, then the new leaders should already be a good fit. However, it is still the responsibility of the manager to ensure the new leader understands the expectations of their new culture. This would include an understanding of the organization's values, beliefs and practices. Any misalignment between what the new leader values and what the organization values can significantly impact success.

Bradt accurately acknowledges that hiring mangers play the key role in onboarding a new executive and that it's one of the greatest investments in their talent they can make. However, there are a few additional important responsibilities of the manager that he missed. The transition process takes a full 12 months in a complex environment, and the hiring manager must play an active role during the entire process.

> **Matthew Walter** is the VP for Bank of America. He designs and develops employee selection, individual assessment, and leader development tools.

George Bradt is spot-on when he addresses the demanding role of the hiring manager by describing it as a multiple role of being a producer, director and stage manager. It accurately describes the complexity and challenge of the onboarding process. However, much more than having a robust process in place, it's essential that the hiring manager knows his or her job. It is about creating a learning culture: where the newly hired will learn about the new company and his or her new role, and the company will learn from the newly hired. This is the only way to accelerate learning, fast engagement and commitment on both sides.

We know the high price that comes with employee and especially executive level derailment during the first years in a new position. Derailment is usually not about lack of intelligence, depth of competencies or experience in the job itself, but rather it is the challenge of integration and assimilation into the new organizational environment.

An effective and well-structured onboarding process is one of the best ways to ensure that organizations avoid derailment of newly hired key people and provide a strong take-off during the first 90 days of being in the new job.

Onboarding That Produces Results

Organizations have varying views on what a powerful induction should include. Some organizations want to do their best to ensure successful assimilation and integration to the new organizational environment; they usually make sure that the onboarding includes multiple actions during a longer period—i.e., systematic meetings and interviews with key stakeholders. Many organizations have found that designating an onboarding coach and/or a mentor can be powerful in under- ➤

> The transition process takes a full 12 months in a complex environment, and the hiring manager must play an active role during the entire process.

standing the unwritten organizational cultural patterns and in the transfer of the tacit knowledge to the newly hired.

Recruitment is the Starting Point

Working with executive onboarding for many years, I have found that the key for making sure the onboarding is a successful transformational leadership experience (for both the hiring organization and the person being hired) starts naturally with the recruitment process. Carefully analyzing the cultural fit of the candidate is crucial. Also, put emphasis on assessing the person's own personal values as well as the organizational values of the previous companies in which the person has spent his or her career.

Often in the many cases I have seen, only the competencies and capabilities matter and drive the decision to hire—especially if there is some urgency involved or if the HR leader involved is not in a power position to take a stand about this issue.

Learning Organizations Learn from the Newly Hired

Doing a first-class job onboarding key people entering the organization can also

By appreciating and utilizing systematically the knowledge and wisdom the newly hired brings, the organization makes the person feel appreciated and valued in an early phase.

benefit the organization tremendously. There is an organizational learning element involved, which unfortunately is not always used to its fullest extent. The situation when you enter a new organization is familiar to everyone. You have a great opportunity to look at the organization from a new angle and from a perspective that is quite different from those who have already worked in the company for quite a while. You can ask fundamental and basic questions, make comments and give suggestions from a different perspective. If there is an understanding and appreciation in the organization to capture these insights, it can increase the quality of the current organizational thinking and lead to significant improvements and new ideas.

By appreciating and utilizing systematically the knowledge and wisdom the newly hired brings, the organization helps make the person can feel appreciated and valued in an early phase. This is usually the stage when he or she is not yet fully up-to-speed and productive in the new setting and does not gain appreciation and feedback for tangible results.

Organizations that truly want to strive toward being a learning organization usually create a learning culture, where they embed learning from newcomers as well as the behavior of key people who play a role in the onboarding process. I have seen how enormously it can empower the individuals to get a jump start on the new job as well as create a strong employer brand for the company.

Successful onboarding requires more than right actions and efficient processes. It is about having a broad organizational learning mindset.

Sonja Weckstrom works as principal consultant within Talent Management for Right Management based in Helsinki, Finland.

People & Strategy 33.2 Point Counterpoint:

Onboarding: An Act of Transformational Leadership

Discovery Questions

- Do you agree with George Bradt's thesis that onboarding is an act of transformational leadership? Explain your position.

- What is transformative in the event of bringing a new employee on board?

- Using the Theater metaphor, describe the players involved in the onboarding transformation, what are their roles? Comment on multiple manager roles, the onboarding employee role; discuss the significance of the larger organizational culture.

- In your experience, do organizations give enough focus and attention to the onboarding process? Comment on examples cited in Charles Forgang's article "Curtain up on the Two Way Transformational Leader Role."

- How common are the approaches that LexisNexis and Bank of America have adopted in their onboarding process? (article by Robert Rigby-Hall and Matthew Walter)

- What are the requirements for a successful global onboarding process?

Selected Facts

- The most common approach to onboarding in companies today remains a "sink or swim" attitude.

- The best-in-class onboarding process requires significant pre-planning and starts "ahead of joining."

- Every successful onboarding process has to follow an "Onboarding Plan" and has to have dedicated people managing it.

- Managers play a critical role in the success of the onboarding process. The HR role is critical in supporting the managers.

- Failure to properly bring a new hire on board leads to a higher percentage of future failure on the job.

- Some schools of thought advocate for 90 day plans (Michael Watkins) and others for 100 day plans (George Bradt)

Key Discussion Points

- What were the key highlights of George Bradt's approach to onboarding?

- What is the role of onboarding in the overall "Talent Management" process?

- What is the correlation between onboarding and success on the job?

- What are the critical roles that a manager needs to assume in the onboarding process?

- What are the responsibilities, strategies and tactics of the employee who is being onboarded?

- What do best practice companies do in the onboarding process? Give examples of LexisNexis and Bank of America.

- What are the challenges involved in onboarding employees globally?

- How do you see onboarding evolving along with the overall evolution of Talent Management?

- Comment on the competencies HR needs to have in order to design, deliver and oversee the onboarding process in their organizations.

Review of Solutions

- Identify 2-3 Practical Ideas that could be implemented in your organization.

- Draft a template "onboarding" plan and discuss its key milestones.

Recommendations Summary

- Identify at least one thing that you will do differently based on what you have learned from this discussion.

Learning Outcomes

- Tell what personally you would do differently based on the information you have received.

Why Leading Sustainability Matters More Than Ever

Daniel Goleman, Psychologist, Author and Lecturer

Sustainability has become a key driver of business growth and innovation. So argues C.K. Prahalad, the University of Michigan-based thought leader, in the pages of the *Harvard Business Review* [September 2009]. Writing with Ram Nidumolu and M.R. Rangaswami, Prahalad contends that the tradeoff between sustainable products and financial costs is a false choice, one that fails to see how the pursuit of sustainability can lower costs, raise revenue and drive growth through innovation.

A concrete sign of this happened July 14, 2009, when Wal-Mart announced it will work with an independent, academic consortium to develop a product-rating sustainability index that the retailer will eventually post next to the prices of products in its stores. Other companies, like BestBuy, also are showing interest, and Wal-Mart hopes Target, Costco and other retailers will adopt the index as well.

If so, one day shoppers will instantly see not only that one item is cheaper than the other, but also which has ingredients that do less environmental damage, generate hazardous by-products, require toxic compounds to make, or contain chemicals suspected of being carcinogens. This, in turn, could make winners of those companies that are most nimble in innovating more sustainable alternatives, and losers of those that fail to do so.

The sustainability index is meant to set an industry-wide standard for ecological transparency. And it will no doubt be a game changer, not just for strategy, but also for people decisions. The dawning of ecological transparency in the marketplace propels sustainability leadership to the center of strategic planning. The position leaps from a "nice-to-have" to a "must-have," putting a new premium on the ability of executives to lead sustainability initiatives.

The announcement put on notice the more than 100,000 Wal-Mart suppliers that they must be prepared to analyze and divulge the ecological impacts of their products in the rating index. Companies that do not do this preparation will become "irrelevant," losing their space on Wal-Mart's and Sam's Club's shelves. Coincidentally, China—home to the bulk of Wal-Mart's supply chain—is devoting five percent of its stimulus budget to innovations in sustainable development.

All these forces for sustainability operate at the B2B level, between retailers and their suppliers. But a parallel force is emerging in the consumer marketplace, where a working

notify their Facebook or Twitter friends wh[en] they just switched shampoos. Some majo[r] retailers are already in conversation wit[h] GoodGuide about posting its ratings next t[o] product prices—getting a jump on the sus[-] tainability index that Wal-Mart announced

These methods for ecological transparenc[y] are disruptive technologies in retailing an[d] manufacturing. For one, such ratings lowe[r] to zero the mental effort (what economist[s] call the "information cost") needed to evalu[-] ate a product's ecological impacts. This wi[ll] make the ecological impacts of products [a] stronger element of their marketability, alon[g] with price and value.

Until now, anyone who wanted to learn th[e] carbon footprint or chemical risks for a prod[-]

> As sustainability proves key to strategy, HR becomes crucial to execution by seeing that the right people are in the critical positions. The big question: What competencies are needed to be effective in leading a company's sustainability initiative?

---

model for a sustainability index already exists in GoodGuide.com. This information system, hatched at the University of California at Berkeley, aggregates more than 200 databases on the environmental, health and social impacts of a given product, and summarizes all that for shoppers in a single score on a 10-point scale. GoodGuide offers an instant comparison of the ecological impacts of competing products, and allows users to

uct has had to track down a Web site that ha[d] the data (if there was one at all), and remem[-] ber it while shopping for the item in question Market surveys find that approximately 1[0] percent of consumers, at best, ever bother Nearly a quarter of shoppers say they couldn'[t] care less. The real action zeroes in on the two-thirds of shoppers who say such data woul[d] influence their choices if it were easy to get[.] And Wal-Mart cites surveys showing that ose shoppers born since the 1980s increasingly are motivated to vote with their dollars for a cleaner, safer and cooler planet.

This development resolves for corporations the long-standing internal debates over sustainability, where voices for social responsibility say practices must change and those for fiscal responsibility counter there is, at best, a lim-

heat water to use its detergent products as a huge negative for global warming. As such, they developed cold-water detergents as more sustainable alternatives.

As sustainability proves a key to strategy, HR becomes crucial to execution by seeing that the right people are in the critical positions. The big question: what competencies

in positions of power to take the sustainability agenda seriously and put it into action.

These findings bring into focus what HR should look for in promoting or recruiting sustainability leadership. The challenges will be both recruiting people with the right skill set for leading sustainability, and sharpening the competencies of those already in the position. An executive's persuasion and cooperation abilities can be honed, as executive coaches will attest.

Business savvy is equally crucial. At every step of the way, leaders must be able to make a strong business case for sustainability if their arguments are to be persuasive.

So what about all those newly minted graduates of "green business" programs? It's well and good that they understand the nuts and bolts of sustainability. But that alone will not be sufficient for them to become effective sustainability leaders. They'll also need those tried and true leadership competencies for getting people motivated, focused and working together. And, as Wal-Mart's Andy Ruben told me, "Graduates of green business programs need first of all to be good at business."

Editor's Note: Daniel Goleman's latest book is *Ecological Intelligence: How Knowing the Hidden Impacts of What We Buy Can Change Everything.* His conversations with thought leaders on ecological transparency can be heard at: http://www.morethansound.net/ecological-awareness.php. The book is being reviewed in this issue on p. 61

> From the perspective of the social intelligence competencies found among highly effective leaders, the specific people skills that typify the best sustainability leaders are telling: the abilities to persuade and influence, and to cooperate as a team player.

ed business case. "Smart companies now treat sustainability as innovation's new frontier," the Prahalad group writes in the *Harvard Business Review.*

Andy Ruben, who has led Wal-Mart's sustainability initiative and now runs its private brands division, sees great advantage for companies able to create value via ecological innovations throughout the supply chain. "This is the largest strategic opportunity companies will see for the next 50 years," Ruben told me. "This is the most exciting time to be in business, with more opportunity to create change in the world than ever."

That reinvention of industry's most basic platforms, processes and chemical palette can be expedited by another new class of information system, designed to spot innovative opportunities in the supply chain. One prototype is Earthster, supply chain management software that uses product life cycle assessments to highlight the most negative ecological impacts—the points where a positive change will boost a product's sustainability rating the most. Procter & Gamble deployed this very strategy that spotted the customer's need to

are needed to be effective in leading a company's sustainability initiative? Some answers come from a global study of executives leading sustainability at companies in dozens of countries, done through intensive interviews by a worldwide team of 17 partners at Egon Zehnder International, the executive recruiting firm.

The EZI team, led by Christoph Lueneburger, used systematic interviewing to assess the unique competencies displayed by sustainability leaders who had scored successes, and compared them to executives in comparable positions who had struck out or just tread water. Those who succeeded showed strengths in two categories of competencies: social intelligence abilities and business skills.

From the perspective of the social intelligence competencies found among highly effective leaders, the specific people skills that typify the best sustainability leaders are telling: the abilities to persuade and influence, and to cooperate as a team player. That makes sense in terms of the organizational chart. Executives leading sustainability are not in a command position, but rather they must exert their influence laterally by convincing others

Daniel Goleman, Ph.D., covered behavioral sciences and the brain for *The New York Times* for 12 years. He has taught at Harvard University, where he received his Ph.D., and was senior editor at *Psychology Today.* His books include *Emotional Intelligence,* Working with *Emotional Intelligence,* Vital **Lies, Simple Truth, The Meditative Mind,** and, as co-author, **The Consumer's Guide to Psychotherapy.**

Caveat Venditor: How Sustainability Is Shifting the Balance Of Power

Christoph Lueneburger, Head, Global Sustainability Practice, Egon Zehnder

We are in the early days of a massive transformation of commerce, brought about by sustainability. Daniel Goleman has sketched this revolution along two dimensions. First, he describes how competent leaders with strong commercial orientation will advance this agenda inside corporations. Second, in what Goleman describes as a "parallel force in the consumer marketplace," consumers are rapidly becoming more sophisticated in their purchasing decisions. Our research and work with global clients aligns with Goleman's analysis, but—as a counterpoint demands—I will counter that the consumer is the primary driver rather than a parallel force in this transformation.

In his book *Ecological Intelligence*, Goleman introduces "radical transparency" as the enabler of the sustainability revolution. As he previously summarizes, radical transparency

Much as nutritional labeling enables informed choices about food (and the extinction of some substances, like trans fats), this consumer revolution will pull even the most recalcitrant companies into the 21st century or else render them irrelevant.

The motto for what's ahead is *caveat venditor* —let the seller beware—and in the generational shift to leaders and employees who understand this transformation, companies face some difficult people challenges. At a recent roundtable discussion we conducted with sustainability executives from leading companies, a Chief Sustainability Officer recounted a recent meeting with his CEO. After listening to a detailed presentation, the CEO countered, "Too much information. Tell me the one thing we have to do to get this right." Without hesitation the CSO responded: "Hire the right people."

He was not talking merely about hiring a few executives for a sustainability function, but about a substantive culture change that will require the right people with the right competencies across the entire organization. He also was pointing implicitly to a phenomenon

CEOs that recognize the immense commercial power of the consumer revolution are beginning to seek new leaders to profitably map the path rather than wait for it to happen or worse, rely on a regulatory compass to chart their course. Those who champion this shift in their own ranks have embraced two lessons that are simple but not easy. First: the customer really is always right. Second (and consequently): sustainability, ultimately, is about the sustainability of their own companies.

Christoph Lueneburger is an Equity & Water Investment Expert at Egon Zehnder International and serves as a member of Advisory Board at Microvi Biotech Inc.

Sustainability Rests in the System, Not the Product

John R. Ehrenfeld, MIT Faculty (Emeritus), and Author, Sustainability by Design: A Subversive Strategy for Transforming our Consumer Culture

Daniel Goleman is on-target in suggesting that new skills will be critical for companies in the sustainability game. HR needs to be especially careful when selecting and supporting personnel tasked to lead efforts in this domain. Further, what have been conventional performance criteria will need to be expanded to include factors related to sustainability. This is where, I believe, Goleman goes astray.

The first part of his article describes emerging sustainability indices and suggests that shoppers will be able to use them to select items that best satisfy their intentions toward sustainability. The story is not quite so simple and direct. Unlike price, which can be easily played off against some set of satisfying factors, sustainability metrics cannot. Sustainability is not a single-valued function; rather, sustainability is a holistic property of a system. A system, like the economic or environmental system, exhibits sustainability when it pro

> As radical transparency reaches even the most casual shopper at the point of purchase, the pursuit of sustainability will shift from a choice companies make to their license to operate, which masses of consumers won't hesitate to revoke.

is the result of convenient access to objective information about products that enables consumers to make uncomplicated decisions about complex issues. As radical transparency reaches even the most casual shopper at the point of purchase, the pursuit of sustainability will shift from a choice companies make to their license to operate, which masses of consumers won't hesitate to revoke.

we, too, have observed: the existence of a "blocking generation" of senior business managers who see that sustainability can't be ignored but don't yet relate to it instinctively the way the next generation will. As Goleman observes, the challenge for HR is to help change the mindset of those executives, which is hard. But they will be helped by a change in generations, which is certain.

ces desirable qualities, like flourishing or curity, over long periods. Sustainability is e result of the interaction of many relation-ips, each of which may be understandable hen looked at in isolation. But it is the inter-eshing of these relationships that matters, d in all-important cases, the tangled web at emerges cannot be described by a set of stractions, formulas or indices.

Systems thinking is the key to sustainability. Today's mess can be blamed on the failure to understand the system within which we are embedded.[1] Unfortunately, systems thinking is given only lip service in most disciplines, espe-cially in MBA programs. HR personnel tend to come from single discipline roots, making sustainability more challenging for them. The usual mantra that guides operations—if you

> ustainability is the result of the interaction of many elationships, each of which may be understandable hen looked at in isolation. But it is the intermeshing f these relationships that matters, and in all-mportant cases, the tangled web that emerges cannot e described by a set of abstractions, formulas r indices.

hat is where the indices to which Goleman fers go astray. They make a valiant effort at pturing the impact of diverse factors on vironmental sustainability, and to a lesser egree, social responsibility. Product life cycle ssessment systems, like Earthster, have been sed for nearly 25 years without much effect n the environment. Even if one combines undreds of separate factors as is done in e GoodGuide system, the result cannot be rrelated with any positive image of sustain-bility. These measures can be useful in the ther direction, pointing to products that ay create smaller negative effects than oth-rs. Even so, the outcome on the world we ve in is not likely to be satisfying. As Gole-an writes, these indices may be disruptive nd, and as a result, would demand highly killed, innovative personnel to maintain cor-orate leadership.

he significance for HR departments is to real-e that they will need personnel with more an analytic skills along with the kind of per-asive powers to which Goleman points.

can't measure it, you can't manage it—doesn't apply to sustainability. The challenge is to attain it and get the system right.

The real winners in the future will be those firms that truly understand this, and are hon-est and clear in their presentations of their products and services. The shortcomings of sustainability indices will become evident in the future, and firms uncritically adopting them may well lose whatever glitter they have acquired. This situation may be one where the early adopters—the hares—will eventually lose out to the tortoises.

Dr. John R. Ehrenfeld currently serves as executive director of the Interna-tional Society for Industrial Ecology.

Buyer Beware: The Pathway to Collapse Could Be Paved with the Most Sophisticated Consumer Metrics

Peter Senge, MIT and SoL; Author of The Fifth Discipline *and* The Necessary Revolution

I agree wholeheartedly with Daniel Goleman that product sustainability indices like Good-Guide.com and the one that Wal-Mart's and other retailers are working to develop are potential game changers in creating a more sustainable industrial system. But they are only first steps. We all must be careful not to be seduced by "being less bad," and continu-ing to destroy our inherited social and natural capital just a little less rapidly.

The first thing everyone must understand is that most all of these metrics track relative impacts: how one product fares relative to another competing product. But is the prod-uct good? That's a much tougher question to answer.

The bottom line is that nature does not care about the relative impact of one product com-pared to another. Nature cares about our total impact in *absolute terms*. Relative rank-ings may not only fail to convey our impact in destroying ecosystems, depleting water or soil nutrients or destabilizing global climate, they can distort the speed and scope of chang-es actually needed.

To illustrate, consider the real (i.e., absolute) changes needed to avoid the dangers of climate change. The growing consensus among climate scientists is that we need to stabilize green-house gas *concentrations* in the atmosphere at not much above where they are today—which means we need a 70-80 percent reduction in emissions (given the rate of CO_2 sequestered by the biomass) within three or four decades.[2]

1. Senge, P. M., B. Smith, et al. (2008). *The necessary revolution: How individuals and organizations are working together to create a sustainable world.* New York: Doubleday.
2. To see why the changes need to be this strong, try the freeware simulator based on the latest in climate science developed at MIT: www.climateinteractive.org.

What does this mean, for example, for the average mileage for cars? Given continued historic growth in cars on the road, a lot. An 80 percent reduction in emissions would require a five-fold increase in fuel economy—for the U.S. fleet, an average of about 100 mpg. But, if the global fleet of automobiles keeps pace with GDP and grows at about 3 percent annually (some expect new car sales to rise far faster with standards of living growing far faster than 3 percent per annum in China and India), the number of cars on the road will double every 20 years, which means a four-fold increase by 2050. So the average fuel economy would need to be 400 mpg to meet the emissions target. (That figure would have to double again if cars on the road double in another two decades.)

This is what happens when relative improvements in eco-efficiency or ecological footprints for individual products collide with unending growth. None of this is revealed by sustainability rating systems that focus only on relative performance of one product compared with another.

Daniel Goleman is correct that sustainability matters more than ever and that when the customer demand starts to lead the changes, a new chapter in the journey will have started.

But we are, at best, at the beginning of the beginning. Until consumer-facing ratings track the absolute changes needed—not just relative ratings—and the implications of unending business growth, and HR professionals help managers develop the capabilities to do so, the new chapter will turn out to be part of the same old story.

Peter Senge is a senior lecturer at the Massachusetts Institute of Technology. He is also founding chair of the Society for Organizational Learning (SoL).

Why Leading Sustainability Matters More than Ever

Miriam Hawley, CEO, Enlignment, Inc.

When I read the opening line of "Why Leading Sustainability Matters More than Ever," Daniel Goleman's commentary on the research of several thought leaders, I cheered inside. Here was an author I admired quoting from the influential *Harvard Business Review*, saying what I hope for and coach for—leadership from a sustainability perspective.

As I read further about Wal-Mart's commitment to develop a product-rating sustainability index that will help consumers choose products that cause the least environmental damage, I paused.

While "sustainability has become a key driver of business growth and innovation," there is an underlying context and conversation that must be addressed for sustainability to be possible, let alone flourish. The context is *Sufficiency* and the conversation is *What is Enough?*

In my last decade as a professional and activist, I have discovered that sufficiency is present when nothing is wasted, and sustainability is possible only where sufficien thrives. We need a way to gauge what is su tainable in our personal lives, our busine and community lives, and as global citize We could say that when sufficiency is cau sustainability is effect.

While having a measure of ecological tra parency is critical, there are other questio we need to ask. It may be less expensive to b more, but do we need more? What is t impact on the communities whose land is us to build these massive structures? What is t cost to farmers' markets and neighborho stores that offer just enough and no mor What about our growing need for sustainab packaging and fair wages for workers?

What is *enough*? What is enough food, lov sex, money, time or business, clothing, hou ing or support? The answer requir contemplation and can be difficult to discer

According to Lynne Twist, global activist ar author of *The Soul of Money*, we must "co front not only the financial crisis, but also a other crises which stem from the same root scarcity." She asserts that we are in a tranc fueled by the three toxic lies of scarcity: the is not enough; more is better; that's just th way it is.

Becoming leaders of sustainability initiativ involves nothing short of a paradigm shif from not enough to enough, from greed t gratitude, from scarcity to sufficiency, fro dominion over nature to partnership with th natural world. For the earth and all species t flourish, we must completely rework, or eve create for the first time, our ideas about wha is enough.

So what is sufficiency? Buckminster Fulle one of the world's greatest futurists and global thinker, taught that the distinction c sufficiency is not an amount, but an exquisit *experience* of "enough," like satisfaction. Su ficiency is a shift in mindset, a declaratio that we *have* enough and we *are* enough.

Sufficiency is not a point on the scarcity ar abundance continuum (which are two sides c

---

> The bottom line is that nature does not care about the relative impact of one product compared to another. Nature cares about our total impact in absolute terms.

---

e same coin) or a destination. Sufficiency is lively, ongoing process, practice and conversation discovered in the context of community.

he dilemma is that Wal-Mart encourages us one hand to be conscious consumers and the other to consume more than we need. he size of Wal-Mart stores alone exemplifies more is better and that's just the way it is." it? The bottom line is that we can't achieve ustainability without considering sufficiency.

Nancy Miriam Hawley, LICSW, is a co-founder of Enlignment, Inc., a coaching, consulting and training company.

Making Sustainability Part of Everyone's Job

aniel C. Esty, Chairman, Esty Environmental artners, Hillhouse Professor of Environmental aw and Policy, Yale University and Director, ale Center for Environmental Law and Policy nd the Center for Business & Environment t Yale; and Sandra Lauterbach, Managing onsultant, Esty Environmental Partners

)ver the last decade, we have seen a dramatic increase in the number of companies hat view sustainability as a "key driver of usiness growth and innovation" as Daniel ioleman discusses in "Why Leading Sustainbility Matters More Than Ever."

s sustainability consultants for leading cororations, we argue that sustainability should e "an essential component of business strat-gy." But in reality, companies that align usiness and sustainability strategies are rare. /lany executives see sustainability as non-ore to the business, forcing sustainability fficers to rely on persuasion skills, as EZI dentified. To connect sustainability and busi-less advantage, companies need to drive hange throughout the enterprise. In this esponse, we offer examples of leading comanies who are tackling this challenge.

The importance of integrating sustainability into strategy will only intensify as stakeholders, including supply chain partners, pressure companies to reduce environmental footprints. Companies also need to address resource constraints, rising energy prices, more stringent regulations and changing consumer expectations—all of which pose business risks and opportunities.

We agree that an effective sustainability strategy begins with recruiting executives with skills to "persuade and influence." The right leadership is essential.

Yet reducing a company's footprint, using sustainability to drive innovation and redesigning products and processes require the commitment of the entire organization. With the logic of sustainability growing daily, the stakes are too great to leave these issues to a select few or to informal processes.

In the new sustainability context, integration and execution matter. By implementing processes, systems and metrics, executives can ensure that all employees have the capabilities and incentives to capitalize on emerging opportunities. How do sustainability leaders accomplish this?

issues and sharing best practices help build competencies and a sustainability-oriented culture. Some companies, such as Clif Bar, encourage commitment and enthusiasm by educating employees on work- and home-related issues.

- **Increase accountability** – Using its "Session E" process, GE formally reviews the environmental performance of all business units. Plant managers—not environmental managers—provide the updates, and GE uses reviews to hold managers accountable for continuous improvement. Several companies have integrated sustainability into compensation. For example, Shell calculates bonuses based on a performance evaluation scorecard, which includes a sustainable development component.

- **Track and report metrics** – Environmental management systems can track metrics and improve decision making. At Herman Miller, each designer can access a database that categorizes materials' environmental impacts. This enables smart decision making throughout the company. Linking environmental efforts with business metrics, such as cost savings or revenue

Becoming leaders of sustainability initiatives involves nothing short of a paradigm shift: from not enough to enough, from greed to gratitude, from scarcity to sufficiency, from dominion over nature to partnership with the natural world.

- **Include sustainability in planning processes** – Dow ensures that business managers include sustainability goals and plans in their annual planning cycle. Sustainability and business plans are better aligned because the business unit develops and owns both.

- **Educate employees on strategy and issues** – Training employees on environmental

growth, and reporting these metrics also can drive change.

As new business realities and opportunities emerge, the stakes are higher to integrate sustainability thinking throughout an organization. The right leadership—and the right processes and systems—can move the ➤

entire company toward creating business value from sustainability.

Daniel C. Esty is the Hillhouse Professor of Environmental Law and Policy at Yale University. **Sandra Lauterbach** is a managing consultant with Esty Environmental Partners.

Sustainability Leadership & The Real Value of Brands—At the Core

Sophie Constance, Societal Business, Melbourne, Australia

Daniel Goleman focuses on the attributes needed for sustainability leadership. This means not only inculcating the values needed to drive a sustainability culture, but making sustainability an integral part of your business and core brand value. Alignment of Sustainability/CSR with your core business strategy creates organizational, brand and business value. This also engages your employees with the brand and has the potential to unleash their value as human capital. It is the efficient lynchpin to aligning your internal and external stakeholders and business into a cohesive whole, creating a more significant impact.

A "core brand" (or "core organizational brand") must stem from the main business strategies and focus on the total corporate image as a synthesis of all its products and services. This follows the assumption that consumers will select a product or service based on their perceptions of trust in—and the credibility of—that business, as it has been incorporated into the core brand.

Several examples of global companies help illustrate the point. Marks and Spencer (M&S), a major British retailer, has gone through a transformation to become a company demonstrating a holistic integra-

tion of values, embedded in their business operations—both internally with staff and externally through their supply chains. In 2007, they launched a high-profile 'Look Behind the Label' advertising campaign— "Plan A," under which they committed to

> Alignment of Sustainability/Corporate Social Responsibility (CSR) with your core business strategy creates organizational, brand and business value. ...It is the efficient lynchpin to bring internal and external stakeholders and the business into a cohesive whole, creating a more significant impact.

a string of social and environmental targets. It was the first major campaign wherein a retailer concentrated on the way products are sourced and made. Its success reflects the consumer trend for a more ethical way of living, combined with a healthier lifestyle.

The process begins with a thorough employee-engagement strategy that mobilizes shoppers and their expectations through the employees' experiences. Fifteen months after launching their "Plan A" program, M&S said it achieved 17 out of the 100 targets it set for itself, results were positive across the board and focus groups showed consumers were behind it. 'Look behind the Label' is considered the most successful and well-embedded concept of a responsible retailer: In a poll by *The Times* in London, (March 2008), Marks & Spencer was nominated the "the greenest supermarket" and the one most popular with socially and environmentally aware consumers.

When Unilever streamlined its global operations in 2004, it identified a unifying purpose of vitality for its employees and products. "Feel good, look good and get more out of

life" was its core brand message. Unilever was one of the first to use the Global Reporting Index (GRI) framework that sets out the principles and indicators organizations can use to measure and report their economic, environmental and social performance. The

delivered the 'execution' or expression of this core brand message via an interactive guide on their Web site—showing their environmental impacts at every stage of the lifecycle of their products—from concept to consumption, e.g., sustainable fisheries created with the Marine Stewardship Council."

Further to the notion of ecological transparency that Dan Goleman proposes, the way to enable it more effectively is through refocusing on citizenship. People should not be defined primarily just as "consumers." People are first and foremost citizens who happen to consume. Employees are citizens, too. This *citizenship* frame creates a better link to engaging with ecological transparency across the entire value-chain process, as employees with a citizenship perspective can advance the organization's purpose by influencing all its stakeholders.

Sophie Constance is the director of Societal Business-Corporate Social Leadership.

Sustainability: Harnessing the Collective Innovation of All Employees

Shari Aaron, Author and Expert in Sustainability and Market Research

Daniel Goleman makes a very strong case that we are finally coming to a point of convergence where data can be harnessed to support the transition to a more sustainable economy. We see governments moving toward new regulations and citizen consumers seeking out products made in a less toxic, more just and earth-friendly fashion. According to McKinsey, 5 percent of CEOs report that businesses must address the social and environmental pressures of society (McKinsey & Co., July 2007), and evidence shows that employees will drive companies' efforts to address sustainability (MIT Sloan Management Review, Sept. 2009).

Increasingly, companies understand that they can strengthen their competitive advantage and reach new heights through innovation and sustainability. Increased collaboration and cooperation among all sectors will accelerate the pace by which companies can achieve sustainability.

My experiences help me understand why sustainability is one of the hardest issues for business and society. Sustainability calls on business leaders to rethink so many aspects of their businesses and re-evaluate current systems. It implores us to have a sense of moral courage and unwavering conviction. This applies directly to employees who, given our recent financial crisis, face such difficult working environments today. So while it may very well be true, as Daniel Goleman states, that certain employees will have a greater ability to bring forth more sustainable solutions for their companies, I firmly believe that we need to support and encourage all employees to get engaged.

The time is now to empower more employees who work inside corporations to champion sustainability. We could be facing a brain drain where the best and brightest seek alternative career paths away from the corporate sector. We are seeing an unprecedented interest in careers that involve social good, particularly those from the younger generation that Daniel Goleman cites in his article. One of the most popular student clubs at Harvard in 2009 is Social Entrepreneurship. It rivals the ranks of those who join the finance and investment student clubs.

Over the past few years I have been conducting research regarding employees and sustainability. My 2008 Corporate Employee Sustainability Study reveals that 75 percent of employees report that their firms are not investing in sustainability training. This research reveals that many employees want training, as only one in 10 employees feel they have the tools and training needed to help their workplaces become more sustainable. In 2009, for *Climb the Green Ladder: Make Your Company and Career More Sustainable*, my co-author Amy Fetzer and I interviewed 80 sustainability leaders and hundreds of employees who brought successful sustainability strategies to their workplaces. I was amazed by what creative, smart and courageous employees at many organizations—in government, academia, non-profit and business sectors—were able to achieve. Many employees try to live responsibly in their home lives by recycling, composting, buying fair trade and organic, and flying, driving or buying less. They explain that it can be uncomfortable and distressing to feel that during their work lives, they are contributing to wasteful, disrespectful or environmentally damaging behavior—often on a scale that dwarfs one's personal life. Many say they want to do something to impact their company or organization's unsustainable practices, but often don't know where to start.

Companies such as HP and Wal-Mart have active, well-branded employee-engagement programs where they work to bring education and awareness about sustainability to their employees. The theory is to train employees to think like sustainability champions and empower them to find practical, business-building solutions for their workplaces.

The research for *Climb the Green Ladder* uncovers the six key principles that underpin all successful sustainability strategies so that employees can benefit from this knowledge. These include:

1. Get the mindset
2. Make the business case
3. Get your colleagues on your side
4. Have two-way conversations
5. Work together
6. Make it part of the culture

Kristen Thomas from the Phelps Group, Martin Blake from Royal Mail, and Coral Rose from Wal-Mart are all clear examples who bring these six principles to life. Kristen Thomas was concerned about the mound of disposable dishes that was piling up at her firm's holiday party. Her investigation into how to solve this issue led to a tidal wave that greened her company and won new business. Martin Blake helped to show Royal Mail how to save £20 million a year and wipe up to 100,000 tons off its carbon footprint. Coral Rose wanted to help Wal-Mart develop new products and was instrumental in persuading this corporation, now the largest buyer of organic cotton, to first introduce organic clothing.

I have seen firsthand that employees—in any industry and with any job title—can make a difference. The more we learn and share with each other, the more we inspire others to action. So while I agree with Daniel Goleman that some people may be inclined to be more effective in championing sustainability strategies, I vote for using an all-hands-on-deck approach to allow all employees to engage in the process. The more we provide the tools and training and inspire them to action, the quicker we can accelerate the pace to viable solutions. HR departments, focused on employee career development, can champion employee training on sustainability and harness the collective innovation of their employees. **P&S**

Shari Aaron, executive director, *Climb The Green Ladder,* is a market researcher, sustainability consultant, author and strategic thinker

learning guide

People & Strategy 33.1 Point Counterpoint:

Why Leading Sustainability Matters More Than Ever

Discovery Questions

- Do you support Daniel Goleman's assertion that *"Leading Sustainability Matters More than Ever"*? Explain your position.

- Are Sustainability issues being discussed in your organization? Have those issues become an integral part of your business and HR practices? Elaborate as to why. (Argue for either "yes" or "no".)

- Would you agree that Sustainability and Corporate Social Responsibility (CSR) should be aligned with the core business values? Explain how this alignment helps create a more cohesive impact.

- What competencies are important in leading a company's sustainability initiatives? Discuss the competencies as proposed here by Christoph Lueneburger, Dan Esty, and Miriam Hawley. Would you add or take away any of those competencies?

- Please, comment on Lynne Twists' statement that we need to move away from the economy of scarcity that rests on three fundamental "lies": 1) There is not enough, 2) More is better, and 3) That's just the way it is. Do you believe this transition will be possible? Where does Lynne suggest we go from here?

- Do you agree with the statement that "becoming leaders of sustainability initiatives involves nothing short of a paradigm shift: From not enough to enough; from greed to gratitude; from scarcity to sufficiency; from dominion over nature to partnership with the natural world? Explain your position.

Selected Facts

- Wal-Mart announced on July 14, 2009 that it is working on a product rating sustainability index that would be posted on items for ecological transparency.

- C.K. Prahalad claimed in September 2009 that the trade off between sustainable products and financial costs is a false one. The pursuit of sustainability can lower costs, raise revenue, and drive growth through innovation.

- The *GoodGuide.com* summarizes on the 10-point scale more than 200 databases on the environmental, health and social impact of a given product at the consumer level.

- We need a 70-80% reduction in emissions (given the rate of CO_2) in the next three or four decades to stabilize global warming.

- Research by Shari Aaron uncovered that 75% of the businesses are not investing in sustainability training. Does this surprise you?

Key Discussion Points

- Why is sustainability one of the hardest issues for business and society to act upon?

- What were the points of agreement among the discussants?

- What issues generated the debate and divergent points of view?

- Explain the concept of consumer "radical transparency" and how it connects with implementing sustainability in business.

- Discuss Shari Aaron's six key principles of the business change agenda that underpin sustainability strategies:
  a) Get the mindset
  b) Make the business case
  c) Get your colleagues on your side
  d) Have two-way conversations
  e) Work together
  f) Make it part of the culture

Review of Solutions

- Identify 2-3 practical take-aways that could be applied in your organization.

- What are the change management recommendations that could be adopted for your organization?

Recommendations Summary

- Identify at least one thing that your organization could do differently based on what you have learned from this discussion.

Learning Outcomes

- Describe what personally you would do differently based on the information you have received.

Leading the Talent Development Life Cycle:

The First-Ever HRPS Fall Executive Forum

More than 200 HR leaders gathered on October 14-16, 2007, for the inaugural HRPS Fall Executive Forum. The event was built as an enhancement to and expansion of the Society's traditional Corporate Sponsor Forum. Sponsors were invited, as were Society members, and cochairs Dianne O'Connell and Gary McKinney and their working team established a rich and interactive format.

"Our goal was to create a new kind of learning event for the Society—targeted to a high level audience and heavily focused on presentations, discussion, and networking on a single, crucial topic," according to O'Connell. Incredibly enthusiastic reviews from attendees declared that the event exceeded its goal. Participants loved the topic, speakers, discussions, and venue. "Chicago in the fall can't be beat," said McKinney.

The event was designed to follow the talent development life cycle, with segments on talent strategy, acquisition, development, and engagement and retention. Segments included a keynote presentation followed by deep dive case studies, allowing plenty of time for attendees to talk about and apply the ideas they were hearing. As at all HRPS events, attendees had ample opportunities to network and meet new colleagues—a rich source of professional development.

There were so many highlights it is impossible to mention them all, but here are a few that stood out:

■ Tony Rucci, CEO, Ohio State University Physicians, Inc., and a long-time leader in proving the links between employee commitment, customer satisfaction, and value creation, reviewed the evidence demonstrating the economic value of intellectual and human capital. Rucci noted, "Intangible assets add more to the market cap of publicly traded companies than tangible or fiscal assets by a ratio of 4:1 in 2007."

■ Richard Vosburgh, SVP-HR for City Center Division, Mirage Resorts, MGM MIRAGE in Las Vegas, reported on his massive, ongoing project in talent acquisition—the need to recruit for more than 15,000 new jobs to staff the new City Center on the Vegas strip and the domino impacts the new jobs have on 40,000 existing jobs at MGM. Likening it to an employment "tsunami," Vosburgh highlighted the sustainability and diversity aspects of his work. "The world works here" is part of the emerging employment brand, supporting the desired MGM culture and customer experience.

■ Brian Fishel, SVP, Executive & Leadership Pipeline Development, Bank of America, gave a detailed look at the BofA's no-nonsense approach to building leaders. Talent/performance planning is one of the bank's four key processes, along with strategy, finance, and risk management. Line management owns it, and "it's not about programs and metrics, it's about the business."

■ Marshall Goldsmith, co-founder, Marshall Goldsmith Partners, and the number one corporate coach in the world, gave a rousing rendition of key ideas from his new book, the best-selling *What Got You Here Won't Get You There*. As he always does, Marshall got attendees laughing and buzzing about his ideas as they applied his concepts while coaching each other.

■ Jim Shanks, SVP of CDW, Inc., the long-time best place to work in the Chicago area, concluded the meeting with a great summation. Said Shanks, "Being a great place to work isn't enough, leaders have to have a laser focus on talent. The way to do that is to make it personal, for both the leader and the talent."

On that note, attendees left with their learning objectives fulfilled and ready to raise their efforts at talent development in their own companies. In response to the overwhelmingly positive reception that the first Forum received, the Society immediately scheduled the next year's event for Chicago, October 19-21, 2008. As this year's Forum sold out, attendees will want to book early. See you at the 2008 Forum!

Point/Counterpoint

Editor's Note: The Point/Counterpoint feature article: "Competitive Advantage, Human Resource Strategy, and the 2008 Olympics," by Fox, et al., launches a spirited exchange among a diverse group of China experts representing US, European, and Chinese perspectives. The counterpoint format allows the multidimensional presentation of this issue. It fits well with Arthur Yeung's warning at the end of his thoughtful response: "As China is a vast and diverse country with a unique political, economic, and social background, it is often dangerous to overgeneralize the reality based on a snapshot or a single incident."

A second piece, by Dr. Alison Eyring, enriches the China discussion with a look at Chinese talent strategies that Western multinationals are pursuing.

Our focus on Chinese human resource challenges serves as an adjunct to the Asia-Pacific issues that several speakers will address at the HRPS Global Conference in April 2008 in Huntington Beach, California. We hope to see you there.

POINT

Competitive Advantage, Human Resource Strategy, and the 2008 Olympics

Jeremy B. Fox, Ph.D.
Department of Management
Appalachian State University
Boone, NC

Joan M. Donohue, Ph.D.
Department of Management Science
University of South Carolina
Columbia, SC

Jinpei Wu, Ph.D.
Department of Management
Virginia Tech
Blacksburg, VA

China, by hosting the 2008 Olympics, hopes to create not only economic payback, but, more importantly, long-term national public appeal. The following statement by Fowler (2006) gives witness to this "best face" goal:

Sun Weide, a former press official for the Chinese Embassy in Washington, works extensively with Hill & Knowlton (PR consulting). He says his main message is to emphasize China's development and Beijing's technological, social and environmental approaches to running its Games.

An organization hoping to achieve some specific goal must look at the planning and strategies it intends to implement by asking, "Will the actions of our organization serve to achieve that goal?" In the case of the 2008 Beijing Olympics, and considering China's globally competitive labor cost advantage,

we are led to examine a project goal in the context of strategic human resource management. Specifically we consider whether, in the long term, Olympic exposure will allow the country to make a "great leap forward" and become an incubator for top global companies. (See Gadiesh, et al., 2006, for a fulsome discussion of this specific point.)

Ultimately, the measure of "success" in human resources often has been the cost of providing performance, rather than a strategic accomplishment measure of that performance for the organization.

In the example of HR misalignment, explained later, the reader can discern how China's traditional globally competitive advantage of cheap, compliant labor, often supplied with limited government oversight, is now misaligned with China's "hypermission" of favorably impressing the world during its hosting of the 2008 Olympic Games in Beijing.

Hutzler (2005), a columnist in *The Wall Street Journal*, reports:

China's communist leaders want to showcase the country's rising wealth to the world and enhance their popularity with their own people, while local governments are using the event to

promote their own agendas. "Anything that involves a crane is called an Olympics project," says an executive with the China subsidiary of U.S. conglomerate General Electric, a top Olympics sponsor.

China hopes, as do all hosting countries, to show a profit (see Owen, 2005, for a strong contrarian point of view on the potential for profit). More importantly, China wants to show off the country to the world in a light that will put China on the world's stage of important countries for sports, entertainment, and technology, and highlight it as a country that can follow through on projects and "make things happen."

In the face of the nation's excitement over being selected to host the Olympics, a National Peoples Congress (NPC) deputy unconsciously raised the specter of disas-

> Wherever there is substantial construction activity or needed manpower, there is the potential for labor abuse misaligning with a desired PR goal.

trous risk associated with detrimental labor outcomes when he said: "The organizers of the event should exert all efforts to present the best ever games to the world with the minimum amount of expenditure" (*Shanghai Daily*, 2006); however, if, in using this existing globally competitive advantage, China's Olympic HR process utilizes underpaid and poorly treated employees as perceived by the world at large, its "desired goal" may be replaced by another less desired, unintended, and detrimental outcome: a public relations (PR) problem.

Reports have come out about abused Olympic-related labor. The Human Rights Watch (2006) reports substantial worker unrest on Olympic projects because of pay issues. This is not an issue unique to any one country. Recognizing this fact, what emerges is a cautionary tale of strategic HR (mis)alignment. This is, indeed, a worldwide issue: Wherever there is substantial construction activity or needed manpower, there is the potential for labor abuse misaligning with a desired PR goal. From Dubai, for example, Fattah (2006) of *The New York Times* reported:

Far from the high-rise towers and luxury hotels emblematic of Dubai, the workers turning this swath of desert into a modern metropolis live in a Dickensian world of cramped labor camps, low pay and increasing desperation.

In China, at least five entrenched factors establish the risk of abuse of construction (and other) workers that could subsequently mar the public's perception of any large

> With this investment comes increasing concerns . . . that a cheap and ready supply of labor may be accompanied by substantial risks.

project, including the 2008 Olympics. Historically, these five risk factors have provided China with a substantial competitive advantage. With the new Olympic goal not related to low-cost manufacturing, using old competitively advantageous (labor) processes will create an undesirable outcome. The following five factors are manifestations of the current misalignment between prevalent Chinese HR practices and the stated Olympic goal of a glowing PR:

1. China's economic growth has been based on a "low pay model."
2. Cheap labor has been supplied, predominately, by migrant laborers moving from the rural farms across China to the metropolitan areas.
3. Contractors are advantaged by foregoing legally required employee contracts.
4. China has a world image of poor treatment of laborers.
5. China has in place the outdated "Labor Law of 1995."

Three steps could realign HR functions and Olympic goals:

1. China should clean up the existing labor contract situation. All labor carried out on Olympic projects should be done by laborers who have the legally required labor contracts with their employers. Labor contracts that are generally required might best be monitored for their existence by officials of the All China Federation of Trade Unions.
2. Pay rates should be demonstrably at or above average for laborers in the Olympic venue sites and should be policed by the All China Federation of Trade Unions and by outside monitors as well. The Labor Law of 1995 needs to be

interpreted, clarified, and re-codified in its areas of ambiguity.

3. There should be enforcement of contractor compliance. All building contractors associated with any aspect of the Olympic preparation projects should be shown the full range of punishments associated with failure to comply with the required hiring contracts and pay and safety processes.

CONCLUSIONS

By the end of 2002, China had received, since 1992, a cumulative 750 billion US dollars of foreign direct investment (Deng, 2003). With this investment comes increasing concerns, particularly by foreign direct investors, that a cheap and ready supply of labor may be accompanied by substantial risks. These risks are associated with cheap labor the world over and include underage, underpaid, and overworked employees in unsafe work environments. These risks are seen in every developing nation, and in many developed nations, and are often a temporary competitive advantage.

The risks that face China's hosting of the Olympic Games are the same public relations risks associated with using Chinese labor, and these risks are faced by foreign investors as well; therefore, reducing labor risks as discussed herein would also serve to align HR processes (in this case, perceived fair treatment of labor) through careful HR planning, with the country's stated goals of putting forward its best face. China's current and powerful competitive advantage of low cost labor will otherwise not achieve the current goal of its government (and its people): favorably impressing the world with their hosting of the 2008 Olympics. Conversely, with acceptable labor policies and practices in place, China will be strategically aligning its treatment of labor with its goal of looking modern and progressive to the viewers of the 2008 Olympics.

NOTE

A longer version of this article originally appeared in the *Journal of Change Management* as "An Application of a Human Resources Strategic Model to the 2008 Beijing Olympics: A Discussion of HR

Goal Misalignment in Projects," London (Jun. 2007), 7(2): 171.

REFERENCES

Deng P (2003). "Determinates of Full-Control Mode in China: An Integrative Approach," *American Business Review*, 21(1): 113-124.

Fattah HM (2006). "In Dubai, an Outcry from Asians for Workplace Rights," *The New York Times* (Mar. 26): 3.

Fowler G (2006). "China Prepares for Olympic Spotlight, Changing Media Rules, Turning to PR," *The Wall Street Journal* (Dec. 15): B1.

Gadiesh O, et al. (2007). "Preparing for China's Next Great Leap," *Strategy & Leadership*, 35(1): 43-46.

Hutzler CS (2005). "Olympian Extravagance — Beijing Indulges in a Frenzy of Building for 2008 Games: Will Projects Benefit Locals?" *The Wall Street Journal* (Eastern edition, Aug. 23): B1, B4.

Owen J (2005). "Estimating the Cost and Benefit of Hosting Olympic Games: What Can Beijing Expect from Its 2008 Games?" *Industrial Geographer*, 3(1): 1-18.

Shanghai Daily. "Lawmakers Eye Olympic Extravagance" (Mar. 4-5): 1.

COUNTERPOINT

Arthur Yeung, Ph.D.
Associate Dean and
Philips Chair Professor
China Europe Int'l Business School
P.R. China

Based on some reports of labor unrest during the construction of Beijing 2008 Olympics facilities, the authors raise a much bigger concern in their article on whether China's over-reliance on its traditional sources of competitive advantage based on cheap, compliant labor will eventually backfire on the government's intention to showcase China as a progressive country and pose significant public relations risks for top global companies that operate in China because of potential negative publicity. The authors' recommendation is obvious: China should improve its labor management practices so that the competitive advantage in China can be harnessed on the one hand while the risks of negative publicity can be reduced on the other.

As a US-educated HR professor and executive, I can fully understand the authors' recommendations based on the logic of the people-service-profit chain where engaged/committed employees lead to better products or services and, eventually, better financial returns. In this regard, China still has a lot of room for improvement in labor management practices, especially for those migrant workers who are being employed on a subcontracting or outsourcing basis.

The need to further protect employee rights is also recognized by the Chinese government. The authors should be pleased to know that "the outdated Labor Law of 1995" has already been replaced with a labor law, effective in January 2008. Under the new law, a better balance between business interest and employee rights has been maintained; however, such a new labor law is introduced in China not because of external publicity or PR concerns, but because of a more important concern related to internal political stability under the banner of "social harmony" advocated by the Chinese government.

Many Western observers who try to describe and prescribe business or management practices in China exhibit a strong tendency to assess the situation based on a Western frame of reference while neglecting the political, economic, and social differences between China and their home countries. Using the Beijing Olympics as an example, I find the arguments and recommendations of the authors both right and wrong. Sure, China needs stronger enforcement of labor contracts and employee protection. True, labor abuse should be prevented in China as anywhere else in the world. China does, however, have more burning issues to address because of its unique situation. One obvious example is how to ensure employment opportunities for the huge number of workers that enters into labor market every year. As mentioned by Premier Wen Jiabao in 2003:

> China has 740 million people in the workforce, more than United States and Europe's combined workforce of 430 million. China's workforce grows by 10 million people per year, and there is a further 14 million lay-off workers. In addition to the 120 million rural migrants into the cities, China is facing huge employment pressures.

Based on demographic trends, some studies (Niu, 2004) estimate that China has a surplus workforce of 14 to 20 million every year between 2005 and 2010. Clearly, from the Chinese government's point of view, the more pressing issue is how to avoid further polarization of the society ("those who have" and "those who have not") that can lead to major social unrest. Put in this context, labor abuse is important but not so important in China.

For global firms operating in China, a cheap and abundant supply of labor, in addition to huge market opportunity, is still one of the major attractions to invest-ment in China. Again, the authors' concern about potential negative PR risks in association with the use of underpaid and poorly treated employees is low on the priority list of many multinational firms in China. Although labor abuse does exist in China, it occurs more frequently in subcontracting work, in which subcontractors are squeezed to complete a project with little budget (such as the Beijing Olympics construction project); however, for foreign firms that hire and manage their employees directly, the PR risk of labor abuse is minimal unless these firms choose to engage in abusive practices. On the contrary, the major headache faced by many CEOs of multinational firms in China is how to attract, retain, and engage high-caliber talent who are in great shortage in China (instead of labor abuse of those manual labors in excessive supply). In my recent interviews with more than 20 CEOs of multinational firms in China like Coca-Cola, Johnson & Johnson, Philips, Unilever, and Sony, I asked them one question, "What are the most critical factors that determine the success and survival of your firm in China?" Among a list of factors often cited, such as relationship with headquarters, business model innovation in China, supply chain management, and branding, talent management is by far the most consistently and frequently cited factor. The aggressive growth aspiration of these multinational firms cannot be achieved if the companies fail to attract, retain, and develop talent with the right skills, knowledge, drive, and relationships in China. Being an "employer of choice" is a much more important objective for many multinational firms in China, which face severe talent wars every day.

As China is a vast and diverse country with a unique political, economic, and social background, it is often dangerous to over-generalize the reality based on a snapshot or a single incident. The longer I live in China, the more I find how little I know about China.

*＊＊

Xiaoya Liang, Ph.D.
Department of Business Administration
School of Management
Fudan University
Shanghai, P.R. China

Hosting the 2008 Olympics will become one of the most significant events in China. It presents a golden opportunity for China to demonstrate its economic prosperity and technological leadership. At the same time, the Olympics bring about some major challenges. For example, Fox and colleagues argue here that abused Olympic-related labor practices might cause China a huge potential public relation crisis if not handled properly. Taking an alignment perspective, Fox, et al., stated that China's Olympic mission is seriously misaligned with China's human resources practices in various Olympic projects. The authors go on to elaborate five factors to manifest this serious HR misalignment. I comment here on these factors by offering updates and alternative opinions.

1. *China's economic growth has been based on a "low pay model."* China has enjoyed an average growth rate near 10 percent for the past two decades. Many factors can be attributed to China's economic growth; however, no official statistics show to what extent low labor cost has contributed to China's economic success. At least in recent years, labor is not cheap any more. In a recent survey of over 1,800 manufacturing enterprises in the Yangtze River Delta Region, the authors found that on average the surveyed enterprises hired 67 percent of blue-collar workers and faced strong pressure on rapidly increasing labor costs (Wang, et al., 2007). Take the textile industry as an example: Labor cost in Wuxi is about nine times higher than in Vietnam. This year, some enterprises have had to raise the salary of floor workers two to three times. Thus, I would argue that Chinese enterprises have been able to offer low cost products by utilizing large economies of production scale, convenient industry clusters, and favorable government policies (such as tax reduction, subsidies, and land usage). If a "low-pay workforce" drives rapid economic growth, why have we not yet seen countries with even cheaper labor growing as fast as China?

2. *Cheap labor has been supplied, predominantly, by migrant laborers moving from the rural farms across China to the metropolitan areas.* China has a long-established dual structure system. Because of the residence registration system, many people are constrained in rural areas. Because of low productivity, poverty, and high unemployment in rural areas (unemployment in rural areas is estimated at least 150 million), many young peasants go to cities to get a job. Today, peasants comprise 46.5 percent of the employment in the second and the third industries and 80 percent of the building industry. They mostly take the risky and tiring jobs in the cities and receive discriminatory treatment such as unequal pay policy,

low social welfare, low job security, and poor working conditions.

3. *Contractors are advantaged by foregoing legally required employee contracts.* Lin (2006) interviewed 58 employees in 17 domestic enterprises in 2003, and findings on sweatshop practices were mixed. In six of the 17 enterprises, working conditions were poor and basic labor rights were not in place. In the other 11 workplaces, protections against work-related hazards and safeguards of labor rights were adequate and basic compliance with labor law requirements was in place. In addition, the Chinese Academy of Social Science surveyed 1,800 employees in 1998 to investigate the status of labor practices. They reported in the study that:

1. Sufficient protection against work-related hazards was provided;
2. Arbitrary pay cuts and assaults on workers were rare; and
3. Withholding of deposits or the bonus system were seldom adopted.

Finally, *China has in place the outdated "Labor Law of 1995."* The national people's congress issued a new labor contract law on June 29, 2007. The new labor contract law took effect on January 1, 2008, with an objective to prevent illegal employment practices and promote harmonious labor relations. The new labor law will have a significant impact on human resource management practices in China at least from two aspects:

1. From the perspective of individual employees, the new labor law will greatly enhance labor rights protection by making an employment contract mandatory and specifying terms of employment, transferring, and firing.
2. From the perspective of employers, including all types of for-profit and not-for-profit organizations, the direct and most significant effect is that the new labor law dramatically increases their labor costs. Because the new labor law includes terms and penalties if employers do not obey the law, the cost of illegal labor practices will be high.

* * *

J. Stewart Black, Ph.D.
Executive Director
INSEAD Center for Human Resources in Asia
INSEAD, France

In their article, "Competitive Advantage, Human Resource Strategy, and the 2008 Olympics," Fox, et al., argue that China's goals for the 2008 Olympics are misaligned with its labor practices and advantages. They further imply that this alignment carries with it significant global PR risk.

Having just returned from Beijing and toured some of the 2008 Olympic sites, I have a somewhat different perspective. My perspective is not that China's goals for the 2008 Olympics and its labor practices and advantages are misaligned; my perspective is that they are a non sequitur.

Why is this the case? The vast majority of the world will never see the 2008 Olympics up close and personal. They will watch it on TV. Also, they will see virtually nothing during the construction but will only see the finished product. Even then, the facilities or even the infrastructure, such as the two new subway lines going in, will only be a backdrop to the events and the athletes. As in the past, we can expect that, outside of the televised actual competitions, the vast majority of the other televised stories will rightly focus on the athletes. I do not recall from past Olympics, and do not anticipate for the 2008 Olympics, feature stories on the workers who built the facilities.

For the running and televising of the Olympics, the facilities primarily matter if they are not ready in time or not adequate in quality and functionality. If they are over or under budget, no one from the outside world will really care. After all, the foreign visitors or those outside China who watch the events or follow them via other media will not have had to pay for the venues. If they cost too much, none of the visiting crowds will have to pay an extra surcharge to enter the venues. If the facilities are under budget, none of the visitors will get a check in the mail refunding part of their ticket price.

This is not to say that there are not difficult working conditions or that workers might not be paid what some inside or outside China might deem fair. As the authors note, working conditions in many developing countries have aspects to them that those in developing countries would like to criticize. Although fair labor practices, acceptable standards of safety, appropriate pay, requisite training and education, and the like are all important topics, they are unlikely to come into close enough proximity with the traditional focus of the Olympics for any of the associated risks to have much impact on what the world takes away as impressions from the Olympics. Again, this is not to say that China should not examine and potentially change certain labor practices, but it is to say that I highly doubt that the risk that concerns the authors will occur.

If dozens of workers were killed in a collapse of any Olympic structure or even of a subway line being built in part to support moving people to and from Olympic venues, then the world might sit up and take notice; however, any catastrophe of this magnitude would risk not only workers' lives but also the specific venue or the viability of the games overall. Such a risk is not remotely acceptable to the Chinese leaders. They care enough about the viability and visibility of the games to ensure that such catastrophic calamities are highly unlikely to happen. This is not to say that government officials or others do not care about human life, but it is to say that even if Chinese leaders did not care about the laborers, the government's self interest of having people walk away from the 2008 Olympics impressed with the games and with China creates a subsequent interest in constructing the venues and other related projects in ways that do not risk the catastrophic loss of worker's lives.

My prediction is that history will repeat itself. Despite its best efforts, China (like Greece in 2004) will spend more than anticipated. Because of China's best efforts (like Greece in 2004), the venues will be ready on time and will work well—new records will be set. As in 2004 before and 2012 after, people will focus on the games and the athletes. The venues, several of which are quite stunning to see, will be only be a backdrop for the games. They will not be the feature of the games. As a consequence, the workers who built the venues, along with whatever labor practices and pay were employed in building the venues, will be forgotten by the time the visitors arrive and the cameras roll. Whether the workers or the practices should be featured or forgotten is a different question. But my prediction is that they will be. And this is why I say that the point is not that China's goals for the 2008 Olympics and its labor practices and advantages are misaligned, they are simply a non sequitur.

* * *

Jeff Hasenfratz, J.D.
Managing Director
Mindsight Executive Development
Services
Shanghai, P.R. China

The authors of the "Competitive Advantage" article suggest that the Chinese government take steps to ensure that the Olympics-related labor force is more fairly treated, so as to be in closer alignment with the country's goal of putting its best face forward at the 2008 Olympics.

This is a logical suggestion, and the government is indeed intending to enact a labor law soon, which, if it is uniformly enforced, should result in better treatment for the country's labor force as a whole.

I wonder, though, how many foreign onlookers or visitors will really be paying much attention to this aspect of China's "face"? I suspect that many outsiders will be much more interested in how impressive the Games' venues are, how safely the events are conducted, and how rapidly China's external "face" is changing.

***

Doug Guthrie, Ph.D.
Professor of Management and Faculty
Director of Executive Education
Stern School of Business
New York University.
Author of *China and Globalization:
The Economic, Political, and Social
Transformation of Chinese Society* (2006)
and *Dragon in a Three-Piece Suit: The
Emergence of Capitalism in China* (1999).

Professors Fox, et al., raise some interesting issues with respect to labor, the 2008 Olympics, and China's profile in the global economy. Unfortunately, their comments are based more on caricature and half-truths than fact.

To begin, it is useful to note that China's reform process has been based on a gradualist process whereby leaders of the liberal wing of the Party have used economic reform to gradually introduce institutional changes that would eventually transform social and political realms. The lack of sudden political change (as we saw in the Russia and the Eastern Bloc) has led observers to underestimate the significance of the social and political reforms that have occurred in China. The reality is that changes in China have been radical, and the view that significant social and political reforms have not been pushed forward in China is wrong. Unfortunately, these changes—and the politics guiding

them—are often ignored, as scholars and pundits seek simple prescriptions to complex developmental processes.

To give some specifics to this discussion, let us consider, Fox, et al.'s, characterization of the reforms:

1. *China's economic growth has been based on a "low pay model."* Half true. It is certainly the case that China's Coastal Development Strategy (CDS) of the late 1980s was built on exploiting low-cost labor to provide goods for the world. It is absolutely not the case that this has been the only or even the primary engine of China's economic growth. In the 1980s, the main engine of growth was the dynamic Township and Village Enterprises; in the 1990s, in addition to the CDS, the key feature of development was the joint ventures between Chinese firms and foreign investment enterprises. In the last decade, it has come from state investment in and the dynamic emergence of China's homegrown multinationals, like PetroChina, Lenovo, and Jili. Although the export economy has been plagued with problems of labor exploitation, in the other two sectors, which are rarely mentioned in discussions of China's development, the opposite is true. One need spend only an afternoon in any of the major joint ventures with firms like General Motors and Motorola or in the factories of companies like PetroChina and Lenovo to see the ways in which labor standards and practices are mirroring our own highest standards. There is strong evidence that these practices are diffusing across China.

2. *Cheap labor has been supplied, predominantly, by migrant laborers moving from the rural farms across China to the metropolitan area.* True. But, what point are Fox, et al., making here? Every capitalist economy throughout the world depends upon the supply of cheap labor. Societies vary on the extent to which they decide to protect the lowest ends of the labor pools: Sweden and Holland score high on this front; the United States and China score in the middle of the pack. Before we pass judgment on China, we probably need to take a look at our own migrant labor pool, migrant laborers who work the farms in Florida and California and occupy a second-class citizenship position similar to that of China's "floating population" of migrant labor.

3. *Contractors are advantaged by foregoing legally required employee contracts.* Half

true. Although some contractors forego employee contracts, and those that do gain advantages from it, many contractors do not. A great deal of change in this area often goes unacknowledged by the foreign research and press community.

4. *China has a world image of poor treatment of laborers.* True. But it is largely because the research, media, and political communities have advanced caricatures of the process of changes that have driven China's reforms forward and have failed to report accurately on the changes that have occurred.

5. *China has in place the outdated "Labor Law of 1995."* False. This is like saying the United States is governed by the Wagner Act of 1935, without acknowledging any of the amendments that reshaped labor law in the years since. Take, for example, the most recent amendment to this law, the Labor Contract Law, passed by the Standing Committee of the National People's Congress in the Spring of 2007, and long championed by Hu Jintao: This law is meant specifically to protect the very population of worker that Fox, et al., are concerned about.

Because of gradualism, the dramatic change in China often goes unacknowledged. Economic and political changes are well underway and should be duly noted and understood.

Authors' Response to Comments on "Competitive Advantage, Human Resource Strategy, and the 2008 Olympics"

Foremost, we want to thank the journal and the counterpoint commentators for their interesting, informed, and incisive comments on our manuscript. Obviously, two heads (or more) are better than one and, in this case, outside commentary has provided us with much to contemplate. Naturally, however, we are going to wade in and explain our viewpoint. We will not go over each commentator's points, but rather give some generally pertinent responses to the points raised.

1. Knowing how difficult it is to understand another culture, we feel, as much as possible, that we have not incorporated western biases into this discussion. The western authors (Fox and Donohue) have lived and worked in China for about two years total, traveling extensively in a non-western fashion. The first author ➤

has worked with manufacturing plants in China and, having taught "international management," is well aware of cultural biases and sought to free the article from such biases. Further, the third author on the paper, Wu Jinpei, is a Chinese national and was heavily involved in shaping the article's point of view. Something most of the responders did not mention is our point that, in hosting the Olympics, China is exposing itself throughout the world to all the biases existing in the eyes of the beholders (including those likely to invest in China). China needs to overcome those pre-existing biases; strategically, we see the labor issue as misaligned with the future-positive view of China that Beijing wants to create. Although *we* understand the points made by the responders, those experiencing China for the first time (perhaps) may not, and will therefore have only *this snapshot* of China. Hence, we propose the use of the strategic misalignment consideration.

2. We are not trying to tell Beijing what to do. They did not ask us for our opinions; however, management research in HR is clearly applicable in this situation. Setting goals and aligning functional area behaviors are requisite for goal achievement. US management textbooks, college lectures, and Chinese college students' responses in China to both typically all supported the viability of this misalignment concept regardless of cultural differences.

3. We are aware of the new labor law coming into effect in January 2008 and are researching its provisions and possible ramifications. While visiting China in 2006, we were aware of the continual calls from Beijing for comments and suggestions on the new law (publicized by the newspapers); however, this law is too late to influence labor issues related to the 2008 Olympics, which, as one commentator noted, has its venues pretty much in place.

4. We understand that China has a large workforce (not just low-cost labor) that needs employment. This is a difficult issue to handle. One way to deal with this issue is through continued and increased foreign investment.

5. Public relations is not a big issue for most foreign firms because they tend to bring their own standards, as required by the end consumer. The world's overall view of existing labor issues in China may, however, dissuade future investors; therefore, it is important that the Olympics leave the world with a positive view of labor issues in China.

6. The "gradualist" viewpoint is not germane here. We understand this viewpoint and see it in action every day. We see the history and the present as shaping the future in a growing, organic fashion and study this growth; however, Olympic viewers will get not get this snapshot view. Foreign investors may respond viscerally to what they read or see, and this could be the issue that damages goal achievement in China. For example, only tiny samples of toys made in China have been found to be dangerous, yet what has been the public's response? Apparently, avoidance of Chinese-made toys.

7. We are well aware of substantial labor abuse here in the United States. We are not singling out China for criticism in this regard. We are noting only the misalignment of processes and goals; we are *not making a value judgment* of labor conditions in China because we know (through business interaction) of many extenuating considerations surrounding this situation. We are *not* sympathizing with laborers in China or *criticizing* Beijing, nor are we calling out for China to "do things right" for the citizenship. Rather we are using this example of a country's goals and plans to demonstrate the importance of careful strategic formulation (e.g., earlier competitive advantages may no longer be useful toward goal achievement). This article is not a social commentary, nor is it long-term focused; it is about the here and now of aligning strategies and goals.

8. Concerning the prevalence of labor abuse in China, from our exposure to the Chinese press, that abuse seems frequent and well reported. The full-length version of this article substantially documents this reporting in China and elsewhere.

9. Concerning the public's view of labor and goal achievement as a non-sequitur, this point will be answered in a few months; however, considering all of the bad press the Olympics-related labor issue has received in the press already, we recognize this possibility. (Google will supply you with examples.) Olympic TV reports and coverage will possibly not address labor issues, as TV reporters tend to give less than hard-hitting news coverage. Reporters will, however, be reporters and they do not get noticed for being mild mannered. Newspaper reporters, we expect, will be more hard hitting. Again, consider the toy, drug, and pollution issues and their coverage and the subsequent reactions in Europe and the United States. We see this issue as far from a non-sequitur, and well worth addressing even *if* there is little risk simply because the stakes are so high.

Thanks heartily to the commentators for their thought-provoking comments. Thanks especially to the HRPS and Anna Tavis for putting this format together. We believe it will provide for some interesting reading.

Executing Growth Strategies in China:
Perspectives on People and Organization

Alison R. Eyring, Ph.D., Organisation Solutions

Executing strategy is all about people and organization. Nowhere is this truer than in China. Limited pools of key talent, and keen competition for it, make it hard to attract and retain the right people. When this is combined with high levels of growth across highly diverse markets and in a complex and changing legislative environment, executing profitable growth strategies becomes difficult.

We asked more than 20 China country heads and their most senior HR leaders who are living and working in China to share their practical wisdom about growing their businesses. In interviews, the leaders were asked to share their companies' growth journeys over the past five years, to reflect on what helped or hindered them in executing their strategies, and to share what they had learned from their experiences. Most of

innovation, movement into adjacent competitive spaces, joint ventures, green field investments, and acquisitions. In this article, we focus on the two most common themes relating to people and organization that emerged from the interviews—building the talent pipeline and managing interfaces with the rest of the organization.

Building the Talent Pipeline

Attracting, selecting, developing, and retaining talent played a key role in each growth story and is the largest interview theme by far.

Having a strong reputation as a good employer that develops its people is particularly important to attract talent. "If a company has a good name and reputation, it can attract talent. Money is important too—but less important than development,"

standards in selection while facing significant pressure to hire caused by growth and sometimes turnover.

In many MNCs, ensuring that the right country leader is in place is the key to strategy execution. Two companies jump-started their growth by bringing in a country head two to three levels higher than the previous person. In both instances, the leaders had been running a much larger business than the existing China operation. At the corporate level, the driver for this was the decision "to make China work." Two other companies experiencing turnarounds also brought in new China heads. Of the four companies, three of the senior leaders were external hires. Many MNCs are more accustomed to grooming leaders for mature markets, but are not prepared for the leadership demands in emerging, high growth markets.

Retention also is critical and challenging; however, leaders in six of the 10 companies said turnover is not a problem or that it had improved because of focused efforts. 3M, for example, uses a dual career ladder for technical people to help retain its highly valued R&D staff. One of the companies has seen a step change in how it retains people. "Doing more with employee engagement and creating a shared vision really makes a difference to the business," said its head of HR.

Developing local talent also is a priority. This has translated into large investments in classroom training and eLearning. Most companies have formal leadership development programs and many focus on developing the capabilities of their leaders to develop others. The companies that place a greater emphasis on building a shared organization culture also focus more on development using their leaders as talent developers and through planned movements than other companies.

Importing talent from parts of the business outside of China plays a useful role in developing local Chinese talent. Although many of the leaders spoke of a desire for more local Chinese leading their China businesses, only one leader spoke of the intent to reduce foreign employees. Three of the companies are exporting Chinese talent into the regional and global business structure. "China is now seen as a talent pool for global roles," said one of the line leaders. "This has helped people feel part of the larger organization and create greater interdependencies with other parts of the business." One of the barriers to this is the overriding mental model of what a good leader looks like. "It's

> Two companies jump-started their growth by bringing in a country head two to three levels higher than the previous person.

the 10 participating companies are members of the Asia Pacific Top HR Roundtable. Several are US companies, including Cargill, Microsoft, and FedEx.

As business context, almost all of the 10 companies have been in China for over a decade, and some much longer. All had experienced significant increases in top-line growth over the past five years. "Most MNCs (multinational corporations) in China today are seeing double digit growth," said one line leader, "but getting that growth profitably is much more difficult." Most had seen headcount increase drastically. Two had or were experiencing a turnaround focused on improving profits. Their strategies were incredibly diverse and included pure market share growth, share-of-wallet growth from established clients, product

said one HR leader. In the words of one of the most experienced HR leaders we interviewed, "If one invests and focuses on the area of talent, it can become a huge weapon to win in the talent marketplace. Too many companies don't do this. Many also lack a brand name as a learning institute. They need a much higher level of commitment to developing talent."

Investing the time and resources to bring the right people into the organization and onboard them properly is both important and challenging. "Due to the intensity of our interviewing process, testing used, and use of peer-level interviewing, many of our retention and development problems go away," shared one line leader. HR leaders spoke of the challenge of maintaining high easier for a Caucasian to look and act the way others view a 'leader,'" said one of the HR leaders.

Managing Interfaces with the Larger Organization

Managing corporate or business unit interfaces outside of China is the second largest theme in the growth stories. In this area, there are significant differences across the companies. These result from factors such as business complexity, degree of globalization of business unit structures, relative autonomy of the China business, and the stage of business development in China.

For each of the 10 companies, China has become increasingly important to its home office. For some leaders, this has led to an overwhelming amount of attention and initiatives being driven from outside of China—particularly over the past few years. As one of the HR leaders lamented, "There is a lot of business focus on China—and there is a lot of interest. In one year, we had more than 200 executive visitors." According to several of the line leaders, such attention sometimes drives activities that make it harder to maintain business focus and achieve desired results.

Most of the line leaders reported spending considerable time educating executives at the home office about China. "The home front must be managed carefully," said one line leader. "It's important that they take a long-term view, have the right expectations and understand volatility in China." One long-tenured line leader felt it is critical to "have courage to communicate good and bad news." Although whether line leaders are long-time employees or new to the business does not seem to matter, what is critical for their effective engagement with the home office is that they be credible and trusted by corporate management.

These corporate interfaces presented challenges to the China business leaders, but involving corporate executives in communicating with Communist Party officials and meeting with key customers and partners is essential to growth. This often requires having corporate leaders who appreciate the complexities of China. In one company, a member of the corporate leadership team was relocated to Asia to help facilitate corporate relationships.

These China-based leaders show a strong sense of responsibility for helping corporate decision-makers understand China. "Local teams need to make ourselves messengers to communicate how China has moved and

what opportunities this means," said one of the leaders interviewed. Both line and HR leaders highlighted the need to build continuous awareness of changes underway in China to update perceptions of this complex market.

A couple of the companies we interviewed have structured China to be a stand-alone country or region reporting into the home office through a strong country chair, but most of the companies have multiple, global lines of business that reach into China. This has resulted in matrix structures that can bewilder Chinese employees, and is particularly challenging for those who report to both a local boss and another in Europe, the United States, or elsewhere in Asia/Pacific.

Educating employees about how the matrix structures work benefits companies with these types of organization. In one company, employees were trained how to deal with two bosses, and they implemented a practice of three-way coaching with the two bosses involved. In another company, the head of China created an advisory group to facilitate the numerous touch points with corporate functions. He recruited group members and led the group, which met twice a year. This team helped people in the home office better understand local issues and helped the China staff better understand corporate priorities and access support and resources.

Conclusions

As China plays an increasingly important role in global MNCs' portfolios, it will become essential for western MNCs to better understand and be able to support China growth plans. We have only highlighted a few of the lessons of experience from seasoned China leaders, but our information underscores the need for HR professionals working in and with China to create tools and processes that enable their organizations to build their talent pipelines faster. It also suggests that HR can support growth by helping to design and effectively manage interfaces between the China business(es) and the corporate organization.

* * *

About the Author: Dr. Alison Eyring is president of Organisation Solutions, a global consultancy specializing in organization effectiveness and headquartered in Singapore. The company was founded in 2000 and works with global MNCs to achieve and sustain the growth of their business, teams and leaders worldwide.

The **Asia Pacific Top HR Roundtable** was co-founded in 2004 by Alison Eyring (Organisation Solutions) and Julian Dalzel (Shell). Members include 18 global MNCs whose top regional or global HR executives meet quarterly to share and learn together on issues of strategic importance to Human Resource leaders and their businesses.

About the Interviewees: The line leaders, a mix of Asian and Western expatriates, had 20 to 30 years of experience in their industries and had been in China at least three years—several for over a decade. The HR leaders were mostly Asian; four were mainland Chinese. Most had more than six years of experience working in China and many had worked there for one or two decades. Companies in this study were: 3M, Cargill, Cisco, Electrolux, FedEx, Intercontinental Hotels Group, Kraft, Microsoft, Standard Chartered Bank and The Walt Disney Company.

Competitive Advantage, HR Strategy and China

Discovery Questions

- What are we dealing with in our organization today that relates to this content area?

- Be able to better understand the continuing evolution of HR practices in China.

- To recognize when we are using our Western lens to interpret actions without considering large political, economic and social differences.

- To understand the pressures brought on China by the growth of their population.

- Seeing that attracting/retaining high caliber talent is a larger issue than the potential abuse of laborers who are in over-supply.

- Understand the evolving labor strategy evident in China's Coastal Development Strategy, Township and Village Enterprises, Joint Ventures with Multi-Nationals, and Home Grown Multi-Nationals.

- Recognize that the US migrant population of workers isn't so different than China's "floating population" of migrant labor.

Selected Facts

- What new facts that were presented got your attention?

- China's objectives for the Olympics included a focus on national Public Relations.

- Between 1992-2002, China received $750B in direct US investment.

- The Labor Law of 1995 was updated in 1998 with a better balance between employee rights and business interests.

- Change was driven not by external PR concerns, but by a desire for internal political stability and social harmony.

- The US & Europe have 430 million people in the workforce; China has 740 million.

- 10 million new people a year need to join the workforce in China.

- Textile worker labor costs in China is nine times the cost of Vietnam.

- Peasants from rural areas moving to cities account for 80% of construction labor.

- There continues to be a great deal of controversy over the extent of "sweatshop" practices in China.

Key Discussion Points

- What were the key points being made in this Point Counterpoint presentation?

- What are some recent Public Relations successes/failures for our organization?

- Did Olympic exposure allow China to take a "Great Leap Forward" in the business world?

- What has happened with the world economy since the Olympics were over?

- Has China moved away from its traditional source of competitive advantage—cheap, compliant labor? If so, why?

- Will the People-Service-Profit Chain with aligned/engaged employees come to China?

- Were the Olympics a showcase for China's economic prosperity and technological leadership?

- What new practices did the new labor law of 2008 put into place?

- How has the history of political change been different in China than in the Soviet Union?

Review of Solutions

- Identify 2-3 Big Ideas that are worthy of exploring for our organization.

Recommendations Summary

- Identify one thing that we will do differently based on what we learned.

Learning Outcomes

- What one new piece of information did you learn that will be important to you?

Perspectives—Point/Counterpoint

Anna Tavis, Perspectives Editor

We dedicate this selection of point and counterpoints to the crucial, continuing and changing topic of the relationship among businesses and their human resources partners. In the Point article, David Ulrich and Wayne Brockbank update the evolving discussion of what competencies are required of HR professionals to deliver business value and earn a "seat at the table" when strategic business decisions are being made.

For the Counterpoints, we invited the top HR practice leaders from five leading executive search firms to respond to the academic gurus and to share their cross-industry experience of the changing expectations in the CEO suite of their HR departments. To add to the search consultants' observations, we asked three HR practitioners to describe the current status of the HR profession as seen from inside their organizations.

Collectively, our academic, consulting and practitioner writers came up with a composite portrait of an HR leader rising to the demands of the ever-changing business situation. We also want to invite readers to respond with your own observations and points of view to the editors. Please send your comments and thoughts to *People & Strategy* Managing Editor Jay Strother at **jstrother@hrps.org**.

The HR Business-Partner Model: Past Learnings and Future Challenges

Dave Ulrich and Wayne Brockbank, The RBL Group, Ross School of Business at the University of Michigan

The informal business-partner model has existed for well more than 100 years, when effective support functions, including HR, have contributed to business results. Formalizing how HR professionals can create more value as business partners has been our focus for the last 10 to 15 years. Now we can reflect on what we have learned in the past decade about the relevance of the business-partner model and see clearly the challenges that lie ahead.

Looking Back: Nine Lessons Learned

First, the business-partner model is not unique to HR; all staff functions are trying to find ways to deliver more value to top-line growth and bottom-line profitability. If they are not delivering definitive and sustainable value, they have been given the mandate to change, or face elimination or outsourcing.

Second, the intent of the business-partner model is to help HR professionals integrate more thoroughly into business processes and align their day-to-day work with business outcomes. This means focusing more on deliverables and business results than HR activities.

Third, being a business partner may be achieved in many HR job categories, typically in one of four positions:

1. **Corporate HR**

2. **Embedded HR,** working as HR generalists with line leaders

3. **HR Specialists,** working in centers of expertise to provide technical expertise

4. **Service Centers,** building or managing technology-based e-HR systems

Fourth, business success is more dependent today than ever on softer organizational agendas, such as **talent** and **organization capabilities.**

Fifth, just as general managers turn to senior staff specialists in marketing, finance and IT to frame the intellectual agenda and processes for these activities, they also turn to competent and business-focused HR professionals to provide intellectual and process leadership for people and organizational issues.

Sixth, our research shows that the HR profession as a whole is quickly moving to add greater value through a more strategic focus. At the same time, some HR professionals are not able to live up to the new expectations. In any change effort, there is typically a 20-60-20 grouping. The top 20 percent of individuals asked to change already are doing the work that the change requires. The lower 20 percent will never get there. With training, coaching and support, the other 60 percent can make the move. And we see this majority moving toward, rather than away from, business relevance. They see customers as the real, **external** ones rather than the historical internal ones.

Seventh, being a business partner requires HR professionals to have new knowledge and skills that connect their work directly to the business. Traditionally, HR professionals have tended to focus on negotiating and managing terms and conditions of work and facilitating administrative transactions.

Eighth, the inevitable failures in the application of the business-partner model may stem from both personal and organizational factors:

1. Asking HR professionals who have focused on policies and transactions to do talent and organization audits and massive change efforts may be too great a shift for some.

2. Personal interests and abilities may deter some HR professionals from engaging i

the business-partner role. Their focus on administrative detail may not allow them to embrace the larger and more complicated perspective of the business as a whole.

3. Some HR professionals simply may not know how to proceed. Substantial empirical evidence shows that HR professionals who are provided exposure to such information quickly can apply that information in adding greater value to the business.

4. HR's impact on business may vary by business setting: A particular firm's business conditions may not require talent and organization as keys to success. Under such conditions HR professionals who push for alignment, integration and innovation in talent and organization are less likely to contribute to business success.

5. Some line managers have trouble either accepting the importance of talent and organization or accepting HR professionals as significant contributors to these agendas. This may be because of their having a limited perspective on the changing nature of business or because of past bad experiences with a specific HR professional.

Ninth, there are really few other options. The reality is that the HR professionals must evolve into being the best thinkers in the company about the human and organization side of the business. The human side of the business is a key source of competitive advantage.

Looking Forward: Challenges Ahead

As we look forward, we need clear thinking, effective practices and insightful research. Many of the critics of the business-partner model look at today's problems through yesterday's solutions and wonder why they do not work. The HR business-partner model of the 1990s has changed in recent years to adapt to today's business challenges.

Our firm, the RBL Group, in conjunction with the University of Michigan and a variety of HR professional associations from around the world, has studied the competencies and agendas of HR professionals as business partners for more than 20 years. We recently completed the fifth round of this ongoing global study of HR professionals and developed a clear picture of what business leaders expect from their HR business partners. We project five trends that will continue to evolve the HR field and how it delivers value.

1. There has been steady progress in the HR field as it has moved toward greater strategic understanding and relevance.

HR professionals will increase their knowledge of their companies' wealth-creating activities, become more knowledgeable about internal operations and increase their knowledge of critical external realities such as customer requirements, supplier relations, competitive market structures, domestic and international regulatory issues, globalization and the requirements of capital markets.

With this foundation in business knowledge, they will bring to strategy discussions their personal visions for the future of the business. They will work with their management teams to formulate unique business strategies and develop the org-

anizational capabilities to implement the business strategy and serve as the long-term sources of competitive advantage. They will continually innovate to develop HR practices, polices and processes that link directly into the business strategy and create measurable business results.

2. Companies will continue to require fewer HR professionals to do transactional administrative work.

Newly emerging information and communication technologies will continue to be applied to improve the efficiency of HR administrative work, directly facilitate greater transaction processing at lower costs and indirectly promote efficiencies by allowing the transfer of transactional work to internal service centers or to external outsourcing firms. Nice-to-have but strategically unnecessary HR activities will be eliminated.

3. As business partners, HR professionals will increase their focus on creating value for key external constituents: customers, capital markets, competitors and communities.

- They will do this by directly involving **customers** in the design of HR practices such as performance measurement, reward allocation, training recruitment and promotions. They also will provide linkages to external customers by continually conceptualizing and creating the organizational capabilities that influence the buying habits of external customers: this is what we have called "the HR wallet test."

- HR professionals likewise will become more attuned to the requirements of

capital markets. The recent burgeoning research in finance and economics on intangible assets is emphasizing the increasing importance of human capital assets and HR practices that create and sustain those assets. The investment community has begun accounting for practices such as succession planning, leadership development, corporate culture and executive compensation as ➤

> The intent of the business-partner model is to help HR professionals integrate more thoroughly into business processes and align their day-to-day work with business outcomes.

considerations in buy-or-sell decisions. Companies that are able to create a credible leadership brand are more likely to enjoy P/E ratios above those of their competitors. We have suggested that the new ROI for HR is return on intangibles.

> The reality is that the HR professionals must evolve into being the best thinkers in the company about the human and organization side of the business. The human side of the business is a key source of competitive advantage.

- As HR professionals account for customer and owner requirements in the design and delivery of organizational capability and related HR practices, they will do so with greater awareness of **competitors**. They will recognize that forward-looking and innovative HR practices have relatively little value unless they create greater value than those of their dominant competitors. Internal measures of change must be viewed from the perspective of change relative to external competition.

- A final emerging trend in HR's external focus is the role of HR in representing companies to their **communities** and in accounting for community requirements in their companies' value proposition. The mandate for greater corporate social responsibility (CSR), which originated primarily in Europe, appears to be quickly taking root in North America, China, India and in many countries with emerging economies. Concerns about global warming, air and water pollution, local employment regulations, ethical treatment of indigenous populations, endangered species, and land utilization have moved up the list of corporate priorities. HR departments increasingly are given the mandate to work with

local communities in addressing these complex and important issues.

4. As HR professionals become more effective as business partners, they will become more balanced in their approaches to their work.

In the most recent round of our competency research, we found that effective HR professionals function in the following six roles. If HR professionals fail to function in any of these roles, they significantly detract from their contributions as business partners.

- Credible activists build relationships of trust based on business knowledge and have a point of view not just about HR issues, but about business issues.

- Strategy architects contribute to the development, execution and communication of winning strategies.

- Culture and change stewards support the organization in identifying and facilitating important changes that improve the capabilities of the organization to compete and grow by turning what is known into what is done and linking external firm identity to internal employee actions.

- Talent managers and organizational designers provide important support and counsel in building both individual competencies and organization capability.

- Operational executors do the operational work of HR effectively and cost efficiently, using information systems

and external vendors when appropriate to ensure better, faster and cheaper HR delivery.

- Business allies demonstrate a firm grasp on how the organization operates, makes money and competes.

5. HR business partners—as in other key functional areas—will be expected to base their activities on solid empirical research associated with business results.

Because the best HR practices are emerging from all parts of the world, HR research increasingly will be conducted on a global scale, and will focus on the practices and competencies that result in individual and company performance.

By Way of Summary

Many HR professionals are doing exceptional work. We are continually amazed at the number of hard-working HR professionals and leaders who are serving and being recognized as business partners by their company executives. In thousands of companies around the world, HR professionals are making enormous progress toward delivering business value.

In the future, the ways in which HR professionals will serve as business partners will continue to morph. The bar has been raised, and some HR professionals will—and others will not—make the grade. Those that do will help businesses manage the enormously difficult and exciting challenges of the 21st century.

Dave Ulrich and **Wayne Brockbank** are partners at The RBL Group and professors at the Ross School of Business at the University of Michigan.

perspectives – counterpoints

The Good and the Great: Definable Differences

By Stephen P. Kelner Jr. and Manuel de Miranda, Egon Zehnder International

As Ulrich and Brockbank persuasively argue, the HR business-partner model is not only alive and well, but also thriving. Based on Egon Zehnder International's experience of executing more than 30,000 management appraisals conducted in the past five years, we are in a position to go beyond anecdotal accounts using our model of leadership that encompasses the indispensable competencies that top leaders possess. Of the more than 5,000 executives in the database who are at the C-level, more than 360 are chief human resources officers (CHROs) or the equivalent, representing leading companies in 20 industries on four continents.

An analysis of this data produces some interesting conclusions. About 15 percent of the HR executives rank as "outstanding" on our competency scale and 45 percent rank as "good."

other people to become change leaders and creates an agile culture that continually can adapt to change.

2. **Strategic Orientation:** The second largest differentiator between outstanding HR leaders and good HR executives lies in their ability to make strategic contributions. They don't just carry out one- or two-year plans handed to them by others; they convert larger corporate strategy into appropriate HR plans or, in the very best cases, act as a full partner at the C-level, challenging the strategy and helping redefine it.

3. **Results Orientation:** As Ulrich and Brockbank observe, the results-oriented HR leader has the ability to translate HR actions and metrics into business results. The good leader works to meet or sometimes beat goals while the great leader not only works harder, but works smarter and introduces calculated improvements into the way things are done.

In each of these competencies, the great HR leader ranks a full standard deviation, or

cally insignificant in two of them: results orientation and change leadership.

As we looked for further nuances we discovered some other statistically significant data that raises critical questions for the function. Only one-quarter of all HR executives in our database have had line roles at some point in their careers. All of those who had line experience outscored the remaining three-quarters on every single competency. And here the ex-line HR executives rank staggeringly higher in the areas of strategic orientation and driving results than those HR executives who have had only staff roles.

For the HR professional, there is much to ponder in these data, especially the implications for career development. Acting as a business partner requires specific competencies—not simply experience, but demonstrated behaviors. Developing those competencies may require some departures from the traditional HR career path, and on the part of companies, a rethinking of HR executive assessments. Those who aspire to be CHROs will need to adopt a more proactive style and show a larger appetite for helping shape the business. Incumbent CHROs who want to extend their role as business partners increasingly will position themselves as active participants in business debates and provide their business perspective, not merely the implications for HR.

Ulrich and Brockbank rightly conclude that the ways in which HR leaders serve as business partners will continue to evolve. With a clear understanding of precisely what competencies are required and to what degree, there is no longer any reason that individuals and companies cannot greatly increase their odds of success.

> In the future, the ways in which HR professionals will serve as business partners will continue to morph. The bar has been raised, and some HR professionals will—and others will not—make the grade.

Although an outstanding HR leader is, of course, highly desirable, good HR leaders can make a substantial contribution to a business. Nevertheless, there are significant and definable differences between the great and the good when it comes to the three leadership competencies—the demonstrated behaviors—critical for HR leaders:

1. **Change Leadership:** Both the good and the great have the ability to understand and overcome the barriers to change and to adopt new ways of working; but, at the highest level, the great HR leader induces

higher than the good HR executive, which is, of course, statistically significant. A clear picture of the great HR executive comes into focus: a strategic change leader capable of getting business results and inspiring other people to peak performance.

Perhaps most interestingly, our research shows that the top decile of HR performers have a fair amount in common with our dataset defining great CEOs. For example, with respect to the three leadership competencies discussed here, the difference between the great CEO and the great HR leader is statisti-

Stephen P. Kelner Jr., Ph.D. in motivational psychology, is Global Knowledge Manager for Egon Zehnder International. **Manuel de Miranda**, Ph.D., Cambridge, is head of Energy Practice in Egon Zehnder International's New York office.

part V: building a strategic hr function

Change the Terminology!

By Jerry McGrath, Korn Ferry International

I cringe whenever a candidate declares, "I'm a strategic business partner." It drives me crazy. Why not just say I am a business leader? I have never liked the word partner as it relates to the HR function. It is far too passive and too bland.

This is more than just semantics. The phrase "business partner" suggests a weaker, more subservient role of HR as a starting point. The term does the function a disservice. Does anyone ever hear a chief financial officer referring to himself or herself as a business partner? A head of engineering? A head of sales? IT? I like what Ulrich writes about the activist HR professional, but we need to stop referring to ourselves as partners. "Strategic business partner" sounds canned; and the term rolls off the lips of too many marginal HR professionals. People who don't know what it means overuse it. On the other hand, HR professionals, and people in general, don't say that they are a leader if they do not believe it.

A dictionary definition of partner is "a person associated with another or others in some activity of common interest." The word leader is far more powerful and reflects the true role for the CHRO: "someone who shows the way, by going in advance" and "one who has influence or power." It is high time for HR to rid itself of any submissive vestige.

The portfolio that the CHRO possesses is enormous, exciting and vital to the business. The knowledge and data alone that a CHRO has in his or her realm is a powerful base for leadership. An effective HR leader knows the performance, pay and potential of everyone in the company, from the mailroom to the boardroom. This gives the CHRO the golden opportunity to lead and to be the first among equals in the C-suite. A high-performing CHRO is one member of a senior leadership team that others look to for judgment, counsel and advice—all qualities of a strong business leader.

Shifting our terminology from partner to leader will inspire HR professionals to be more commercial, relevant and effective. The HR leader should feel empowered to weigh in on a vast array of strategic issues. The HR leader should act like a CEO, overlapping with that key role as a thought leader, constantly assessing the HR impacts attributable to gaining market share, increasing sales or making an acquisition.

There are significant and definable differences between the great and the good when it comes to the three leadership competencies—the demonstrated behaviors—critical for HR leaders.

Because I work across industries, I like HR executives/candidates who think like a CEO and set the stage for me in terms of the competition, market share, shareholder value, sales, revenue and so forth of their company. A business leader can do that. Too many so-called strategic business partners can't answer those questions.

Leaders are respected, big and wise. This subtle but significant shift in terminology will do wonders for the self-respect and self-image of human resources professionals. This has been one of the main contributions of Ulrich's writing and teaching through the years.

Jerry McGrath is a senior client partner, Human Resources, at Korn Ferry International.

Critical Roles with New Emphasis

By Claudia Lacy Kelly, Spencer Stuart

There is no question that during the past 10 to 15 years companies have been looking to

their human resources leaders and professionals to adopt a more strategic results-oriented approach to HR, whether they are in charge of corporatewide initiatives, regional or business unit programs, or centers of expertise within the function. And indeed, many HR leaders have acquired the business knowledge and developed the skill sets to position themselves as true business partners.

In recruiting senior human resources leaders for our clients, there is demand for HR executives who are able to participate in discussions on business strategy from both an HR perspective and a shareholder perspective, translating the human capital ramifications of business changes. Increasingly, companies want their HR leaders to be champions of business performance who take a holistic approach to motivating and developing talent and know how to use all the available levers to achieve business objectives. These leaders have a commercial mindset and the influencing skills to partner effectively with business leaders.

Though I largely agree with the trends outlined by Ulrich and Brockbank and their implications for the roles that HR professionals increasingly must play as full business partners in organizations, a few areas require additional comment.

First, human resources executives have a key strategic role in managing compensation. Compensation—in the form of payroll, benefits, incentive programs and pensions—is not only the largest or one of the largest expenses for most companies; it is also one of the most effective levers in linking employee behaviors to the business' strategy and objectives. HR business partners must take the lead in designing compensation programs that reinforce desired behaviors and drive the key objectives of the business.

Recent events have underscored the importance of a well-structured compensation program. In the current environment, more boards and CEOs are looking to their HR executives to reexamine and, in many cases, overhaul compensation practices to achieve a better balance between the organization's short-term, top-line goals and its broader and longer-term business objectives. For example, in the wake of the credit crisis, HR leaders at many financial services firms are examining new compensation formulas meant to ensure that organizations do not reward short-term successes that end up having negative consequences over time.

Second, HR executives serve the interests of capital markets—more specifically, the company's investors—by ensuring that the company remains vigilant in planning for the

response to performance problems or emergency situations.

Despite widespread agreement about the importance of succession planning, it is an area with which many boards struggle. Human resources executives help the board navigate potential obstacles to CEO succession planning by helping define the succession process and keeping ongoing succession planning high on the board's agenda. The most sophisticated organizations have well-established succession planning and talent-development processes encompassing all high-level executives.

While the top HR executive of the past reported exclusively to the CEO, the modern-day head of HR—since the passage of the Sarbanes-Oxley Act—has assumed a fiduciary responsibility to the investor community and the board of directors to ensure that the company is planning for the succession of the company's top leaders.

they are not trained to serve in the business-partner role. This requires companies to be disciplined about exposing HR professionals to the business from very early in their careers; for example, by inviting them to strategic planning meetings, and applying the same talent-development and succession approaches to the HR function that are used to identify and develop other high-potential professionals in the business. HR professionals aspiring to become true business partners must be committed to learning about the business and its issues—pushing to be invited into business and strategy meetings, learning to read the company's financial reports and pursuing a business education. If they do not build an understanding of how the business is planned, developed and executed, HR professionals cannot be effective business partners.

Claudia Lacy Kelly is global practice leader, Human Resources Practice at Spencer Stuart.

> It is high time for HR to rid itself of any subservient vestige…shifting our terminology from partner to leader will inspire HR professionals to be more commercial, relevant and effective.

succession of the CEO, CFO and other critical senior executive roles. A comprehensive, objective and ongoing succession planning process is not merely a good governance practice; an organization's ability to place the right leaders in these top roles has emerged as a key investor concern, directly related to a company's performance and sustainability.

In the case of the CEO, shorter CEO tenures add urgency to succession discussions, as a leadership transition is an issue all boards are likely to confront. Companies must plan for long-term succession needs and be in a position to accelerate a CEO transition in

Third, HR business partners will continue to be more aware of competitors—as well as best-in-class organizations in other business sectors—as part of their efforts to benchmark senior talent. Through competitive talent intelligence, HR leaders can better determine the level of talent within the company relative to other organizations, potentially revealing talent gaps or the need to enhance development plans for key executives.

Finally, for companies to have the HR business partners they need for the future, they must commit to training HR professionals about the business. The truth is HR professionals cannot become business partners if

Additional Hurdles

By Joanna Miller, Russell Reynolds Associates, Inc.

I congratulate Ulrich and Brockbank on an excellent summary of the evolution of the human resources business-partner role, challenges pertaining to the role and future trends as the role continues to evolve in response to changing business needs, demographics and other factors. I have been assessing and recruiting senior human resources professionals for the last 15 years, and it truly is gratifying to see how many organizations have grown in their recognition and reliance on human resources professionals as key strategic resources.

Several points bear further highlighting regarding the challenges facing the new human resources business partner, now relieved of transactional responsibilities. To the authors' eighth point, on personal and ➤

organizational factors leading to failure of the business-partner model, I would add three additional hurdles that frequently need to be overcome:

1. **The fear factor:** Many human resources professionals have built successful careers by focusing on fixing administrative and transactional problems for the business leader(s) they support. In the shift to the new model, they sometimes can be afraid that if their old role is eliminated by moving the more transactional functions to a shared services organization or outsourcing firm, or more recently to an e-resource, they will be left without a visible way to add value and continue to be a hero in the internal client's eyes. Even when the human resources business partner has the motivation, skills and training to make the shift from transaction and process orientation to strategy and results, he or she may still lack the self-confidence and courage to make the leap. One solution to this problem is to seed the organization with strategic business partners who can be role models.

2. **Lack of business acumen:** Through the years, the sought-after competencies in specifications for senior human resources executives increasingly have listed business acumen at the top of the list. A limitation to success in the business-partner role can be a lack of the understanding of key business drivers and financial metrics, and the ability to interpret financial and strategic analytics, let alone understand their link to human resources issues. Companies that encourage or require financial and accounting education for their human resources professionals are headed in the right direction.

3. **Internal competition:** Some companies that have converted to a business-partner model struggle to develop productive collaboration and teamwork between the generalists and the specialists. Human resources business partners can sometimes be reluctant to give up the trusted adviser role they held with business-unit leaders in the past, and sometimes resist the direct contact and involvement of specialists with their internal client. Specialists need superb emotional intelligence, maturity and relationship-building skills to develop the required collaboration. It also helps if they have low ego needs and are willing to work behind the scenes without needing obvious credit.

The incentive to overcome all these obstacles to success comes in the form of the bright future that awaits the effective human resources business partner as senior attract, assess, develop, compensate, promote and retain key line talent across the organization is a powerful contribution. As the talent guru, the HR executive must bring the understanding of how all functions interrelate to drive good outcomes—as any other functional or business leader. But the further expectation is that these HR executives will translate their business savvy into actions that go beyond traditional HR and advance the organization's larger objectives.

A few areas require additional comment: managing compensation, planning for succession, being aware of competitors for talent and training HR professionals about the business.

leaders—including boards of directors—increasingly recognize strategic talent and organizational issues as key business drivers, risks and opportunities.

Joanna Miller is managing director at Russell Reynolds Associates, Inc.

It is Time to Take a Different Seat at the Table

By Lauren Doliva, Heidrick & Struggles

In consulting with business leaders with respect to HR talent, there is no question that Ulrich and Brockbank have captured the key expectations in the six roles they outlined in the challenges ahead. Now that many top executives recognize that talent drives success and are taking ownership for it, they are, in parallel, requiring human resource officers to have broad business competencies to maximize people assets across the enterprise.

Talent management is a step in the right direction. Establishing a holistic system to identify, As a consequence, many executives are putting line leaders into top HR jobs. And clients are insisting that HR professionals have operational or customer-facing experiences. A small but developing trend in recruiting is the request to see candidates from both the line and human resources career paths. The good news for the profession is corporate recognition of the critical need to integrate all aspects of talent management into business goals. The challenge is the size of the pool of business-savvy HR executives who are prepared to effectively use the levers of business, both within and beyond the traditional scope of human resources.

Though the authors estimate that 80 percent of the function is not yet fully prepared to take on the role, the term "HR business partner" already has been widely adopted in the business vernacular. Candidates typically describe themselves as HR business partners and insist they only want to work where the business values HR as such. But just saying it, as Ulrich and Brockbank suggest, does not make it so. And those of us who are trying to help our clients fulfill their HR needs with such talent concur.

he astonishing notion reverberating in this rticle is that the human resource function is ;ill coping with its identity as being part of ne business, so much so as to label its leaders s HR business partners. The HR function is business function. Though it has distinct rofessional responsibilities as does finance, Γ or marketing, the other support functions

Though we can appreciate and value the need for research to validate best practices and approaches, each professional (as does each business person) has an enormous opportunity and obligation to go beyond expectations, to broaden himself or herself as necessary, and to exercise creativity to transform business in the context of this new

However, in many cases, this takes place with little thought about how the new function can best be established and how the individuals themselves need to change for it to be successful. The transition from working in a transactional manner to operating as a strategic business partner within an organization requires new tools and techniques. We have seen and continue to see within HR that it is tempting to revert to familiar activities, which then hamper personal and functional credibility. The change requires skills and confidence to obtain a seat in the boardroom as a strategic partner and as a commercial contributor.

sn't it time to take up the implicit charge of the key oles defined by the authors, and be an innovator and visionary with respect to meeting these challenges? sn't it time to take a different seat at the table?

re not insisting on a similar modifier. Has HR limited its power and influence by this inguistic insistence?

Admittedly, every business is not yet ready to ake advantage of an HR business partner as o well defined by the authors, but it is incumbent on every employee, especially HR, o influence, work and strive to achieve business objectives in the context of the whole while balancing the case for his or her own contribution.

HR grew as a business function out of the need to manage the relationship between management and labor, a critical business issue. Yet after 100 years the profession still seems to be struggling to prove, according to this article, its connection to corporate goals. Are there things, in the language of Jeff Katzenbach, that the function needs to "unlearn" to be able to move ahead?

Ulrich and Brockbank call on the profession to continue to evolve. But should the profession simply settle for evolving in this time of rapid change, economic stress and global complexities? Isn't it time to take up the implicit charge of the key roles defined by the authors, and be an innovator and visionary with respect to meeting these challenges? Isn't it time to take a different seat at the table?

transform business in the context of this new world. It's time for everyone to calculate his or her own ROI and find ways to freshly contribute to the bottom line.

Lauren Doliva is managing partner, Chief Advisor Network at Heidrick & Struggles.

Understanding the Elephant

By Amy A. Titus, BearingPoint

One challenge for HR professionals today is to deliver efficient and reliable HR operations and support. As such, HR professionals also act as business partners and strategic advisers to the senior team.

Organizations are changing the structure of their internal service departments such as HR and finance, forcing them to take a more consultative and strategic role within the company. Executive expectations about what HR delivers have expanded, using concepts such as "employee engagement and commitment to drive productivity," and "combining compensation and other forms of recognition to influence behaviors and level of effort."

HR business partnering is not a new business concept—in fact HR transformation has been a priority for organizations for more than a decade. However, HR transformation in the past has been more theory than reality and has been focused on outsourcing and changing titles. Determining what it actually means to be the HR business partner has been a search for many human resource professionals. Dave Ulrich and Wayne Brockbank address this question by starting with the identification of nine learnings about HR in the business-partner role. They then outline challenges ahead for the field encapsulated in five trends. All points make sense and provide a good source of confirmation and guidance regarding the business-partner role.

What this article does not do is pull together the various items needed to provide a path for how individuals grow into the six roles that the successful business partner plays. For HR practitioners to become commercial contributors, a framework is essential that outlines how to arrive at business acumen, how to lead and facilitate senior leaders, how to attain the ability to influence key people and, finally, how to build credibility and position HR as a valued service in the organization.

The authors, however, immaculately place the elephant on the table. This elephant is critical to understand clearly for those HR practitioners who aspire to be business partners. Some business leaders are not ready and lack the capability to team with human ➤

part V: building a strategic hr function

resources. There also are other businesses that are not organized to value HR and, in some cases, they do not need a strong HR business partner to be successful. In these situations, the proper perspective on the part of the HR professional is required to define success.

This article convincingly outlines the role of the HR business partner during times of economic growth. There is limited guidance for times of recession and crisis. In the current down cycle, the HR business partner has to undertake a new role and assist in identifying the employees and programs that are not priorities and guide the business in how to efficiently make changes and downsize where and as needed. Grasping the organization's new evolving agenda is essential for HR to provide senior leaders with honest feedback about plans for the recession. HR needs to support managers to make tough decisions as well as challenge them to articulate clear messages about the future of the organization. HR business partners have a more critical role than ever before, one that is only partially charted.

Amy A. Titus is managing director, Global Human Resources, at BearingPoint.

gy architects, culture and change stewards, talent managers and organizational designers, operational executors and business allies. Yet successful execution of these roles often relies on competencies not described by the authors.

In my own experience as an HR business partner at all levels, and as sponsor of a project to implement such roles, I have found three high-impact competencies often sought in HR business partners—coach, conscience and catalyst (it is a coincidence that these all begin with "c"). These competencies are necessary for actualizing Ulrich and Brockbank's six roles, and they enhance the likelihood that an HR business partner's contribution will make a real difference. The partner's belief in his or her own efficacy is a key success factor in demonstrating these competencies.

Coach: Leaders often desire critical feedback from HR partners. HR professionals who lead with business acumen can be the trusted mirror in which leaders see themselves and see more clearly the impact of their actions. Skilled

ners help leaders understand the gaps tha employees may perceive between what is sai and what is done. By acting as conscience, H business partners help the organization ope ate more efficiently by avoiding missteps an staying on course around both business an people objectives.

Catalyst: Every responsible leader will agre that managing performance and monitorin engagement levels are critical to managin the business. But it can be hard for them t commit to accomplishing things they know are important in managing people but tak long-term planning and leaders' time t implement. Effective HR business partner link the work of developing an effectiv workforce to strategic business objectives greatly enhancing the likelihood that thi critical work will get done.

Effective HR business partners confidently display the competencies of coach, conscienc and catalyst and proactively assume th responsibility of ensuring their own compe tence as business—as well as HR—leaders.

A small but developing trend in recruiting is the request to see candidates from both the line and from human resources career paths.

Essential Competencies

By Joy Wyatt, Franklin Templeton Investments

In business-partnering models, as explained by Ulrich and Brockbank, HR professionals support organizational strategy by leading with their knowledge of the business, linked to their knowledge of human resources practices. For HR professionals to succeed in this position, they must understand and help to champion the business agenda of their business-unit colleagues, not simply be HR's voice at the table. They also must assume weighty roles that are essential to business-unit success. Ulrich and Brockbank cite these critical roles: credible activists, strate-

HR business partners who are effective coaches and communicators, and whose agendas align with those of leaders, are supportive and credible sources of truth. They help leaders avoid making mistakes and reinforce what they are doing right, thereby saving time and wear and tear on the organization.

Conscience: Leaders often need to be reminded of promises they've made to employees. HR business partners are in a unique position to re-ground leaders in organizational values and guiding principles when they are caught up in the need to meet immediate business needs. The most effective HR business part-

Joy Wyatt is vice president, Human Resources–Organizational Effectiveness at Franklin Templeton Investments.

Lasting Competitive Success

By Cheryl Thomas, Johnson Financial Group

Though it is interesting to review the historical perspective of the business-partner model, I think current and future business allenges create opportunities for even eater differentiation of the HR role from her staff support functions. Only our heres of responsibility offer the chance to uild lasting competitive success.

usiness success always has been about culure, talent and organization capabilities, gardless of whether they were influenced or anaged by an HR professional. Elements of e business-partner model are universal to l staff functions, but the key differentiators r HR are the roles of culture and change ewards, talent managers and organizational esigners. The article's description of five HR rofessional failures in the application of the usiness model makes this point. Yet, all but e fifth failure could be failures of any aff professional.

fail. As we continue to see dramatic changes in political, economic and social environments, the human side of the business is continuing to emerge and enlarge as the key source and differentiator of competitive advantage. Whoever forgets the key impacts of culture, talent and capability is doomed to fail in the marketplace.

As the article aptly points out, the distinguishing characteristic of HR leaders is to be the best thinkers in the company about the human and organization side of the business. This thinking requires knowledge and understanding of the business' vision and strategy, organizational and individual capabilities, and the cultural attributes that best support leveraging these capabilities to achieve strategy. All support-area professionals, whether

tive work may get things done. But if these players are not efficient, or they are not contributing to positive business results, they are not sustainable—competitive pressures will demand change. However, today, and certainly in the future, as businesses have more access to bigger and ever-changing markets, and technology impacts productivity, it is the human element that is the constant in creating and adapting to change.

Best practices are emerging from all parts of the world, and this further supports the growing opportunity for HR professionals to differentiate their roles. Where other functional support areas may apply processes, technologies and systems on a global scale, I believe HR's opportunity is to translate, align and support changes locally, taking into account the uniqueness of individuals and each local organization's strategies, plans and capabilities. We can create competitive advantage for our companies by our knowledge of, unique thinking about, and good stewardship of particular cultures and competencies. The human element is still the most unpredictable and exceptional weapon in the arsenal of each business. **P&S**

---

he transition from working in a transactional manner
o operating as a strategic business partner within an
rganization requires new tools and techniques.

Iowever, when the HR professional or the nterprise as a whole doesn't accept or recogize the importance of culture, talent and rganization capability, then HR has failed to istinguish itself for the value it brings to the usiness, and, very likely, the business will

in HR, finance or IS, are moving toward greater strategic understanding and relevance to the business, and companies will continue to allow fewer professionals—not just in HR—who do not understand and who are not relevant. The transactional, administra-

> **Cheryl Thomas** is senior vice president, Human Resources at Johnson Financial Group, one of *Fortune's* 100 Best Companies to Work For.

learning guide

People & Strategy 32.2 Point Counterpoint:

The HR Business Partner Model:
Past Learnings and Future Challenges

Discovery Questions

- What are we dealing with in our organization today that relates to this content area?

- Understand the essence of the Business Partner model and what needs to change.

- Know the difference between Corporate HR; Embedded HR; HR Specialists and HR Service Centers.

- Recognize the importance of involving the external customer in the design of internal HR processes.

- Understand how HR must play a role in Corporate Social Responsibility.

- Learn the six roles required for effectiveness as an HR Business Partner.

- Articulate the submissive downside of the "Business Partner" term.

Selected Facts

- What new facts that were presented got your attention?

- All staff functions, not just HR, are struggling with how to ensure they contribute.

- There has been steady progress in HR becoming more involved in the business.

- Companies are requiring fewer HR people to do transactional administrative work.

- Companies with a credible leadership brand are more likely to have P/E Ratios higher than those that do not.

- Role requirements for effective HR Business Partners include: Credible Activist; Strategy Architect; Culture and Change Steward; Talent Managers and Organizational Designers; Operational Executors; and Business Allies.

- In a global study of 360 CHROs, only 15% rank as Outstanding and 45% as Good; the key differentiators being Change Leadership; Strategic Orientation; and Results Orientation.

- Great CHROs have these abilities in common with great CEOs: Change Leadership and Results Orientation.

Key Discussion Points

- What were the key points being made in this Point Counterpoint presentation?

- The "human side of business" can be a key source of competitive advantage. How?

- What is "the HR wallet test"? Would our organization pass that test?

- The "new ROI for HR" is Return on Intangibles. Give some examples of that.

- The assessment of the effectiveness of change initiatives must be viewed in comparison to how the competition has also changed to compete more effectively. Do we have examples of that?

- The improper design of compensation incentive systems can motivate what types of negative behaviors?

- In what way is succession planning a legitimate fiduciary responsibility?

Review of Solutions

- Identify 2-3 Big Ideas that are worthy of exploring for our organization.

- How could a focus on Talent and Organizational Capability improve business results?

- How does the 20-60-20 Model relate to our organization and its issues?

- Discuss the individual and organizational reasons that a Business Partner model fails.

- Identify examples where we've used external customer feedback to design internal HR processes.

- How can HR play a greater role in the community via Corporate Social Responsibility?

- Assess what we can do to better meet the role requirements for effective HR Business Partners: Credible Activist; Strategy Architect; Culture and Change Steward; Talent Managers and Organizational Designers; Operational Executors; and Business Allies.

- What can HR leaders do to learn more about the business and financials of the company?

- How can we overcome the following hurdles to becoming an HR Business Partner: The Fear Factor; Lack of Business Acumen; and Internal Competitiveness?

- How do the roles of Coach, Conscience and Catalyst relate to the new HR?

Recommendations Summary

- Identify one thing that we will do differently based on what we learned.

Learning Outcomes

- What one new piece of information did you learn that will be important to you?

Point/Counterpoint

One cannot discuss the role of the CEO without talking about what and how they get paid. Though at HRPS we usually leave that to other professional associations, we know many of our members are involved with issues of executive compensation, from working with boards to determine pay levels to worrying about the impacts of executive pay on employee engagement. In this issue we take two looks at executive pay, here in the Point/Counterpoint and later in an excellent article by Steven Van Putten and Aubrey Bout. This Point/Counterpoint leads with a new way of measuring CEO pay effectiveness by Ross Zimmerman of Exequity, LLC. A diverse group of commentators weigh in on Ross' methodology and recommendations, as well as other key aspects of CEO pay.

POINT

Are You Getting A Bang Out of Your Executive Pay Buck?

Ross Zimmerman
Founding Principal and Senior Attorney
Exequity, LLC
Libertyville, IL

Executive pay is so complex that all parties involved struggle to establish a clean way of discerning whether an executive team is being fairly or extravagantly rewarded. One would think that this would be easier, particularly with the intense focus on the issue from all sides.

Adding to the confusion are the many different ways in which executive pay is disclosed, measured, and critiqued. The press tends to sensationalize executive pay by spotlighting individual extremes, and exacerbating these extremes by adding together the elements of pay that imply the most egregious waste of corporate money. Executive pay critics tend to sniff out the pay practices that they see as most incendiary, and hold the recipients of this largesse up to public ridicule. Companies often anticipate and respond to this dynamic by employing opaque disclosures to throw the critics off the scent.

The government has jumped into the fray with Goliath-sized boots, regulating executive pay from a variety of angles. The regulations have come with mixed results: in some cases, adding clarity through transparency of executive pay disclosures, and in others adding fuel to the fire of escalating pay levels.

Most agree that the governmental actions that have been imposed with the legislative agenda of restricting executive pay—for example, the tax limits on the deductibility of executive pay over one million dollars and the golden parachute excise tax rules—have backfired by provoking companies to make pay changes that have contributed to substantial increases in executive pay. On the other hand, regulations that have focused on the transparency of executive pay (through public disclosure of pay levels and programs) are generally agreed to have helped constrain pay levels.

The jury is still out on the impact of the most recent changes to the proxy disclosure rules. These rules, applicable for the first time in 2007, seek to require companies to provide greater clarity of complex executive pay arrangements. Although the mandated uniformity in tabular and narrative disclosure has enhanced the understandability of many elements of companies' executive pay programs, the sheer volume of the disclosures has frustrated many proxy readers. Further, the reliance on disclosure of accounting charges associated with long-term incentive awards and the blending of disclosures related to various incentive arrangements have muddied the picture for many.

So how does one gain a better insight into whether an executive team is effectively shepherding a company toward enhanced shareholder value? We believe that the best measure of an executive team's effectiveness is the company's executive pay spend—the total value made available to the executives in a given period of time—not a blend of multiyear accounting charges attributed to incentive vehicles together with true dollars delivered, such as is front-lined in the summary compensation table (SCT) of the proxy disclosures. If pay-for-performance is the ultimate benchmark of executive pay effectiveness, then the most pertinent focus is a comparison of the true dollar value made available to executives in relation to the company's increase in total shareholder value.

Just as companies often judge the effectiveness of operational leaders based on the returns generated versus the investment in creating those returns, we believe that top executives should be evaluated by comparing their contribution to shareholder value in light of the money spent paying the executives. We at Exequity call this metric the company's "return on executives," or ROX, for short.

An Overview of the ROX Index

At the core of the ROX index is a summation of value made available to executives by the company. Some elements of pay are easy to tally in this regard: base pay, bonuses earned, and long-term incentives that are earned during the test period. We add these into the mix regardless of whether the amounts are deferred, as our focus is the value credited to executives within the period.

In the case of equity-based awards, we include two aspects of incentive value:

1. The actual value reaped by an executive during the period. In the case of stock options, this value consists of in-the-money gains associated with options that are exercised during the period. In the case of restricted stock and performance shares, this is the full value of awards that vested during the period.
2. To this we add the appreciation (or depreciation) in value attributable to awards that were not exercised (in the case of options) or did not vest (in the case of restricted stock and performance shares) during the period.

This focus on actual value delivered (and/or accruing) to executives highlights the true value transfer from the company's shareholders to executives. This represents an important distinction from the disclosures in the summary compensation table of the proxy, as the SCT showcases the accounting charge attributable to all unvested long-term incentives that are outstanding (not just those that delivered actual value to the executives). By focusing on the accounting charge, the disclosure fails to capture true dollar value transferred to the executives, and instead portrays the *expected* value (often measured solely at the grant of the award) accruing to the executives.

Other tables in the proxy reveal the true value received by the executives during the year (e.g., the "Options Exercised and Stock Vested" table), but the reader is required to extract these disclosures and add them to the base pay and incentive numbers provided elsewhere in the proxy. In truth, the new proxy rules obscure one of the most important contributors to executive pay: the annual appreciation in unexercised options held by executives. In order to make sense out of option appreciation the proxy reader is required to make a number of calculations on all outstanding option tranches and compare these calculations to similar math applied to options outstanding in the prior year.

We believe that the executive pay spend is best understood by deriving the value that becomes available to an executive in a given period, where that value was not paid-for by the executive. This truly represents the wealth accumulation to the executive and the corresponding opportunity cost incurred by the company in directing money to executives as compensation instead of to shareholders as stock price gains or dividends.

In our view, determining the total company spend on the executive team is half the battle in understanding whether the company is getting the best bang for its executive pay buck. The other half of the equation is the company value created (or destroyed) under the executive team's stewardship. This one is easy: We merely measure the total shareholder return during the period, that is, the summation of stock price appreciation and dividends distributed during the measurement period (see Exhibit 1).

The ROX score of a company helps provide a comparative metric that can be used to evaluate the efficiency of a company's cost of delivering executive pay, through all pay vehicles offered. Just as a company's return on capital can be used to gain a better understanding of returns in relation to investment in capital, ROX can be used to gain insight into the return on the company's investment in its leaders.

We believe that the ROX score of an executive team is a better metric than a narrow focus on sheer amount of pay delivered to executives. By comparing total value accruing to executives in relation to increases in company value, we can assess whether the company's results have merited the pay.

Everyone understands that if a company wants to secure the services of an executive team that has the potential to perform like a Mercedes Benz, it cannot spend as if it were buying a Yugo. The ROX index provides a convenient barometer to determine whether the executive team the company has cultivated is justifying the company's investment through its executive pay programs.

In addition to helping the compensation committee calibrate pay levels versus its peers and establish the right mix of pay, the ROX score can help provide further insight for making incentive award decisions in the context of the executive team's

EXHIBIT 1

Determination of ROX Score

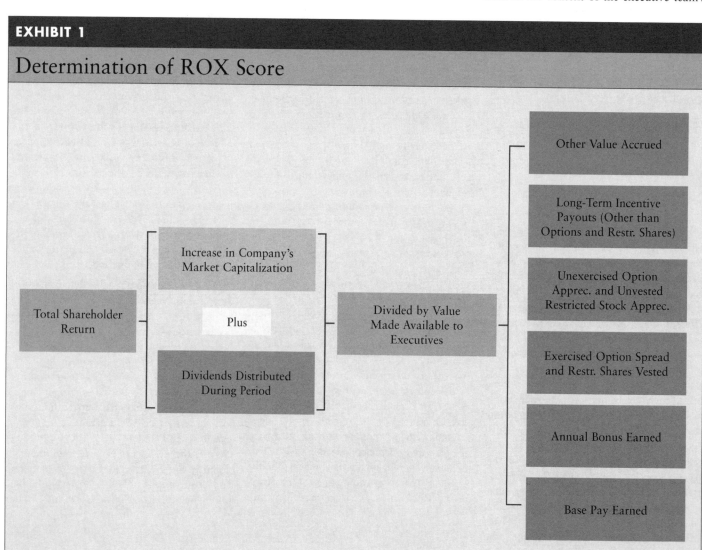

EXHIBIT 2

ROX Scores for Companies of Varying Sizes

Company Size	Highest CEO ROX Score	Median CEO ROX Score	Lowest CEO ROX Score
Large Cap	$24,665	$633	$119
Mid Cap	$2,586	$73	$13
Small Cap	$659	$66	$17

overall wealth accumulation. There have been increasing calls for executives' wealth accumulation to be incorporated into the determination of incentive award design and pay levels. By evaluating an executive team's past ROX performance, the committee can make judgments about the past effectiveness of reward structures, and can recalibrate the pay mix and design to better correlate pay delivery and company performance.

A strong ROX score also provides support for a company that has been criticized for the overall pay delivered to its executive team. One of the most surprising findings from Exequity's review of ROX scores is that some of the highest returns for each dollar of executive pay delivered were garnered by companies whose top executives have been heavily criticized for executive pay bloat. In our view, the best defense to the allegation that executives have been overpaid is evidence that the executive team has delivered greater company value for each dollar spent on executive pay than have executive teams that received lower overall pay.

Findings of Exequity's Review of ROX Scores of Leading Companies

Exequity reviewed the executive pay packages and company performance of the top 20 S&P companies, based on 2007 proxy filings. The results of the study were surprising in that many companies that received sharp criticism for their executive pay practices actually delivered far better returns on their executive pay spend than did companies that received acclaim for the moderation of their executive pay packages. Before we present the findings of the ROX study, a couple of cautions are important:

1. The ROX scores represent only one year of pay and company performance (2006, as reflected in 2007 proxies). This one-year focus was necessary because the

new proxy rules first applied in 2007, so earlier-year comparisons are made challenging by the different disclosure frameworks in prior years. As additional proxy years unfold, multiyear ROX performance can be monitored so that the current relationships between executive pay and company performance can be reviewed in a broader context.

2. ROX scores are generally positively correlated with company size. It is important to make comparisons between companies of similar size. Similarly, given the unique market forces that can affect companies within a specific industry sector, it is important to exercise caution in drawing conclusions when comparing companies in different industries.

The correlation between company size and shareholder returns under an executive team is demonstrated by the comparative ROX scores of the CEOs of S&P large cap, mid cap, and small cap companies (the numbers in Exhibit 2 represent the total shareholder value gains for each dollar spent on the CEO's pay during the year).

The ROX scores of executive teams presiding over the 20 largest S&P 500 companies are noted in Exhibit 3 (the ROX scores appearing in Exhibit 3 reflect the return on the executive pay delivered to all of the top five executives, as opposed to the CEO-only ROX scores in Exhibit 2).

We find it interesting that three of the companies that received some of the heaviest criticism in 2007 for their executive pay practices (Pfizer, ExxonMobil, and Verizon) actually delivered some of the greatest returns on their executive pay spend. This indicates to us that a narrow focus on amount of pay alone can lead to questionable conclusions about the appropriateness of a company's executive pay program. The compensation committees that preside over executive pay programs that become the subject of public

attack may also have at their disposal effective (and easily determined) defenses against these criticisms.

Summary

The ROX index provides companies with a useful tool in evaluating the performance of the top executive team in relation to the total value made available to executives. Assessing executive performance in the context of total value delivered to the executive team adds insight into the cost efficiency of achieving shareholder value gains. The focus on executive pay efficiency yields some interesting results when applied to companies that have been criticized for the sheer volume of pay delivered to their executives.

Considering a ROX-based pay link not only for the top executive team but also for directors has merit. Introducing a focus on pay efficiency would result in executive and director pay that is positively correlated with both shareholder returns and containment of executive pay costs. In cases in which the ROX index is not used as part of the incentive structure, the index can be used as an apples-to-apples benchmark to help compare a company's executive pay costs and share performance to those of the company's competitors.

COUNTERPOINT

Getting Beyond Share Price: The Truer Measure of Corporate Value

Donald P. Delves
President and Founder
The Delves Group
An Independent Executive Compensation
Consulting Firm
Chicago IL
and
Author
Stock Options and the New Rules of Corporate Accountability

Reading Ross Zimmerman's article, "Are You Getting A Bang Out of Your Executive Pay Buck?," I found several points of common ground: the need for better methods to compare total executive pay to total performance; examining the total cost of management instead of limiting ourselves to how individual executives are paid; and the courage to rank companies according to how much they pay relative to how much performance they generate. I also find his assessment of how to calculate total

EXHIBIT 3

ROX Scores for Top 20 S&P Companies in 2006

Company	Total FY '06 Comp from Summary Comp Table ($M)	Total "Real" Dollar Comp Cost (Value Made Available to Executives)	TSR in 2006 (%)	Increase in Total Shareholder Value ($B)	ROX Score (Shareholder Value Increase for Each Executive Comp Dollar)
Pfizer	$37	$28	15%	$26	922
Google	$10	$15	11%	$14	904
ExxonMobil	$45	$166	39%	$130	782
Verizon	$58	$49	34%	$30	610
Coca-Cola	$64	$48	23%	$22	451
IBM	$49	$57	20%	$25	438
GE	$73	$84	9%	$34	405
Citigroup	$79	$132	19%	$46	347
AT&T	$123	$156	52%	$50	321
Chevron	$65	$139	34%	$42	299
Bank of America	$71	$146	21%	$43	296
Johnson & Johnson	$65	$82	12%	$22	269
AIG	$63	$56	6%	$11	191
Altria	$96	$160	19%	$30	188
JP Morgan Chase	$148	$203	25%	$35	172
Wachovia	$52	$67	12%	$10	156
Wal-Mart	$67	$63	5%	$9	151
Wells Fargo	$60	$150	17%	$18	118
Conoco Phillips	$70	$264	26%	$24	92
Intel	$34	$(32)	-17%	$(25)	N/A

Notes

1. Shareholder value created is derived by taking the average common shares outstanding during the period and multiplying that by the share price at the beginning of the period, further multiplied by the total shareholder return during the period.
2. The "real" dollar cost of the executive team is derived by taking the CEO, CFO, and the next three most highly paid executives who were employed at the end of the most recent fiscal year. Their "real" compensation cost is derived by taking their total compensation from the summary compensation table with the following adjustments: (i) stock options are included based on the increase/decrease in spread value year-over-year plus gains recognized at exercise; (ii) restricted stock is included based on the increase/decrease in value year-over-year plus the value of shares vested during the year; and (iii) performance shares are included if earned during the year.

compensation to be accurate and sensible.

Where we part company, however, is the use of annual total shareholder return as the ultimate measure of a management team's performance. Focusing solely on short-term stock performance, to me, is anachronistic and will only lead us to repeat the sins of the past. Over-emphasis on stock performance is what led us to multiple bubbles in the market and to excessive risk-taking by companies to boost their share prices, which puts the health of the corporation and job security for employees in jeopardy.

The movement of stock price, in both directions, is only partly determined by the performance of a company and the actions of its management team. A host of other factors, from the overall health (or malaise) of the market to industry trends to commodity price swings, have dramatic effects on stock performance, especially over periods as short as one year. For example, Zimmerman's ROX analysis pinpoints Exxon as a company with one of the highest "ROX scores" because its market value increased so much relative to how much executive pay increased. With oil prices at over $100 a barrel, one can argue that management had little to do with the company's huge increase in market value (which means they should have a high ROX score—even a medium-level ROX score would probably mean they had reaped too much benefit from a windfall they did not produce).

Paying-for-performance means rewarding management for those things over which it does have direct control; such as profitability, margins, return on capital, growth, and the overall well-being of the enterprise. Companies that keep putting good numbers on the boards in a consistent and reliable way deserve notice—and their management teams should be well compensated for their efforts.

My view of stock performance as an inferior arbiter of corporate performance was crystallized when I interviewed former Federal Reserve Chairman Paul Volcker for my book, *Stock Options & The New Rules of Corporate Accountability*. In our discussion, Mr. Volcker challenged the prevailing view about stock performance with his comments about the role of the stock market, which ultimately is to provide a source of capital. He further stated, "There are a lot more important things to the company than the day-to-day movement of the stock price."

In recent decades, Fortune 500 companies not only have stopped using the market for capital, but on a net basis they have bought back more shares than they have issued. So if corporations are not using the market to raise money, why are they so interested in stock price? (A good guess would be high levels of stock-based compensation.)

Using stock price as a proxy for how well the company is serving all its stakeholders—including shareholders, customers, employees, and the society in general—can be short-sighted. As Mr. Volcker explained, "The purpose of the company is really to provide goods and services at the best possible price, at the highest level of productivity, and in a way that serves society and communities. That is the purpose of the company. The stock is just the way that we get there."

That interview caused me to rethink the nature of what we are measuring and paying for with executive compensation. Clearly, it should not be share price appreciation (and dividends) alone. I favor a more balanced approach. This includes measuring those factors mentioned earlier: consistent cash flow, return on capital, margin improvement, and growth; however, these tangible components of corporate performance ultimately involve paying for the past. Equally important in today's competitive environment is for companies to pay for future growth by way of innovation, new product development, building a quality management team, implementing a great succession plan, and developing employees.

Admittedly these are less tangible aspects of performance, but we need to do a better job of quantifying and paying for them in order to build stable companies that create sustainable long-term value. Companies that can balance consistently strong and stable financial performance with innovation, succession planning, and employee development will produce long-term value for shareholders, employees, customers, and communities.

A European View

Michelle Holmes
Owner
M Rewarding
A Total Compensation and Executive
Compensation Consultancy Company
Zurich, Switzerland

"Executive pay is complex" begins Mr. Zimmerman in his article "Are You Getting A Bang Out of Your Executive Pay Buck?" Executive pay is also cultural and the information available, the way it is presented, and the ability for it to be understood are as much, if not more, a factor of geography, culture, and psychology as they are of accounting and mathematical formulas.

The establishment of a return on executives (ROX) score is an interesting approach, and, although the potential distortion of looking at a one-year time horizon is noted, it could have its merits once tested on a multiyear period. The article states the importance of making comparisons between companies of similar size and industry sector, but what about geography? Could the ROX score be applied globally?

From a European perspective, large, publicly quoted companies are operating more globally, are managed by ever-diversified executive teams, and have compensation committees whose members are from a variety of geographic and cultural backgrounds; therefore, the ability to evaluate and compare proxy information in a similar manner on a global basis will surely become increasingly important. Comparisons can be made to the increasing prevalence of relative as well as absolute performance measures such as total shareholder return (TSR) as criteria for performance-based long-term awards. Relative performance against a defined peer group can factor in size, industry sector, and geography.

Take a specific example. What if I, as an investor, an executive, or a member of a compensation committee, wanted to compare the "bang for the buck" of a large US-based financial services organization with that of a similarly sized Swiss-based financial services organization? Although there is clearly a global trend toward increasing transparency on executive pay disclosure, some jurisdictions are leading the way while others are very much in the stages of infancy. The difficulty is that legislation that determines the amount and type of disclosures required on executive pay is regulated at a national level and therefore is typically reflective of that country's cultural state of readiness to open up the Pandora's Box of compensation.

Across Europe, there is no commonality of approach despite the European Union (EU) Commission's having issued in 2004 a recommendation for "fostering an appropriate regime for the remuneration of directors of listed companies." Although the EU Commission closely monitors how its recommendations are being applied, they are legally nonbinding for member states. In the United Kingdom, disclosure requirements on executive compensation are comprehensive and covered by a mix of statutory requirements, stock exchange regulations, and institutional investor guidelines. In Germany, listed companies were required as of 2006 to disclose the individual components of remuneration paid to the members of the executive board on an individual basis. An opt-out clause can apply, however, when at least a three-quarter majority of shareholders agrees to disclose only the remuneration to the executive board members on an aggregate basis, and the ability to apply the opt-out clause can continue for a maximum of five years.

In Switzerland, the increased public attention on executive compensation practices and levels has contributed towards a revision to the Swiss Code of Obligations through the implementation of the new Transparency Act as of January 1, 2007. This requires individual disclosures by name of the total compensation for each member of the board of directors as well as that accorded to the highest paid member of the executive board.

The biggest challenge facing both Swiss and German quoted companies is the move from aggregate to individual disclosures on executive pay. This is a huge cultural shift. Switzerland is renowned for its banking and financial services industries, and banking secrecy is a reality not a myth. In a culture of nontransparency it is not surprising that all of the research done on degree of readiness to comply with these new disclosure requirements would indicate that the majority of quoted companies in Switzerland are not.

It is, however, just a question of time. The intense focus that has come to bear on US companies, particularly from the press, is building in Switzerland. The key now is to take the opportunity to plan proactively rather than react defensively and get a company ready, before the inevitable opening of Pandora's Box.

This Approach Deserves More Research

Michael Schuster
Professor Emeritus
Syracuse University
and Professor of Management
United States Coast Guard Academy

Mr. Zimmerman is to be congratulated for his thought-provoking contribution to executive pay. He offers a novel way of evaluating the overall compensation of America's corporate leadership. As no one paper or theory is going to settle this complex issue, several aspects of his analysis—both good and bad—are worth considering.

Several salient points raised deserve to be underscored:

1. The focus on the executive team rather than just the CEO suggests a fruitful area of investigation. Although the press is subsumed with the sensationalism of some executive pay packages, thoughtful students of this subject may find consideration of the compensation of the leadership team an interesting area for consideration and research.

2. Executive team turnover deserves more attention than it is commonly given by the critics. Zimmerman rightly points out that the costs of severance for poor performance or inadequate cultural fit, as well as the cost of acquisition of talent, are significant. We would like to hear more of his thoughts in solving for that.

3. Director compensation should be tied to executive stability, according to Zimmerman. We agree; however, if there are long-term incentives to improve executive continuity, they must be paid out only when continuity equals business performance.

4. Zimmerman demonstrates the greater

contribution of performance units/shares as providing enhanced incentive value in his sample. Performance units are shares of stock delivered to executives when corporate goals are achieved, such as earnings per share. Zimmerman contrasts this with stock options, wherein the executive has the right to purchase (exercise) the company's stock at the granted price by a defined expiration date. When stock prices increase in value, options add to executive wealth; declines make options worthless. Thus, performance shares are more valuable. More importantly, from my perspective, because performance units can be used when targets are achieved, they potentially can be deployed to enhance the effectiveness of a balanced scorecard by allowing metrics (e.g., diversity or sustainability) beyond earnings.

Look at annual performance a bit closer. I attempted to work with the ROX model using two of the top companies. A comparison of Exxon and Pfizer is shown in Exhibit 4 (including an additional year). For simplicity it excludes dividends (part of the ROX model) and shares outstanding, which would be used to calculate the change in market capitalization.

Although the return on shareholder value for each executive compensation dollar was higher at Pfizer than Exxon, as an Exxon shareholder I felt a lot better about my return than I suspect most Pfizer shareholders did. The next year's results (2007) speak for themselves; however, pure stock price (i.e., shareholder value) does not capture the details of how results were achieved or not achieved. In Pfizer's case, the removal of a high profile drug in development and a questionable pipeline suggest difficulties beyond the one-year timeframe that Zimmerman suggests as appropriate. At Exxon,

EXHIBIT 4

Year Over Year Change in Share Price: Pfizer vs. ExxonMobil

	Exxon	*% Change*	*Pfizer*	% Change
12/30/2005	56.17		23.32	
12/29/2006	76.63	36.43%	25.90	11.06%
12/31/2007	93.69	22.26%	22.73	-12.24%

directors will need to isolate the stewardship of the executive team in a volatile market from the increase in shareholder wealth derived from speculation, the terrorism premium, and a higher market multiple.

Zimmerman's model is useful, but represents only the first step in what would have to be an exhaustive study combining multiple years of data, a larger sample of companies, and sufficiently diverse economic conditions that better test its predictive value. Further, this approach would gain considerably more credibility if it was evaluated by university researchers, whose research design, statistical competencies, and absence of economic motive could be deployed.

Compensation: One of Many Critical Factors in Executive Effectiveness

Douglas R. MacGray, J.D., C.F.P.®
Senior Vice President of Financial Planning
EGE Advisors, Ltd.
King of Prussia, PA

A goal of a corporate board is to pay executives as much as is necessary, but not more, to ensure that an executive team is in place that will deliver appropriate shareholder value. Mr. Zimmerman provides an important contribution to this overall discussion. Clearly, data is needed to measure the performance of the board in meeting this goal. Mr. Zimmerman's ROX Index serves to provide a helpful method of comparing a common data point for various corporations. In my view, boards should avoid a narrow focus on an economic metric when they assess the effectiveness of executive pay. Such a singular focus actually can be detrimental to maximizing the value of dollars spent in compensating executives.

Corporations can make more effective use of their executive dollars if they:

1. Ensure that the executive clearly understands the specific elements of the value of his or her compensation package;
2. Connect compensation directly to expected performance; and
3. Focus more effectively on the nonfinancial aspects of motivating and retaining key talent.

In my experience, top executives typically have surprisingly little understanding of the value of the various components of their compensation. Many executives have an overall sense as to the magnitude and the "fairness" of the compensation, but they do not have a detailed grasp of the various components, how they work, or how to maximize their value. When I first meet with an executive, it is common for him to admit to being embarrassed by a lack of understanding of various components of his compensation.

With the exception of some CEOs, executives rarely speak as though their future compensation depends on their personal effectiveness. They often speak in terms of doing better if their division has a good year or if the overall economy causes their stock price to increase.

If the executive does not understand her compensation and benefits, or critical components concerning them, and if she does not see a connection between her behavior and her incentive-based pay, how can such compensation and benefits possibly be effectively motivating or retaining the executive?

Compensation is just one of many factors determining whether an executive team will perform effectively. Nonfinancial factors motivating an executive team include:

1. Leadership that the executive respects;
2. Crystal clear corporate vision, mission, values, and key priorities;
3. Opportunities to shape the corporation's priorities;
4. Obvious and direct link of the executive's contributions to the corporation's ability to meet its vision and priorities;
5. Frequent feedback, in the form of public recognition and private correction—by financial and nonfinancial methods—regarding the executive's performance against the key priorities;
6. Support in tough times;
7. Positive overall work environment; and
8. Freedom to make prudent mistakes.

Financially, executives want to be compensated in a manner that allows them to achieve their personal financial objectives, and they want to feel that the corporation is treating them fairly.

Compensation is one of many critical factors, albeit the one most easily quantified. If corporations focus on the financial aspect of executive pay only, and not on other facets of what it takes to build and retain a talented team, then the financial cost becomes enormous. The cost to retain an executive who is working for a CEO she does not respect is expensive. Similarly, if the executive is working for a corporate enterprise to whose mission and values he does not subscribe, it will be costly to retain that executive.

One of the most respected business researchers of our day, Jim Collins, asserts that how you compensate executives has little to do with the success of the enterprise. Mr. Zimmerman supports this notion when he states: "a narrow focus on amount of pay alone can lead to questionable conclusions about the appropriateness of a company's executive pay program."

Companies need to work harder at connecting individual behavior and future pay effectively, and in communicating the intricacies of the various forms of compensation and benefits awarded the executive. In addition, the enterprise needs to create an atmosphere in which the noneconomic factors are closer to optimal. If closer attention is paid to these areas, it may be less expensive to motivate and retain key executive talent, and its overall ROX index score will improve.

Be the Sixth Highest Paid Executive!

Paul Kirincic
Executive Vice President, Human Resources
McKesson Corporation
San Francisco, CA

Although the ROX index provides companies with a useful tool to understand top executives' pay, it is only a tool . . . one of many that can be useful. The goal of any executive compensation tool, such as ROX, should be commended when it helps compare "apples to apples." Today, the summary compensation table, even with its faults, makes a credible effort to do just that. It might include accounting values, but the end result is more transparency than we have experienced in the recent past and is no more complex than an income statement or a balance sheet is.

As an EVP of HR at a Fortune 20 company and a board member of a publicly traded retail company (and member of the compensation committee), my biggest concern is putting the compensation practice in the proper context within the marketplace in which we compete for talent. The financial health of the company, the general health of the economy, the industry in which it competes, the impact of the true competitors upon the industry, and many more factors, affect the performance of the company and the fit for executive pay. Has the company been a strong or weak performer within its industry? Is it in a turnaround? Is the industry going through fundamental economic change? What is the track record of the top ➤

management team? Was a substantial change in top leadership necessary? Is there a strong bench in place? Does the compensation decision-making process include an external compensation consultant, an outside legal counsel, and a competent internal executive compensation department? Does the company have a realistic, achievable strategy upon which to base its compensation practice? At the heart of the compensation practice, is the practice rewarding measurable, fact-based performance, performance that is crucial to the long-term financial health of the company?

The answers to these questions need to come together in a smart and candid story. That story should be told in the compensation discussion and analysis section of the proxy. If the story hangs together, is logical and authentic, constituents will be open-minded. What might make no sense for one company may make perfect sense for another. Some measures might be chosen in a particular year that seem odd, but are crucial to the long-term success of the company. That dilemma must be faced with courage. Sometimes, success cannot be driven in one year. Sometimes, decisions are made that will only show results in periods longer than a year. Look at pay levels in start-ups, for instance. They must be made to ensure the success of the company . . . long term. Our focus on quarterly or annual results sometimes negatively affects compensation decision-making.

Lastly, a company might quiet some critics by using a tool like ROX, but fail to answer "hot button" compensation issues like change-in-control pay. This is another important compensation lever not addressed by ROX. What if it is in the best interest of the company and its shareholders to sell it, either to another company or to private investors? How should pay influence shareholder interests in those complex decisions? The answer should seem obvious enough, but how should the top team's personal compensation (and futures) enter into their thinking? Should compensation committees take personal financial concerns out of the equation entirely? How many good deals are lost and how many bad ones get done because of individual incentives?

With regard to director pay, I believe directors are the true stewards of the corporation. Too much short-term pay-for-performance could also result in selling the long term for the short term. Although a ROX tool might alleviate some concerns, it cannot address all the important compensation questions we face today.

As a tool, ROX is one more useful model. But, do not look for these tools to tell the whole story. Context, characterizing the strategy over a longer period—and painting an accurate picture of an industry undergoing subtle or obvious change—can provide the insight in which important compensation decisions are made. In the end, the shareholders will decide if the story hangs together. If it doesn't, they will take their investment to a company whose story does.

The bottom line on all this? Be the sixth highest paid executive in the company and you will never have to explain your compensation to anyone, including your wife—or husband.

A Matter of Optics

Chuck Csizmar
Principal
CMC Compensation Group
Apopka, FL

Who are they, those who question the pay-for-performance credentials of executive pay? Every spring, like daffodils popping through the warming ground, investigative articles appear challenging the validity of how the executive suite is rewarded. Critical commentaries by notable compensation experts, as well as a financial analyst here and there, will question whether job performance has warranted the amount of financial rewards reported in proxy statements.

What follows is usually a series of back-and-forth speeches and written pieces both criticizing and defending the logic of the executive reward process; however, those who press their divergent viewpoints seem unable to reach consensus on an equitable process, so next year the cycle of debate repeats itself. Such has been the case for years.

In my mind, the proverbial "man in the street" or "court of public opinion" is what truly matters. If you take the point that it is the general public who needs to be convinced that our corporate leadership is not unfairly gorging itself on financial largesse like hogs at a feed trough, then the article touting the advantages of a "return on executives" (ROX) falls disappointingly flat.

Unfortunately it is not the negative impressions of the general population that are being addressed by the ROX article, but instead a complex argument is presented supporting those who are being challenged, the executive leadership themselves. This is a circle-the-wagons article crafted to refute challenges to the current executive reward process by providing a technical defense that would not be understood by that same general population.

A CEO I admire and respect once told me, it's a matter of optics: The present system of determining executive suite reward *looks bad* to the general public. No amount of explanatory formulae or charts and graphs is going to change that impression; the more complex the defense, the more skepticism that will be generated.

Another senior executive cautioned that if I could not make my point on a single sheet of paper, including a lot of white space, then my arguments would not convince him. In other words, keep it simple, keep it clear, and keep it brief.

That has not happened here.

The ROX system is presented as a formulaic methodology that can be utilized through consultant intervention by corporate leadership to refute their critics; however, even as the ROX calculations try to make their point, the wider audience will remain unconvinced, so how has the argument been advanced? The reward system will still *look bad*.

Viewed in its entirety, the article presents an apologist viewpoint for current reward practices. Criticisms are only generally mentioned, without specificity, and the press and critics are considered biased and uninformed in their attempts to sensationalize individual extremes. Broad and unsupported statements ("most commentators" and "everyone understands") tend to offer up generalized assumptions cynically in support of a point of view. This is not dissimilar to an orator's working an audience to nod their heads repeatedly in advance of the controversial message point.

I like the idea of measuring performance to gauge the amount of reward. Who can argue with that? But the process being described here is flawed by its complexity, by its inability to explain itself in laymen's terms, and by an apparent sleight of hand (the author says the system works, but with "a couple of cautions") for the casual observer.

While holding up the ROX index as a useful tool to measure executive performance, there are several disturbing acknowledgements that would suggest the data "could" be skewed ("one year ROX scores can be distorted" and the data set "is too limited to support firm conclusions").

Even as an apologist for executive pay determinants, the author makes no mention of "how high is up" or how much is "enough" reward. Given that for similar performance nonexecutives receive considerably less, it is surprising that this disconnect was ignored. A large portion of the *looks bad* environment is the "amount" of the reward. Should those on "mahogany row" have parameters to their reward, like the rest of the population? This key issue is not addressed.

The problem connecting a pay-for-performance concept with examples of executive pay excesses is an optical one: It looks bad! Attempts to rationalize the practice with complex terms, charts, and theorem will not convince anyone outside of the board room. The way to change that negative impression is to challenge the convoluted methods that executives use to rationalize their reward structures. The general population (not the financial analysts, proxy readers, or specialists) wants to see a direct cause and effect (simple, clear, and brief), as that is how they are rewarded in their own lives.

Nice Idea, but Hard to Apply in Practice

Eric Hosken
Client Partner
Executive Compensation Advisors
(A Korn/Ferry Company)
New York, NY

Wouldn't it be great if the assessment of the effectiveness of an executive compensation program could be reduced to a single measure providing the equivalent of a report card grade for each company's program? Executive compensation is at times overwhelmingly complex and any effort to simplify its evaluation is to be applauded. As we have seen from the enhanced compensation disclosures under the revised rules, more information does not always enhance understanding and can actually further confuse an already complicated issue.

In his article, "Are You Getting A Bang Out of Your Executive Pay Buck?," Ross Zimmerman proposes such a measure. He calls the measure the "return on executives," or ROX for short, and defines it as the total value made available to executives in a given period of time relative to the company's increase in total shareholder value.

Is ROX the hoped for measure that will simplify our understanding of the effectiveness of executive compensation programs?

Unfortunately, it is not that simple. In theory, ROX is a potentially useful input in assessing the effectiveness of a company's compensation program, but there are a number of practical challenges to its implementation.

The underlying rationale for ROX as a measure is promising. All else being equal, a company that pays its executives $100 million over a period of time and increases shareholder value by $10 billion will likely feel it get a better bang for their buck than a company that pays its executives $100 million over the same period of time and only increases shareholder value by $1 billion; however, there are a few fundamental problems with the measure:

1. Company scale;
2. Timing of measurement; and
3. Differences in company circumstances.

Company Scale

As Ross Zimmerman mentions in his article, "ROX scores are generally positively correlated with company size." This poses a problem for using this measure as a basis to compare companies that are not very close to one another in terms of market capitalization at the beginning of the measurement period. The reason for this is that pay levels do not increase on a one-to-one basis with a company's market capitalization (i.e., executives at a $10 billion company are not necessarily paid twice as much as executives at a $5 billion company). Instead, pay levels tend to increase less than proportionately with a company's market cap. Unless pay levels increase proportionately with market cap, ROX scores will generally be better for companies with higher market capitalization. For example, if the management team of a $1 billion dollar market cap company was paid $10 million for doubling its market value to $2 billion, its ROX score would be 100 ($1 billion/$10 million), even though its shareholder return was 100 percent. By comparison, the management team of a $2 billion company that is paid $10 million for increasing its market value to $3 billion will also have an ROX score of 100, even though its shareholder return was 50 percent.

Timing of Measurement

Conventional wisdom is that executive compensation should focus on long-term performance, rather than short-term swings in company performance. As a result, for ROX to be a useful measure in evaluating compensation programs, it needs to be

measured over the long-term. This adds complexity to calculating the ROX score and in using it for relative comparisons. Over a long period of time, many things can change that complicate relative comparisons (e.g., changes in management teams, different industry economic cycles, and different timing of long-term incentive grants/option exercises). Depending on the arbitrary start date and end date of the ROX measurement period, very different results for the ROX score will likely be obtained. To be sure that a program was working well on the basis of ROX, the ROX score would have to be analyzed over multiple time periods for nearly identical companies. This sensitivity to timing limits its practical utility as a measure.

Differences in Company Circumstances

Another challenge in using ROX is that different companies face different circumstances. Consider two hypothetical companies as an example. Company A is in a declining industry in which relatively flat shareholder returns represent remarkable management performance. Company A has not created any shareholder value over the last five years, but its industry peers have lost half of their market value over the same five years. Company B is in a booming industry. Its annual shareholder return has been 15 percent per year over the last five years, above the broader market average of 10 percent per year for that same period of time. Company B's most direct industry competitors have provided a 30 percent shareholder return over the last five years. Relative to its industry, Company A's performance is better than that of Company B relative to its own industry; however, Company B's ROX score will be higher than that of Company A.

Conclusion

ROX is a nice idea in theory that is hard to apply in practice. Unless two companies are nearly identical in terms of the following company factors: market capitalization, industry, growth prospects, and management tenure; it is difficult to use the measure as the basis for relative comparisons. Use of ROX as the basis for assessment where firms are not identical in terms of the preceding factors may lead to false conclusions that are not justified once company specifics are taken into consideration.

learning guide

Are You Getting the Bang Out of Your Executive Pay Buck?

Discovery Questions

- Do you agree that any conversation about management of 21st century corporations will inevitably lead to a discussion of executive compensation? Explain why.

- What recent changes have occurred in executive pay that exacerbated the fierce debate between companies and their critics?

- Ron Zimmerman postulates that pay-for-performance (pay efficiency) should be the ultimate measure of total executive compensation. Do you agree?

- Explain what goes into the ROX according to Zimmerman?

- What are the broader implications of measuring executive pay efficiency based on ROX?

- Summarize criticisms presented by Donald Delves (especially ROX's focus on shareholder value).

- Explain what cultural context is necessary to consider in order to evaluate the appropriateness of executive pay allocations. (See Holmes' European Perspective.)

- Explain why Chuck Csizmar does not find convincing "attempts to rationalize the practice with complex terms, charts, and theorems." He considers ROX to be a matter of optics. Explain how.

- What Counterpoints focus on measures of executive success that are not financial. What are they? Cite examples from Michelle Holmes, Paul Kirinic, Douglas MacGray and others.

Selected Facts

- What new facts about Executive compensation were presented in this article?

- Does the assumption "pay-for-performance" hold? (Review facts presented by Ron Zimmermman.)

- Donald Delves claims that "stock price" as a proxy for how well the company is serving all its stakeholders (including shareholders, customer and employees) is short sighted and flawed. Explain his reasons.

- Michelle Holmes points out that from the European vantage point "comparisons can be made to the increasing prevalence of relative as well as absolute performance measures such as total shareholder return (TSR) as criteria for performance-based long-term awards. Relative performance against a defined peer group can factor in size, industry sector, and geography." Review this argument and compare it to a ROX approach.

- Douglas MacGray points out the importance of non-financial factors, among them:

  1) Leadership that the executive respects; 2) Crystal clear corporate vision, mission, values, and key priorities; 3) Opportunities to shape the corporation's priorities; 4) Obvious and direct link of the executive's contributions to the corporation's ability to meet its vision and priorities; 5) Frequent feedback, in the form of public recognition and private correction by financial and nonfinancial methods regarding the executive's performance against the key priorities; 6) Support in tough times; 7) Positive overall work environment; and 8) Freedom to make prudent mistakes.

- Paul Kirincic is an EVP of HR for McKesson Corp and his objection to ROX is based in on-the ground experience. "In the end, the shareholders will decide if the story hangs together. If it doesn't, they will take their investment to a company whose story does." What facts does Paul present to explain his position?

Key Discussion Points

- What were the key points debated in this Point Counterpoint presentation?

- Review the quote from Mr. Paul Volker: "The purpose of the company is really to provide goods and services at the best possible price, at the highest level of productivity, and in a way that serves society and communities. That is the purpose of the company. The stock is just the way that we get there." (Donald Delves.)

- The European Context complicates the issue. How is executive remuneration being handled across the EU? According to Michelle Holmes: "Across Europe, there is no commonality of approach despite the European Union (EU) Commission's having issued in 2004 a recommendation for fostering an appropriate regime for the remuneration of directors of listed companies."

- Discuss the broader context of the Executive Pay discussion based on the insights of Paul Kirincic and Douglas MacGray.

Review of Solutions

- Identify 2-3 Big Ideas that are worthy of implementing in your organization.

- Create a list of all the Point arguments for ROX.

- Create a list of all the Counterpoint arguments. How many of them were useful?

Recommendations Summary

- Has this discussion changed the way you see executive compensation? Explain how and why.

- What would you do differently in your current approach having reviewed all Points and Counterpoints in the article?

Learning Outcomes

- Who would you invite to the discussion of executive pay in your organization?

- How would you go about communicating executive pay based on what you have learned in this article?

What's Next?

Ed Gubman, PhD, Strategic Talent Solutions

Now that you've read the best, current thinking by *People & Strategy* thought leaders from around the world, you likely are asking yourself what comes next. Where do we go from here? And, more specifically, what can I do to make a positive difference?

I wouldn't be so bold or presumptuous to suggest a particular answer for any reader. But it is possible to get ready for the future and make a bigger contribution if we know what's coming. We conclude this Point Counterpoint collection by examining some of the macro trends that impact us now and will continue to shape us, and how we might be effective leaders in such a demanding environment.

Big Five Trends

Let's begin with the Big Five. There is no escaping these, and most of us are very familiar with them: Globalization, Technology, Efficiency, Demographics and Green. These have been rocking the world for quite some time, and there is no end in sight to the roller coaster ride they've created.

- **Globalization**—the world continues to get smaller and more interconnected. When a banking crisis in Iceland helps to destroy Britain's biggest home lender or when street riots in Cairo drive down the U.S. S&P index by 2 percent, there's no denying that we are all in this together. Some folks might like to turn back the clock to a more idealized, isolationist time, but that door is locked shut.

- **Technology**—Twitter, Facebook and instant messaging made those anti-government riots in Cairo, like the ones before them in Iran and Tunisia, and the others that surely will come, possible. Without Web 2.0, nobody knows where to gather or what the grievances are. Stop and consider that the United States biggest, recent success stories, and our most notable exports, come from companies that develop new technologies for communications and information. Staggering.

- **Efficiency**—nothing stops the drive to push down labor and other costs of doing business through outsourcing, automation, new sourcing, restructuring, etc. There is no bottom, only brief pauses on our way down. No surprise that Barack Obama appointed GE's Jeff Immelt to head the President's Council on Jobs and Competitiveness, when more than half of GE's sales and workforce are outside the United States. If it's too expensive to make stuff in China, we head to Africa. When it's too costly to answer phones in India, let's put our call center in the Philippines.

- **Demographics**—the great thing about demographics is they're inevitable. By the time we realize what changes are coming, they're already set in stone. The developed world is aging, the developing world is adding huge numbers to its workforces and consumer markets, and there are millions without productive work in the stagnant economies of the Middle East. Most of the time we just react to these determinants; we almost never plan ahead, though we should.

- **Green**—there may still be some enthusiastic climate change deniers out there, but most of the world, including American businesses, get it. The world is getting hotter, and weather changes are more extreme as a result, in both summer and winter. 2010 was the hottest year on record, and the last decade was the hottest too, and our weather just keeps getting weirder. That's why polar bears are searching frantically for ice floes to stand on, why Mexican frogs and lizards are showing up in California for the first time and why New York is suffering through record snowfalls. Meanwhile, many businesses have taken up the green mantle because it's good for the bottom-line, through new products and/or cost savings.

Diversity and Divergence

What about some other trends that will impact our organizations and our lives but which may not be so obvious? To describe some of these, let's keep staring at the big picture. Later the implications will become more visible.

Capitalism is Spreading But We May Not Recognize It

Capitalism has conquered the world, but it's getting more diverse. We are used to thinking about capitalism as our economic system and ours alone. Not true anymore. We can identify at least four kinds of capitalism in the world:

1. **Democratic capitalism**—that should really be small 'd', the kind we practice in the United States, with a political democracy and free markets accompanying it. The emphasis, for the most part, is on the "I's": incentives, initiative, innovation and individualism.

2. **Social welfare capitalism**—the kind they like in continental Europe. There is much less focus on the "I's" and more on the larger community. The entrepreneur may see less upside, but the larger citizenry is protected on the downside. That's why Germany didn't suffer the same fate in the Great Recession as the United States or Great Britain. The German safety net kept most everyone employed even during the country's slowdown.

3. **Authoritarian capitalism**—what's happening in China, Russia and a few other places. This came as a big surprise to many; the accepted doctrine was that you couldn't do a market-based economy without democracy. Leave it to those nations that never had a history of democracy but wanted the riches that capitalism brings to figure this out. Here the government plays a heavy, directive role setting policy, controlling currency, managing markets and seizing property if necessary, all the while ensuring that its friends are well cared for.

4. **Micro-capitalism**—The World Bank and others would say this is what's happening at the "bottom of the pyramid." Capitalism is sprouting up in some of the poorest places in the world as local entrepreneurs respond to mostly local needs. Opening ➤

up a store or small job shop requires help from family and friends, as well as micro lending from individuals and institutions. But big corporations are getting into the act too. To ensure its long-term dominance in Africa's nascent market, Coca-Cola is funding local refreshment stands, cafes, warehouses and distributors. As people throughout Africa work to become more affluent, Coke wants them to stop for "the pause that refreshes."

The question is how will these forms of capitalism co-exist. Will they converge? Will they compete? What happens if you are doing business in more than one type of economy? How do you make adjustments to thrive in each?

The Rich are Getting Richer, Much Richer

For the last 30 years, almost all of the growth in wealth and income in the United States has accrued to the top 1 percent of the economic ladder. The top 1 percent now control 24 percent of the nation's income. This exceeds, by a lot, the level of concentration the United States experienced during the gilded age era of robber barons, and resembles the time in the 1920's right before the Great Depression. Since 1980, more than 80 percent of the increase in Americans' incomes went to the top 1 percent.

There are a lot of reasons for this: educational differences, tax policies, the continuing growth of giant, global corporations, increasing productivity through the replacement of labor by capital, the decline of unions and so on. Nobody is quite sure which causes are most influential or how to slow it down. And, people of different political stripes disagree on how problematic it is. What is clear is that the United States is now one of the most unequal societies in the world, and, historically, this level of inequality causes social strife, fear of immigration and hyper partisanship in politics, the latter we can hear every night on TV.

A typical story, "ripped from the headlines": Walt Disney rewarded its CEO, Bob Iger, with a 35 percent jump in salary and bonuses for 2010, from $12M to $16.3. By what passes

for standards in the world of executive compensation, the raise was well deserved. Disney net income rose 20 percent on a revenue increase of 5 percent, there were hit movies in "Alice in Wonderland" and the magnificent "Toy Story 3," and three of its TV networks—ABC Family, ESPN and the Disney Channel—delivered record ratings. So it's not that he didn't earn it. It's that his raise for one year is more money than almost all Americans will ever earn in their lifetimes. And you can bet that the Disney rank-and-file who contributed to all this success didn't see anything near 35 percent increases. In fact, Disney announced major layoffs in 2009 and early 2011.

Americans are just starting to scream about this stark level of inequality. That's part of the energy behind the Occupy Wall Street Movement. Yet no one is quite sure what to do about it, and we retain our deeply ingrained belief in social mobility. Work hard and you'll be rewarded is something we all hear from birth, and the media still loves rags-to-riches stories, mostly about athletes and celebrities. Unfortunately, no matter how hard we hold on to this belief, it's becoming less of a reality. We often think of "the Old World" of Europe as class-bound and stuck. But real, measured social mobility is much greater in Germany, France, Spain, Denmark and Sweden today than it is in the United States.

The big fallout from growing inequality is the shrinking of the middle class. This is hard to measure, but the shape of our economy now resembles Argentina more than it does most other places. And Argentina is recognized as a place where the middle class collapsed in the early 2000s when its currency experienced its great devaluation.

The other fallout is the growing size of the U.S. welfare state. That appears to be the trade-off, fewer people make much more money, so more people get benefits through unemployment, social security, Medicare and now, healthcare reform. If U.S. corporate profits can reach record levels, while hiring remains depressed and unemployment high, it's hard to argue that people should be left to suffer. And, ultimately, the rich, who gain

the most from big corporate profits as managers and investors, will pay more in taxes to cover everyone else.

Now you might be thinking that Tea Party activists will keep this from happening. Fat chance. Ultra-rich conservative activists opposed to increased taxation and regulation fund a lot of Tea Party activities behind the scenes, and many of the activists may be sincere in their beliefs about smaller government, but they don't want their benefits cut either. Every well-constructed opinion poll shows that four out of five Americans, including Tea Partiers and Republicans, would rather raise taxes than cut social security or Medicare. As one infamous and ill informed Tea Partier yelled at a health care town hall meeting in 2009, "Keep your government hands off my Medicare!"

Your Future, and Your Company's Future, Are Going in Two Very Different Directions

The global economic meltdown accelerated these trends of rising capitalism and rich getting richer. In Europe, France and Germany, with their strong social safety nets, weathered the Great Recession pretty well and helped many Europeans think they have the right answers economically. Home ownership isn't a key retirement asset in countries with well paying national pension and savings schemes, so renting is okay and housing bubbles don't attract so many into something they can't afford. Meanwhile, high social benefits kept consumer spending up. The currency troubles now plaguing Europe are largely a function of countries who aren't good capitalists needing to be bailed out by those who are.

Likewise, China, with its authoritarian capitalism, was able to pick up even more foreign assets cheaply, think Volvo and Hummer among others. It also absorbed more of the world's debt, thereby gaining additional political power.

And rich people are okay with a recession, what they hate is inflation, which devalues their assets. During recessions, they have more places to shelter their money, aren't dependent on any one particular asset class, like real estate, and have the money to snap up bargains at falling prices. Spending on Mercedes and at Tiffany's slowed down for a while, but luxury goods came roaring back in 2010.

Another thing the Great Recession did was to cement a 30-year trend of sending your career trajectory and your company's future on very different paths. For the past 30 years, companies have shifted more risk onto their employees—think 401(k) plans instead of pensions, bonuses instead of merit pay increases, and flatter organizations instead of promotions, etc. We are on our own now. At the same time, corporations, at least big ones, have gotten larger, more powerful and even more secure. "Too big to fail," as well as too globally inter-connected, meant our tax dollars went to saving the likes of AIG, GM, Citigroup, etc. You know the list by now.

While we were bailing out the big guys, U.S. companies shed 8 million workers during the recession. But, helped by government bail-outs, a tsunami of cheap money by the Federal Reserve and aggressive cash hording, cost cutting and layoffs by management, big businesses have prospered. For example, more than 200 community banks were shuttered or seized in the last two years, while the biggest banking institutions now manage more assets than ever. Acquisitions of smaller companies by bigger ones and industry consolidation are occurring rapidly throughout the American economy.

It's a great life if you are "in the club" in one of these large institutions; top managers get taken care of and protected. Just look at what you can get paid as a failed CEO at places like Hewlett-Packard, Home Depot or Lehman Brothers. But for most employees, life isn't like that at all. Lose your job and start scrambling, since it's likely to be many, many years before employment is back at pre-Great Recession levels.

Consider the careers of professionals today in most fields. If you are a competent petroleum engineer you still can work your whole career at Chevron or Shell. But for most in marketing, architecture, accounting, human resources, finance, nursing, technology, law, sales, graphic design, you name it, your career

security is in your own hands. You may spend some time in a large company, in a small company, on your own and back again to another small company or startup. You can stay as long as you are making money for the organization. If your work can be done more cheaply in some other way or place, it will.

What lies ahead for HR, and for you as an HR leader?

You now live in a "gig" economy, with its emphasis on tasks and projects, not jobs. The same technology that your company uses to move functions to Mumbai enables you to make yourself available worldwide, so you can "hook up" quickly with someone who has paid work for you. You can collaborate around the world with people you've never met and will never see again. All of this can be quite stimulating and energizing, as long as you can handle the risk, pay your bills and save for the future. It's a lot harder, more uncertain and probably much less lucrative than a 40-year career at IBM.

This is not a problem, and there is no solution for it. It just is. Get used to it. Today you may be a human resources VP, with a salary, bonus, benefits, perks and stock, but tomorrow you may be consulting, hoping to sell your expertise to keep your home, lifestyle and self-respect. You need the skills for both, and you need to acquire them through your own ingenuity.

The Path Ahead

What lies ahead for HR, and for you as an HR leader? From here, the road ahead looks like driving through the mountains in a snowstorm, loaded with switchbacks, curves and bumps making the destination uncertain. You need to be prepared for anything and everything—agility and resilience are the watchwords of the foreseeable future.

The starting point is staring reality right in the face.

What's Happening Now

It should be pretty clear by now that we live in a world where being a "best place to work" isn't important to very many companies. Sure, *Fortune* still publishes its list, as do several other smaller and local publications.

Have you noticed it's mostly the same companies year after year? Of the 2011 *Fortune* list of the 100 best, 87 companies appeared on the 2010 list, and several of other 13 had appeared in prior years.

I worked on the *Fortune* list for its first three years and even then, during the midst of the "talent wars," we had trouble getting many companies to apply. The same was true during my time helping Winning Workplaces compile its list of best small and family-owned businesses. Being a best place to work is a key strategy or a point of pride for a relatively small (and shrinking?) number of companies. Congratulations to you if you work at one of them—try to keep that job. Still, the vast majority don't care. They'll do just enough to be able to hire and retain the people they need; that's really what being "competitive" means.

And, if you reflect back on the Point Counterpoint perspectives you've just read, you should be impressed by how little they address tactics. Most deal with new directions for established practices, like rethinking talent management, or heading off into newer frontiers, like neuroscience or sustainability. **That's because your success in HR lies in grasping the big picture and translating it into concrete realities that fit your company, not how well you administer HR.**

Yes, you need to get the basics done right and efficiently, and you need to keep up with the trends. You have to get ready for healthcare reform because that's coming in some form, ➤

a closing perspective

no matter what. The job market will pick up eventually, and now is a good time to get your recruiting and hiring processes in fighting shape so you'll be ready.

Beyond those, pick a few areas to experiment. Moving your total rewards statement from the secure portion of your website to a personalized smart phone app will generate enough "gee whiz" to keep you employed for a while. Shortening your talent management paperwork down to a few pages will earn you sighs of relief and kind words from your peers. But neither of these, or similar fine-tunings, will get and keep another customer for your business, improve your earnings or boost your stock price.

Maxing Out

So, what to do to maximize your contribution and satisfaction, while building your career, not job, security? Here's a very short list for your consideration.

1. Get smart about the bigger financial, social and political trends we've been discussing. Most business people don't have the time they'd like to read anymore. Since HR is about influence, and influence is a function of knowledge, become the fount of wisdom in your company about the outside world. Read *The Financial Times*, *The Economist*, *The Week* and other sources that look at the world, not just the United States. Did you read *The Big Short* or any of the other good books about the recent financial collapse so you could really understand it? What was the last, serious piece you read about value creation or innovation? When your fellow executives start to prize your observations about the world in which you do business, you will have gone a long way to becoming a valued advisor.

2. Think through how these trends impact your total business, not just HR. It's been said before but bears repeating, people are an end-to-end resource in business, just like money and information. Nothing happens without employees doing the right things for the business, products and customers. Have an opinion about how a new manufacturing process or information tool will play throughout your organization and voice it. Become a confident consultant to your business.

3. Continue to advocate for employees. It's pretty clear, if you look at some of the big, scandalous recent failures in business, that HR became a tool of the CEO, as opposed to a leader of the organization. Some of our colleagues took being a business partner too far and were seduced by the money and power that can accompany it. If you are going to be in HR, be in HR. Have the courage to stand up for all the people in your company, not just the powerful. When proposals are forwarded that will ruin morale or culture or trample on people, say no.

4. Understand the few, pivotal metrics that dominate your company. In every successful organization I consulted with more than 35 years, there were a few numbers that were more important than any others. These were the operational metrics that drove the bottom line: revenue per user, income per producer, return on sales, inventory turns, capacity utilization, days to market, etc. Know what these are and focus your muscle behind them. Design your HR systems and spend your limited HR dollars on helping operational leaders improve them, even if you have to ignore some other, useful things. Too many times HR tries to be all things to all people in a company and ends up being ineffective at most of them.

5. Do the same thing with talent. Not all talent is equally critical to a company. Know what talent really moves the key needles, those few powerful metrics we just mentioned, and make them your priority. In some companies it's a particular function, like R&D or sales or engineering. In others, it's a few people in pivotal roles throughout the organization. In some places it's your stars. In only a few companies, where the majority of people meet the public, is it everyone, or almost everyone. Develop a deep understanding of what your crucial talent is and stay focused on keeping that supply chain well stocked.

6. Take care of your own development. The odds that you will finish your career in the job or company in which you currently reside are low and getting lower all the time. So be prepared. Get the feedback you need to round out your skills so you can be ready for whatever the future brings. If you don't know how to sell, learn. If you

don't like public speaking, figure out how to get better at it and enjoy it, at least a little. If you can't work a spreadsheet, ask for help. If technology scares you, talk to your kids. The starting point for development has always been and will always be accurate self-perception. If you truly know who you are and what you are good at, you know which strengths to build on and which weaknesses to minimize. On the day you have to face some kind of dramatic job change, you'll be much better prepared if you have tended your own garden and can cultivate some new growth.

7. Finally, pick an area that you are passionate about and learn everything you can. Become an expert. It could be sustainability, organization design, neuroscience and leadership, marketing, innovation, etc. It could be something slightly outside of your normal business but that may have some application—like art and design, communications technology, acting, etc. It could be completely unrelated, like tango dancing or painting. Do it because it's fun and energizing to have something you can call your own, and it leads to a richer life. Maybe you can bring some elements of it into your current job. Maybe you can't. Perhaps you can use it later in another career or during retirement. Likely it will change the way you think and give you a broader perspective. Most importantly, it will make you happier, and that brings health and productivity.

This list could be longer but that would violate a major principle of "don't get distracted." Too much gets thrown at those of us in leadership positions, so much that we often lose sight of what's vital. HR always has been too susceptible to fads and false promises. If you look at many of the biggest name contributors to our Point Counterpoint articles, they have been focused on the same key questions throughout their careers—Marshall Goldsmith on building better executives, Marcus Buckingham on improving individual and team performance, Dave Ulrich on HR business partnering, etc.

That's a powerful model. Stay very aware of all that's happening in the world, but keep true to your own few core principles. That's the best way to drive through the storm and get to where you want to go. **P&S**